LITURGICAL LAW TODAY:
New Style, New Spirit:

LITURGICAL LAW TODAY:
New Style, New Spirit:

by

Thomas Richstatter O.F.M.

FRANCISCAN HERALD PRESS
1434 WEST 51st STREET • CHICAGO, 60609

©1977

FRANCISCAN HERALD PRESS
1434 West 51st St. Chicago, Illinois 60609

Library of Congress Cataloging in Publication Data

Richstatter, Thomas.
  Liturgical law, new style, new spirit.

  Bibliography: p.
  1. Canon law. 2. Canon law—History. 3. Catholic Church. Liturgy and ritual.
I. Title.
Law   262.9   77-3008
ISBN 0-8199-0672-7

February 28, 1977

IMPRIMI POTEST:
  Andrew Fox O.F.M.
  Minister Provincial

NIHIL OBSTAT:
  Mark Hegener O.F.M.
  Censor

IMPRIMATUR:
  Msgr. Richard A. Rosemeyer, J.D.
  Vicar General, Archdiocese of Chicago

MADE IN THE UNITED STATES OF AMERICA

The original version of this book was presented to the faculty of the Catholic Institute of Paris on July 5, 1976, to obtain the degree "Doctor of Theological Science." The work was titled "Obedience to Liturgical Law: A Historical Study of the Theological Context of Roman Catholic Liturgical Law before and after the Second Vatican Council." The thesis was directed by Fr. Pierre-Marie Gy, O.P., director of the Institut Superieur de Liturgie. The jury consisted of Fr. Gy, president, Mgr. Pierre Jounel, assistant director of the institute, and Fr. Jean Passicos, Dean of the faculty of Canon Law.

TABLE OF CONTENTS

INTRODUCTION

I was ordained a priest in 1966. It was an exciting time to begin the ministry. The council was over; the bishops had returned to their dioceses and the work of implementation had begun.

A large part of my time was spent explaining the new liturgical rites in parishes and schools, working with the laity and the clergy of the diocese of Cincinnati. It was an enjoyable and fulfilling ministry.

However, it soon became evident that not everyone had the same opinion on what the new rubrics meant or on how they were to be applied. There were those who were very hesitant to accept the new liturgy and some who were overly enthusiastic for change. Liturgical obedience became a subject of discussion, confusion, and often, the cause of division among priests and among the laity.

When I was given the opportunity to study for the doctorate in theology at the Institute Catholique in Paris, the question of obedience to liturgical law seemed to be an interesting topic for a dissertation. A study of this problem would be useful for my own teaching, and might prove informative to other priests and those concerned with the implementation of the Constitution on the Liturgy.

I thought that a careful study of the new rubrics, noting where freedom is given and where it is not given, and a comparison with the previous rubrics would help solve the misunderstandings in this area. However, as I investigated the problem, I realized that the principal change is not at the level of the rubrics themselves but at the theological level. The rubrics are different now, but the context from which they are given has changed also. We are called upon not only to give obedience to new rubrics, but to give a new type of obedience.

The purpose of this study is to trace historically this change. The study begins with the encyclical "Mediator Dei" (Chapter I.) and examines the theological context of this document. We will then look at the major reforms in the liturgy before the Council (Chapter II). In the Constitution on the Liturgy (Chapter III) and the other documents promulgated by the Second Vatican Council, we find a change in the relation of the Liturgy to the Church—a change which has much influence on the liturgical legislation published after the Council (Chapter IV).

Evidently a study such as this is related to many other problems and changes in the Church and in the world. It is an attempt to trace the history of a change in the way the Church thinks about herself.

A SUMMARY OF THE HISTORY OF LITURGICAL LAW

This present study begins with the encyclical *Mediator Dei* which forms the subject of Chapter I. Readers who are familiar with the history of liturgical law are invited to turn immediately to this Chapter. However, for those readers who would like to see the context of the problem, we have included here a brief history. This history is neither complete nor original. The divisions into different periods are those given by Dom Botte, Msgr. Jounel, and Fr. Gy.[1]

1. St. Paul: First Letter to the Corinthians.

The need for regulating the liturgical assembly came early in our history. Already in the First Letter to the Corinthians, Paul gives two basic principles for ordering the assembly: tradition and order. We will find, in fact, these two principles form the basis of liturgical law down to our own day.

St. Paul's first principle, tradition, is made necessary by the way God has chosen to reveal himself. Christianity is a historical religion and we must be in constant contact with the events which form the very basis of our faith. Paul writes: "You have done well in remembering me so constantly and in maintaining the traditions just as I passed them on to you (11:2).[2] "For this is what I received from the Lord, and in turn passed on to you: that on the same night that he was betrayed . . . (11:23)." "Brothers, I want to remind you of the gospel I preached to you, the gospel that you received and in which you are firmly established . . . (15:1)." "I am the least of the apostles; . . . but what matters is that I preach what they preach, and this is what you all believed (15:11)."

St. Paul's second principle, order, is made necessary by our human nature. When we assemble as a community, we cannot all talk at once. As human beings, we are uplifted by the beautiful and repulsed by the ugly. We communicate by symbols. We are all members of the assembly, but we do not all have the same abilities or capacities. We do not all have the same liturgical role. There is a need for order. Paul writes: "I hear that when you all come together as a community, there are separate factions among you; . . . I cannot congratulate you on this (see 11:17–22)." "Now you together are Christ's body; but each of you is a different part of it. In the Church, God has given the first place to apostles, the second to prophets, the third to teachers (12:27)." "At all your meetings let everyone be ready with a psalm or a sermon or a revelation, or ready to use his gift of tongues or to give an interpretation; but it must always be for the common good (14:26)." "God is not a God of disorder but of peace (14:33)." "And so, my dear brothers, . . . let everything be done with propriety and in order (14:40)."

Both of these principles, tradition and order, admit of a variety of interpretations. Throughout history we find that the community has ever been watchful to preserve this tradition, especially in those things which are most central to the mission of Jesus, particularly the Eucharist and the other sacraments. Yet, this tradition is capable of finding expression in the rites and symbols of many different cultures. The Church is solicitous to remain faithful to its origins and at the same time to allow this tradition a universal expression.

The principle of "good order" also admits of a large range of interpretation. The context in which we find the quotation "God is not a God of disorder but of peace" used in *Mediator Dei* and the highly organized liturgy of 1947 is different from that in which the words were first read some 1900 years earlier:

> What do we propose, brothers? When you assemble, one has a psalm, another some instruction to give, still another a revelation to share; one speaks in a tongue, another interprets. All well and good, so long as everything is done with a constructive purpose. If any are going to talk in tongues let it be at most two or three, each in turn, with another to interpret what they are saying. But if there is no one to interpret, there should be silence in the assembly, each one speaking only to himself and to God. Let no more than two or three prophets speak, and let the rest judge the worth of what they say. If another, sitting by, should happen to receive a revelation, the first ones should then keep quiet. You can all speak your prophecies, but one by one, so that all may be instructed and encouraged. The spirits of the prophets are under their prophets' control, since God is a God, not of confusion, but of peace (I Cor 14:26-33).

We give this rather long quotation because it is important for a balanced understanding of liturgical law and "order" in the assembly, and it is perhaps good to quote it here in full as this is one of the passages of First Corinthians that is never read during the Eucharistic assembly according to the new Lectionary.

With these two principles in mind, the need to be faithful to the tradition and the need for order in the liturgical assembly, we will briefly examine the history of their application.

2. The First Four Centuries.

Those who took the place of the apostles assumed in their turn the responsibility for announcing the gospel and caring for the Churches entrusted to them. The bishop called the people together into a liturgical assembly, he announced the word of God and offered them the bread of salvation. There were no laws as to how he should do this other than the implications of his office. As bishop he was responsible for the faith and good order of his community. The bishop/celebrant had to improvise the liturgical prayers even as he had to improvise many other aspects of his office.

This improvisation led to a great diversity of liturgical formulas. A study of these early liturgies shows differences even in things that today we might consider "essential"—for example, the words of institution of the Eucharist, the formula for Baptism. Dom Botte says of this period:

> We should not go looking for a unique "apostolic liturgy" which later becomes diversified. Undoubtedly each Church had its oral traditions for the essential rites but these were not yet fixed in any uniform way. This liberty gave birth to a wide diversity of discipline and liturgical practice to which the early historians and the Fathers would point with pride. This diversity only serves to show more clearly the strength of the underlying unity of the churches in their preservation of the traditions.[4]

3. The Fourth to the Eighth Centuries.

During this period there was much liturgical creation, however only a portion of it has come down to us. Some of these texts have been incorporated into our tradition and are prayed today as a living witness to the continuity of our belief. Sometimes these prayers were composed by the bishops themselves—often with a catechetical or doctrinal purpose in mind. During this period, although the bishops continued to compose liturgical prayers, they also began to use written texts. Perhaps it was as difficult then as it is now to continually create new texts for the assembly.

At the end of the fourth century, we find St. Augustine complaining that some bishops are using prayers composed by incompetent authors, even by heretics. The bishops, responsible for the faith of their Churches, saw the need for discipline in this most important matter and the third Council of Carthage forbade the use of liturgical formulas which had not been previously approved by a synod. In one sense we can see this as a limitation of freedom, but in fact it is not—freedom outside the realm of orthodoxy is obviously meaningless.

Up to this point one and the same minister, the bishop, is the one who is concerned with the regulation of the liturgy and the one who is the leader of the liturgical assembly. However, the question soon arises as to what to do liturgically in those churches which do not have their own bishop. The answer given is that they are to conform to the mother-church. But, as we see in the case of Rome and its surrounding Churches, sometimes an interval of several generations can come between an innovation in the papal liturgy and the conformity of the subordinate churches.

It is important for our study to see the relation between "Church," "liturgy," and "law" during this period. In an address to the assembly of French bishops on their responsibility in relation to liturgical law, P.-M. Gy stated:

> In both the local and general Councils of this period and in the papal responses to bishops' questions, that which occupies the most space, together with the defense of the faith, is the law regarding the sacraments, and more precisely, the law concerning the fundamental elements of the sacraments, what we would call today "those elements which pertain to the divine institution" or to the intimate relation between the sacramental practice and the sacramentality of the Church, for example, the admission of non-catholics to communion, the presidential structure of the eucharist assembly, or the discipline of Penance. We can say, I believe, that the fathers were profoundly aware of the fact that it is the sacraments which give the Church its very structure.[5]

The fact that the law of the Church is rooted in the liturgy and in the understanding of the Church-sacrament-of-salvation will form the key element in the understanding of the context of liturgical law before and after the Second Vatican Council. Y. Congar points out that this doctrine forms the basis of the Council's teaching on the Church.[6] We mention this fact here, only to point out that the idea is not a novelty of the Council but a return to the thinking of the Fathers.

4. The Eighth to the Sixteenth Centuries.

From the second half of the sixth century, we find less and less liturgical creativity and the beginning of the collection of formulas. "Sacramentaries" begin to appear. Dom Botte says that the work of original creation, and the compilation and adaptation, is finished by the thirteenth century and the various liturgies have by then taken on the form in which they will remain down to our own time.[7]

The unification of the Western liturgy which took place during this time can be traced to the respect of the local Churches for the liturgy of Rome and to the desire for unity throughout the empire on the part of the Carolingians.[8] To these two factors is added a third, found in the ecclesiology of Pope Gregory VII (pope from 1073-1085). The unity of faith invites a unity in liturgical practice. And as the other churches are to have the same faith as the Church of Rome, they ought to have the same liturgy. We see here a change in the perspective of the fathers who considered the diversity of liturgical practice to enhance the unity of the churches by showing each of the churches' concern with preserving the heritage. Gregory felt that he could regulate the liturgy of the other churches, and the popes after him became more and more aware of their right and duty to legislate liturgical matters for the entire Church. In 1171, for example, we see what we would call today the "papal reservation" of the right to canonize saints. Yet papal intervention was rare during the high middle ages. P.-M. Gy writes that "the medieval liturgy was regulated not so much by the Pope or by the bishops as by the customs of the different Churches."[9]

The mentality of the period is important for the understanding of their attitude toward liturgical law. Y. Congar, in an article on the "False Decretals," speaks of this mentality and says that the middle ages did not have our concept of man-made law. For them, law, like truth, comes from God and exists in itself, independent of human decisions. Consequently, we can hardly ask "who makes liturgical law?" Law, the right thing to do, is "what has always been done."[10]

To introduce something "new" into this system, it must appear to be something "old." E. Champeaux, in "The learned legends of old Alsace," writes:

> During a period when tradition formed the basis of law, a new act is unjust because it is new. A just "novelty" implies a contradiction in terms. Justice is that what has always been done. But, even though this be the case, we have to admit certain novelties

in order to live. We can reconcile these new practices with the traditional theory if we present the new acts as the reappearance of earlier, very old acts. In order to allow an infant to enter this museum of antiquities which constitutes the institutions of the Middle Ages, we must first of all give him a long white false beard. This "beard" is a false document or a legend.[11]

This is the reason why, at this period, we find so many fabricated documents. Congar writes:

> Like law, the truth was taken as an objective and transcendent value. It is not regulated by facts but by the purpose and will of God. The truth of a thing, and thus what we can say about it, depends on its relation to the order willed by God. If it is necessary to change a name, or a date, or to fabricate a document in order to affirm and establish this order, we are not doing anything else by this act than simply aiding the triumph of truth.[12]

To the question "who makes liturgical laws?" the Middle Ages would answer: "God, of course." And where are these laws found? In the customs of the local Church. The role of the bishop is to verify that the customs exist and that they are reasonable. The source of the law is not the bishop himself, but the customs of the Christian community.

During an age which placed such a high value on custom, we are not surprised to find the appearance of books containing exact accounts of how the liturgical rites were to be performed—that is, records of how they had been performed in the past. From the eighth or ninth century onward we find liturgical books with the text written in black ink and the indications of ceremonies and gestures written in red ink (*rubrica,* in Latin).

Books explaining the customs and rubrics also begin to be written. But as many of the customs find their origins in the distant past, these didactic books often give allegorical interpretations to the rubrics rather than the true significance of the rites.

As the liturgical customs and rubrics become more and more complicated and esoteric during the last centuries of the Middle Ages, the liturgy becomes progressively the affair of the experts— the monks and clerics. The liturgy moves away from the people. An important change of mentality takes place: the liturgy is no longer thought of as the prayer of the community, but it becomes "a public service, fulfilled by the clerics, for the benefit of the laity."[13] And the laity turn more and more to (what we would call) "private devotions" for their prayer.

5. The Sixteenth to the Twentieth Centuries.

The state of liturgical decline, which had no little part to play in the Reformation, was such that it could only be corrected by a Council. The Council of Trent opened December 13, 1545 and continued (with two interruptions) through the reigns of five popes until December 4, 1563. The Council initiated the work of the liturgical reform. After treating the question of justification the Council set down a list of canons containing the Church's teaching on the sacraments, for the sacraments are the means by which justification either begins or is increased or is restored when lost by sin. The 13th canon states that the ministers may not change the sacramental rites.

> 13. If anyone says that the accepted and approved rites of the Catholic Church that are customarily used in the solemn administration of the sacraments can, without sin, be belittled or omitted by the ministers as they see fit, or that they can be changed into other new rites by any pastor in the Church: let him be anathema. [14]

The reform of the breviary and the missal had been prepared by a commission and was to be presented to the Council; however many of the bishops were eager to return to their dioceses and in their final session, December 4, 1563, they decided to let the pope with the responsibility of promulgating the breviary, missal, catechism, and index of forbidden books.[15]

The breviary was published in 1568 and the missal in 1570. In these books we find, according to the use of the Roman Curia, the list of rubrics printed at the beginning of the book—a practice that continues to our own time.

The success of these books—aided by the invention of the printing press which enabled the Roman liturgy to be introduced much more economically than ever before when the printed book became other than an object for the rich—inspired the revision of the other liturgical books. The calendar was revised in 1584 during the pontificate of Gregory XIII. Pope Sixtus V gave the task of correcting the liturgical books to the newly formed "Congregation for Sacred Rites and Ceremonies" in 1588. The new edition of the pontifical was issued in 1596, the ceremonial for bishops in 1600, and the Roman ritual in 1614.

The three centuries which follow the revision of the liturgical books are marked by very little liturgical change. In this period of liturgical stability, much emphasis is placed on the rubrics. Many commentaries on the rubrics are published. Private interpretations and explanations multiply. The decisions of the Congregation of Rites were first collected by Aloysius Gardellini in 1807 and by 1887 this collection contained 5,993 decrees.[16] In 1898, Pope Leo XIII substituted a new and official collection in five volumes issued 1898-1901 with the title *Decreta Authentica Congregationis Sacrorum Rituum.* This collection contained 4,051 decrees. Supplements have been published in 1912, 1927, and again in 1947.

When the bishops, at the end of the Council of Trent, left it up to the pope to issue the new liturgical books, we enter a new period of liturgical law. The liturgy is no longer regulated by the authority of the local bishop but by the central authority. the pope. The authority of custom gives way to the central authority which issued the liturgical books and their rubrics. The element of authority becomes prominent in the definition of liturgy.[17]

After the Council of Trent we again witness a growing division between the liturgical prayer of the Church and the devotional prayer of the faithful. In the liturgical prayer itself, the central mysteries are obscured by the celebration of saints' feasts and votive offices. Msgr. Jounel states that if the development of the cult of the saints can be explained in part by the continual flourishing of Catholic sanctity, it was no doubt principally caused by the desire to substitute a festive mass and office for the ferial because they were shorter.[18] By 1883 the priest was able to celebrate a votive Mass and office each day of the week during the entire year, except Ash Wednesday, passion time, and the week preceding Christmas. The "Ordo" for the Latran basilica for 1909 shows that the Sunday Mass "of the year" (that is, with green vestments) was only celebrated twice during that entire year. H.E. Jung, in his thesis on the renewal of the liturgical year, compares the Franciscan calendar for 1904 with that of 1974 and shows that the former contained only one Sunday "of the year." All the other Sundays of the Year were not celebrated because of the feast of a saint or a votive celebration.[19] "At the close of this period of the rubricists, the liturgy is in a state of profound decadence."[20] (Evidently the mere fact that the rubrics allow the choice of texts and votive masses is not automatically a sign of "progress" in the pastoral adaptation of the liturgy.)

Various attempts were made to reform this situation. However it was at the beginning of the 1900's that we find the origins of what we have come to call "the liturgical movement." A history of this period would mention such names as Dom Prosper Guéranger (1805-1875), Dom Lambert Beauduin (1873-1960), Dom Odo Casel (1886-1948), and Pius Parsch (1884-1954). The movement sought to rediscover the pastoral dimensions of the liturgy and to re-unite the liturgy and the devotional life of the church so that the liturgy might once again be the source of the Christian spirit.

When Pope St. Pius X (1835-1914) began his pontificate in 1903, he chose as his guiding principle the moto "To restore all things in Christ," (Eph 1:10). He undertook not only the reform of Canon Law (promulgated under Benedict XV in 1917), but also many pastoral and liturgical matters. The decree "Tra le sollecitudini" (1903) speaks of sacred music and the restoration of Gregorian chant, and also "the active participation of the laity" in the liturgical action. The decree encouraging frequent Communion follows in 1905, and the decree lowering the age for first Communion in 1910. The liturgical books begin to be reformed, a work continued during the pontificate of Pius XII. These reforms bring us to the state of liturgical legislation at the time of *Mediator Dei,* with which we begin our study.

THE WAY IN WHICH LITURGICAL LAW WAS TAUGHT IN AMERICAN SEMINARIES AT THE TIME OF MEDIATOR DEI

After giving a short history of liturgical law, perhaps one more consideration is in order before we begin our study of *Mediator Dei.* The way in which liturgy is taught in seminaries has changed so radically that it may be difficult to understand the mentality of *Mediator Dei* and the liturgical reforms of the years immediately before the Council unless we recall the way in which liturgy was taught, and thus the theological and moral context in which this legislation was received and understood.

These few pages are not a scientific survey of the seminaries of the period; they are only an attempt to recall an underlying mentality. Obviously these observations may not apply to all seminaries of the period.

1. Threefold presentation: Doctrine, Discipline, Ceremonies.

The Mass and the sacraments appeared at several different places in the seminary curriculum. Their doctrinal aspects—what we believe about the sacraments—were presented in the course of dogmatic, or systematic theology, often in a cycle of courses such as: apologetics, church, God, redemption, grace, and sacraments.

The disciplinary aspects of the sacraments—the laws governing their administration and reception—were treated in the course on canon law; the dimension of these laws being treated in the course on moral theology, often in a cycle such as: general moral principles, commandments, justice, sacraments, marriage. Sometimes this matter was divided between the two disciplines; for example, the moral teacher presenting Mass and the sacraments, and the canon law teacher presenting marriage (due to extensive canonical treatment of this matter).

The liturgy course treated the rubrics—the rites and ceremonies to be observed by the priest in saying the Mass and administering the sacraments. With the liturgical movement this situation changes in that the liturgy courses begin to include not only the rubrics but the history of the liturgy and the meaning of the rites and prayers.

When Dom Botte was asked in 1961 to write an article for *La Maison-Dieu* on "The necessity of a liturgical formation for seminarians which goes beyond merely teaching the rubrics," he first thought the request a joke, for surely all seminaries had moved beyond this stage by the 1960's. However, he wrote the article because "these ideas are often implemented slowly." He states that he can recall when "rubrics" and "liturgy" were virtually synonymous. "I remember in 1922 a university professor criticizing the liturgical movement saying that it is not possible to get the people interested in the rubrics." The liturgy courses taught the making of gestures and the saying of words, the sense of which was of little importance.[21]

Fr. Gy states that this threefold distinction (doctrine, discipline, ceremonies) first appears in the papal magisterium in the brief of Pope Benedict XIV titled "Quam ardenti studio," (1752) which promulgated the new ritual, pontifical, and ceremonial for bishops.[22] These books were revised by experts in doctrine, discipline, and liturgical matters (that is, the rites and ceremonies).

In this threefold framework, liturgical law, and obedience to liturgical law were usually studied in the seminaries in the courses of canon law, and moral theology.

2. Canon Law Courses and the Presentation of Liturgical Law.

The current code of canon law was promulgated by Pope Benedict XV in 1917 and went into effect the following year. The Code is (at the time of this writing) being revised to incorporate the spirit and the legislation of the Council. However, the Code of 1917 is still the law of the Church, except for those canons which have been explicitly abrogated or emended by the Council and the legislation implementing the Council.

The index of the Code reveals another threefold division: persons, things, processes (that is, juridical processes). This division is reflected in the five books of the Code:

Book I.   General Rules
Book II.   Laws concerning Persons
Book III. Laws concerning Things
Book IV.   Trials
Book V.   Offenses and Penalties

The sacraments and divine cult are treated in Book III: Things. This division of the Code influences the presentation and understanding of the sacraments.

Before looking at Book III, we might mention that Book II: Persons, contains 639 canons. After 21 canons on persons in general, there are 574 canons for clerics and religious, and 44 canons on the laity. This fact might be recalled later when we discuss the Vatican Council II and the rediscovery of the role of the laity of the Church and the liturgy.

Book II also treats of the Sacred Congregations of the Curia; here we see again the distinction "doctrine-discipline-ceremonies" reflected in the fact that the liturgy is the concern of the (then) Congregation of the Holy Office which guards the doctrine of faith and morals (Canon 247). The Congregation for the Discipline of the Sacraments has charge of the disciplinary regulations of the seven sacraments, with the exception of matters reserved to the Holy Office in canon 247 and to the Sacred Congregation of Rites in reference to the rites and ceremonies which are to be observed in the administration of the sacraments. (Canon 249). The Congregation of Sacred Rites has authority to supervise and regulate all matters pertaining directly to the sacred rites and ceremonies of the Latin Church (Canon 253).

Book III of the Code, on Sacred Things, begins with legislation on simony (the "selling" of sacred things, canons 725-730) and then begins the treatment of the sacraments. The first of these canons states that:

731. As all the Sacraments instituted by Christ our Lord are the principal means of sanctification and salvation, the greatest care and reverence should be employed in their suitable and proper administration and reception.

The sacraments, at the beginning of the Book on "Things," are presented as "means of grace." The note on this canon refers us to the Council of Trent, session VII, (1547).

Jean-Claude Dhôtel, in his study of *The Origins of Modern Catechetics,* lists about a dozen examples of the definition of "sacrament" as found in catechisms between the years 1554 and

1659.[23] Dhôtel makes two observations with regard to the presentation of the sacraments in these books: first, the definition of sacrament is one of the most consistent definitions in books of this period. Sacrament is uniformly described in terms such as: visible sign, instituted by God, means of grace. Dhôtel also observes: second, the definition of sacrament is not related to the Church. The church is absent from these definitions.

This same context for the definition and teaching on sacraments was found in the Baltimore Catechism, which served as the basis of religious instruction of many priests of the United States during their grade school years. The Baltimore Catechism first presented the Apostles Creed—what we must *believe*. The ninth of the twelve articles treated of the Church (I believe in . . . the holy catholic Church.) The second part of the catechism presented the Ten Commandments—what one must *do* as a Catholic. The third part of the book explained the sacraments—the means of grace.

The division between the treatment of the Church and the sacraments—often Creed, Commandments, and Sacraments were taught during three successive years—obscures the fact that the Church is the principal means of grace. The distinction between the ideas of "Church" and "sacraments" in the minds of most Catholics was evident in the difficulties and confusion which resulted when the Council began to speak of the Church as a sacrament (SC 5; LG 1).

Dhôtel states that the division of "Church" and "sacraments" is related to the fact that once the catechism had taught us what we must believe, it then became a code of conduct for the individual Christian—teaching us the sins to avoid, the prayers to say, the sacraments to receive to stay in grace, or to restore grace once lost by sin. The Church remains outside the economy of the sacraments from the viewpoint of the laity.

Elisabeth Germain, in her study of the history of catechisms, *The language of the faith: mentalities and catechetics,*[24] gives another implication of this way of presenting the Church and the sacraments. The Church is seen, not as a sacrament, or a means of salvation itself; rather, the Church becomes the authority which must safeguard the sacraments. The role of the Church is to protect our heritage. The Church is seen under the aspects of authority and power, an authority to whom we owe obedience.

From the view of the Church as authority and power, it is only one step further to identify the Church with the governing hierarchy. Germain quotes a French catechism from Nancy of 1924 as saying: "The body of the pastors are called 'The Teaching Church,' or simply, 'The Church.' "[25]

As Church and liturgy become separated, the laity lose their place in the Church.

· The treatment of the sacraments in book III of the Code, "Things," can emphasize this aspect of the sacraments to the neglect of the dynamic aspects of the sacraments: the sacraments are not only visible signs, means of grace . . . but also a personal encounter between Christ and man.[26] This aspect of the problem is examined by Fr. J. Rotelle in an article "Liturgy and Author-ity."[27] Rotelle finds the root of our contemporary problem of obedience and liturgical law in the change in the role of the min-ister. He compares the role of the bishop/celebrant in the writings of the fathers with the role of the bishop after the Council of Trent. In the former period the bishop was the true and active leader of the liturgical assembly. It was in the person of the minister that the word comes to the material element and the sacrament comes into being. The emphasis was placed on the agent rather than on the thing, that is, the matter and form. Rotelle states:

A sharp contrast is evident as we compare this period with the post-Tridentine era, when the celebrant was regarded as "the one who fulfilled the rubrics of a liturgical ritual." A sacrament, or outward sacramental sign, was effected through accurate application of a well-determined "matter" and "form" which were its two con-stitutive elements. Hence the insistence on observance of the rubrics by the liturgical agent. On account of this exclusive preoccupation with the material side, a sacrament was no longer viewed as a symbolic *action* but as a symbolic *thing,* and there was predominant stress on the matter and form which were considered the essence of the sacrament. Such an understanding of the sacraments does not take into account the role of the celebrant.[28]

This way of viewing the sacraments, described above by Fr. Rotelle, is reflected in the Code.

We have seen that part one of Book III on "Sacred Things" is devoted to the discipline of the sacraments. The second part of the book treats of sacred places (churches, altars, cemeteries . . .) and sacred times (feast days, times of penance . . .). Part three is titled "Of Divine Worship." This arrangement is unfortunate in that it divides "sacraments" and "cult" and also it emphasizes the identification of "cult" and "liturgy" with the merely external aspects of the liturgy. After ten general canons, the other titles treat of the care given to the reserved Eucharistic species, the honor given to the saints and statues and relics, processions, and sacred furnishings. The homily given at Sunday Eucharist is treated not

with the Eucharist, nor with "Divine Worship," but in the fourth
part of the book on the "Teaching Authority of the Church"
which treats of sermons and catechetical instruction. When "sacraments," "worship," and "homily" are separated for pedagogical
reasons, there is the danger that they may never be re-united in
the way in which the priest considers them after he leaves the
seminary.

Among the canons introducing part three "On Divine Worship,"
canon 1256 distinguishes between *public* and *private* cult.

> If the cult is given to God, the saints or beatified persons in the
> name of the Church by persons legitimately appointed for this
> purpose and by acts (forms of worship) instituted by the Church,
> it is called *public* cult; otherwise it is called *private*.[29]

If liturgy is to be defined as "the public worship of the Church,"
the relation to this canon caused liturgy to be viewed as those
cultic acts which are a) performed in the name of the Church,
b) by an appointed minister, c) using the approved rites. In this
sense, canon 1256 reinforces the view that the liturgy is not the
prayer of the laity but the official prayer of delegated ministers performed in the name of the Church. The Church is not viewed as
"the Church at prayer" but the "Church as authority" which ap-
proves and regulates the prayer. The following canon (1257) reads:
"The Holy See alone has the right to regulate the sacred liturgy
and to approve liturgical books."

E. Jombart, in his article "Culte" in the *Dictionnaire de Droit
Canonique*, states that the "public cult" spoken of in canon 1256
is not to be identified with liturgy. One of his reasons reveals
another aspect of the thinking about liturgy during this pre-conciliar
period. Jombart states that "cult" is directed toward God and the
saints. Consequently, that part of the liturgy which pertains to the
sacraments can not be called "cult" in the strict sense "because
the sacraments are not orientated primarily to the honor of God but
to the salvation of man."[30] With the identification "liturgy" and
"public cult," the liturgy is seen primarily in its function of giving
worship to God; it is only with the Second Vatican Council that
we will find the balance restored by an emphasis on the fact that
all liturgy is also pastoral and educative (SC 33).

For those priests who received a formation with regard to liturgy
and liturgical law which was based on the Code, the Holy See was
understood to be the only authority in making liturgical law; as
we have seen above, "the Holy See alone has the right to regulate
the sacred liturgy and to approve liturgical books (c. 1257)."

The usual minister of the liturgy (except for special cases such as confirmation or ordinations) was the priest. The bishop is somewhere between the priest-minister and the Holy See-authority. Canon 1261 states: "It is the duty of the local Ordinaries to see that the precepts of the Sacred Canons regarding divine worship are faithfully observed." A previous canon (1259) gives an indication of the limits of their power when it states that they cannot even approve new litanies to be recited publicly. Such a view of the role of the bishop/celebrant needs to be balanced by the patristic view of the bishop as an active liturgical agent, as explained in the article by Fr. Rotelle quoted above.

Conclusion:

At the very beginning of the Code, Canon 2 states that liturgical law in general is excluded from the Code, except in those cases where it is explicitly mentioned. McManus writes:

> The laws of the liturgy have never been analytically codified in any form other than that of the liturgical books. When the Code of Canon Law excludes from its legislation the mass of liturgical law, there is perhaps a suggestion that such a codification of the law of worship is not necessary or feasible.[31]

Although the Code does not contain the major portion of the liturgical laws themselves, the Code does give, often by implication, a certain theological context in which liturgical law was understood. We have pointed out above some of the unfortunate aspects of this context. They may be briefly summarized as follows:

1. "Liturgy" is separated from "Church."

2. The sacraments, removed from their ecclesial context become more private—individual means of grace for personal salvation.

3. The sacraments are viewed more as objects than as actions.

4. The major emphasis is on the "matter and form" and not on the role of the minister.

5. The Church is seen primarily in the role of "authority" rather than as "sacrament."

6. The Church tends to be identified with the authority of the hierarchy and the laity are seen apart from the Church and from the liturgy which is performed by delegated ministers.

7. The liturgy can be too easily identified with the external ceremonies of these priestly acts and their rubrics.

8. The laity turn to private prayers and devotions for their spiritual nourishment; the liturgy is performed primarily for God.

9. The liturgical authority is not the person of the bishop but the Holy See. The ordinary leader of the liturgical assembly is not the bishop but the priest. The bishop is seen as the one who must enforce the laws.

10. The liturgical law is one aspect of the law of the Church. It is not viewed as itself structuring the Church. Liturgy is also subordinated to faith and discipline and the "rule of faith" determines the "rule of prayer."

In this context, we will find that *Mediator Dei* was a very positive influence in giving balance to several of the above viewpoints. However, others find their resolution only at the time of the Council. The history of this change of theological context forms the subject of this study.

Before turning to *Mediator Dei* itself, we will look briefly at the manuals of moral theology which were in use at the period in order to see the importance that was given to obedience to liturgical law. An understanding of the seriousness of the rubrics is helpful in understanding the surprise and shock which certain contemporary "disobedience" causes those formed by these books.

3. Manuals of Moral Theology and the Presentation of the Obedience Called for by the Liturgical Laws.

The serious obligation to fulfill the rubrics carefully and exactly is derived from the seriousness of their object: the Mass and the sacraments. However, the manuals teach that not all the rubrics are binding with the same obligation.

1. Essential and Accidental Rubrics

The basic division found in the manuals is that which we see retained in *Mediator Dei* and the Constitution on the Liturgy. The Constitution on the Liturgy states that:

The liturgy is made up of unchangeable elements divinely instituted, and elements subject to change. The latter not only may but ought to be changed with the passing of time if features have by chance crept in which are less harmonious with the intimate nature of the liturgy, or if existing elements have grown less functional. (SC 21)

Mediator Dei expresses this distinction between changeable and unchangeable elements:

> The sacred Liturgy does in fact include divine as well as human
> elements. The former, instituted as they have been by God, cannot
> be changed in any way by men. But the human components admit
> of various modifications, as the needs of the age, circumstance and
> the good of souls may require, and as the Ecclesiastical Hierarchy
> under guidance of the Holy Spirit, may have authorized.[32]

It is these "unchangeable elements" which the manuals identify
as "essential rubrics." Their binding force is evident from the consideration that no one would dare change something that God
himself does not want changed.

The changeable elements of the liturgy are called "accidental
rubrics." However, the manuals sometimes develop the distinction
in such a way as to identify "essential rubrics" with the matter
and form, those elements necessary for the validity of the sacrament. When these identifications are made it is difficult to see
how the post-Conciliar legislation can change the form of a sacrament or alter prayers which were considered essential and unchangeable. The constitution states that there are divinely instituted, unchangeable elements, but these are not identified further.
The manuals take great care to identify the matter and form of
the sacraments and to indicate those rubrics which are "essential"
to safeguard the matter and form, so that we are assured of
the validity of the sacrament, and consequently its effectiveness.[33]

The fact that the other rubrics are called "accidental" does not
mean that they do not oblige under pain of sin. On the contrary,
the manuals teach the seriousness of the rubrics and that the non-
observance of the rubrics is a mortal or venial sin, depending
on the seriousness of the matter and the other criteria ordinarily
applied for determining mortal or venial sin. The category "accidental rubrics" is composed of rubrics which are "prescriptive,"
that is, prescribed under pain of sin.

Besides the "prescriptive" rubrics we also find "facultative"
rubrics, that is, rubrics which permit a choice to be made. The
facultative rubrics are easily determined by their wording. For
example, the rubric before the procession of palms at the beginning of Holy Week formerly read:

> 18. As the procession forms, some or all of the following antiphons
> may be sung.[34]

However, such rubrics which give a choice are rare during this
period for the rite is generally described in great detail.

Some authors[35] make another distinction, "directive" rubrics. The directive rubrics do not bind under sin, but appeal to a filial spirit of obedience and a sense of good order. The distinction is made principally because the authors do not want to say that *every* rubric binds under pain of sin. However, the distinction between prescriptive and directive rubrics is not easy to apply. The Code states that

> The celebrant must observe the rubrics of his liturgical books accurately and devoutly, and beware of adding other ceremonies and prayers of his own choice. All contrary customs by which other ceremonies and prayers are introduced into the Rite of the Mass are disapproved.[36]

Prumer states that although the distinction between prescriptive and directive rubrics is generally given by the authors, it is often very difficult or even impossible to tell which rubrics are prescriptive and which are only directive.[37] McManus says: "It must be insisted that it is almost impossible to find rubrics in the liturgical books which are merely directive, that is, which give a direction or command while leaving complete liberty of action."[38]

Yet, the authors do not want to find sin in insignificant matters. F. Cimetier, a canon law professor from Lyon writing in a popular liturgical encyclopedia in 1931, states that the rubric indicating that the priest must put on the alb starting with the right sleeve rather than the left is a "directive rubric."[39] However, it is not easy to find explicit indication of "directive rubrics" in the manuals.

To limit directive rubrics to "insignificant matters" is not a solution. Martimort writes: "The distinction between prescriptive and simple directive rubrics is sometimes founded on the wording of the rubic, but the problem is much larger than this. . . Often the meaning of a rubric can be discovered only by going back to the original source used by the redactor."[40]

2. The Seriousness of the Rubrics

We mentioned above that prescriptive rubrics bind under pain of mortal or venial sin depending on the seriousness of the matter. However, we must remember that, in general, nearly all rubrics were "serious matter" because of their relation to the cult which we offer to God. During a liturgical conference of the pre-*Mediator Dei* period. Dom de Puniet said: "In the cult which we offer to God, there is nothing of little importance, nothing of light matter."[41]

For example, Noldin states that one must have a missal to say
Mass. Without a missal, there is grave danger that the priest
would make a mistake. To put yourself in grave danger of making
a mistake is a mortal sin. Furthermore, in so important a matter,
if you must say mass, and have the text memorized, and cannot
use a missal, you must place some other book on the altar if
there are people present so that they would not be scandalized by
a priest celebrating without a missal.[42] Or again, a priest must
have two candles to celebrate Mass. To celebrate without any
candle is a mortal sin; to celebrate with only one is a venial sin.
If the candle should go out during Mass and another cannot be
found, the Mass may continue if this happens after consecration,
but if it happens before consecration, the Mass must be discontinued.[43]

The faithful observance of every rubic assured the validity of the
rite, and further, it allowed the rite to possess a certain dignity and
etiquette. Although this way of regarding the rubrics is open to
the danger of an excessive legalism which can lessen the fruitfulness of the rites, an exact observance of the rubrics can also
be seen as a virtue. The sacrifice of one's own will and one's
own preferences to observe the rubrics faithfully is a participation
in the sacrifice of Christ himself. However, here too, there is
danger of constructing an ideology which places an excessive value
on the rubrics themselves. However, to give something of a feel
for this way of regarding the rubrics, we give here a rather long
quotation from a conference given at Louvain in 1914 which explains the value of the rubrics.

In the cult which we offer to God, there is nothing of little importance, nothing of light matter. Our entire being should celebrate
its God. The soul, of course; but also the body by its attitudes.
"All you works of the Lord, bless the Lord." Our entire being is
in the service of God, and if the soul be under the guidance of
divine grace, this service of God easily and naturally extends to
every detail of our lives.

The liturgical man par excellence encompasses in his sacrifice all
that he has, all that he is. That is why the religious who offers himself entirely—even to the extent that he no longer possesses his own
will, or even his own body (according to the forceful expression of
Saint Benedict)—is the liturgical ideal; his entire life is nothing
else but a continual sacrifice of praise.

But the simple priest can also attain this ideal if in the recitation
of the office, in the celebration of his private Mass, in the adminis-

tration of the sacraments, each of the acts prescribed by the rubrics takes on the character of an act of religion. He can make constant acts of religion without ever falling into formalism. This ideal constitutes the nobility and distinction of the priest. This ideal is the enemy, of all lack of etiquette and vulgarity, as is the case of any gentleman, but in a most supernatural sense, as with the holy Cure d'Ars.

This attitude can also be characteristic even of the Christian people, if they are well instructed as to the value of the smallest ritual prescriptions and if they are faithful to practice them in the measure that it is theirs to do so.[44]

The teaching of the manuals of moral theology and their application by the liturgists and priests in general is to be viewed in the light of the theological context of the laws and rubrics which we have examined above: the emphasis on matter and form, the view that sacraments are objects more than actions, the lack of emphasis on the active role of the liturgical leader in the person of the bishop or priest, the tendency to identify liturgy and ceremonies, or liturgy and rubrics. We have seen the historical and theological context of liturgical law at the time before *Mediator Dei.* We will now turn to the encyclical itself.

NOTES

[1] The divisions we will quote here are taken in part from "Esquisse d'une histoire de la Liturgie" in *L'Eglise en Prière,* 3rd. ed. 1965. The period to the Council of Trent is by Dom B. Botte; the period after Trent is by P. Jounel. Also see the summary by P.-M. Gy in LMD 112 (1972) 13-19.

[2] These quotations use the *Jerusalem Bible* translation, New York: Doubleday, 1966. The final quotation and all the following scriptural quotations in this study are taken from the *New American Bible,* New York: Catholic Book, 1970.

[3] 1947 NOV 20. MD. (All references to the documents of the Holy See which are used in this study will be given by date. The exact reference and publishing data can be easily found in the chronological listing in the bibliography.) AAS, 594. NCWC, 69.

[4] EP, page 35.

⁵ P.-M. Gy, "La Responsabilité des évêques par rapport au Droit Liturgi·
que." LMD 112 (1972) 15-16.

⁶ Congar, "Rudolf Sohm nous interroge encore," RSPT 57 (1973) p. 282.

⁷ Dom Botte, EP p. 39.

⁸ Y. Congar, *L'ecclésiologie du haut moyen âge,* Paris 1968, 267-271. Cited
in P.M. Gy, "L'unification liturgique de l'Occident et la liturgie de la curie
romaine," RSPT 59 (1975) 601.

⁹ Gy, LMD 112, p. 16.

¹⁰ Congar, "Les Fausses Décrétales, leur reception, leur influence." RSPT 59
(1975) 281-282.

¹¹ E. Champéaux, "Les légendes savantes de la vieille Alsace." cited by Congar, Ibid., 281, note 6

¹² Congar, Ibid. p. 282.

¹³ Gy, LMD 112, p. 17.

¹⁴ Denzinger. *Enchiridion,* 737. Translation: *The Church Teaches* (St. Louis
and London: Herder, 1955) p. 264.

    Can. 13. Si quis dixerit, receptos et approbatos Ecclesiae Catholicae
ritus, in solemni Sacramentorum administratione adhiberi consuetos; aut
contemni, aut sine peccato a ministris pro libito omitti, aut in novos alios
per quemcunque ecclesiarum pastorem mutari posse; A.S.

¹⁵ Jounel, EP, page 44.

¹⁶ F. McManus, *The Congregation of Sacred Rites* (Washington: Catholic University, 1954). The decrees of the Congregation are treated on pages 131 to
154.

¹⁷ Gy, LMD 112 (1972) p. 18.

¹⁸ Jounel, EP, page 48.

¹⁹ Hans-Erich Jung, *Le renouveau de l'année liturgique dans son enracinement historique.* Thèse. Institut Catholique de Paris, 1975. Page II.

²⁰ Jounel, EP, p. 48.

²¹ Dom B. Botte, LMD 66 (1961) 70-71.

²² Gy, LMD 124 (1975) 8-9.

²³ Jean-Claude Dhôtel, *Les Origines du Catéchisme Moderne* (Paris: Aubier,
1966), pp. 322-323.

²⁴ Elisabeth Germain, *Langages de la foi a travers l'histoire* (Paris: Fayard-
Mame, 1972), 166, gives reference to Congar, *L'ecclésiologie du XIXe siecle,*
(Paris, Cerf, 1960).

²⁵ Ibid., p. 167.

²⁶ E. Schillebeeckx, *Christ the Sacrament of the Encounter with God* (New
York: Sheed & Ward, 1963).

27 John E. Rotelle, O.S.A., "Liturgy and Authority," *Worship* 47 (1973) 514-526.

28 Ibid., p. 516.

29 Can. 1256. Cultus, si deferatur nomine Ecclesiae a personis legitime ad hoc deputatis et per actus ex Ecclesiae institutione Deo, Sanctis ac Beatis tantum exhibendos, dicitur *publicus;* sin minus, *privatus.*

30 E. Jombart, "Culte," *Dictionnaire de Droit Canonique*, IV, c. 863.

31 McManus, *Congregation of Rites*, pp. 4-5.

32 MD, AAS 541-542. NCWC 22.

33 For example, the following authors make the distinction Essential-Accidental rubrics: Coelho, *Cours de Liturgie Romaine*, p. 37. Aigrain, *Liturgia*, p. 42. Sporter, *Theologia Moralis*, III. p. 25. Prumer, *Manuale Theologiae Moralis*, III, p. 58. Noldin, *Summa Theologiae Moralis*, p. 30.

34 Dominica II Passionis seu in Palmis. 18. Incipiente processione, cantari possunt Antiphonae sequentes, omnes, vel aliquae, pro opportunitate.

35 Noldin, p. 30, p. 45. Prumer, III, 58. Airgran, p. 42. Hebert, *Lecons de Liturgie* I, p. 14. Callewaert, *Liturgical Institutions*, I, 107. Haegy, *Ceremonial selon le rite Romain*, I, 2. Coelho, p. 80.

36 CIC 818. Translation: Woywod. Also see canon 733.

Can 818. Reprobata quavis contraria consuetudine, sacerdos celebrans accurante ac devote servet rubricas suorum ritualium librorum, caveatque ne alias caeremonias aut preces proprio arbitrio adiungat.

37 Prumer, *Manuale Theologiae Moralis*, p. 58.

38 McManus, *The Congregation of Rites*, p. 136.

39 F. Cimetier, "La Liturgie et le Droit Canonique," in Aigran, *Liturgia*, p. 43.

40 Martimort, in EP, edition of 1961. In the revision of the article in the third edition of EP, 1965, p. 85, there is no mention of prescriptive or directive rubrics. Compare with p. 73 of the first edition.

41 P. de Puniet, "La methode en matiere de liturgie," *Des Semaines Liturgiques* (Mont-Cesar: Louvain, 1914), p. 60.

42 Noldin, *Summa Theologiae Moralls*, p. 30.

43 Ibid.

44 P. de Puniet, Loc. cit.

I.

Liturgical Law In The Theological Context Of The Encyclical *Mediator Dei,* 1947 Nov. 20

The Historical Context of the Encyclical

Mediator Dei is situated historically in the context of the liturgical movement which had begun at the grass roots and which had been developing in various countries for nearly 50 years. In the introduction to the encyclical Pius XII states:

> You are of course familiar with the fact, Venerable Brethren, that a remarkably widespread revival of scholarly interest in the Sacred Liturgy took place towards the end of the last century and has continued through the early years of this one. The movement owed its rise to commendable private initiative and more particularly to the zealous and persistent labor of several monasteries within the distinguished Order of Saint Benedict. Thus there developed in this field among many European nations and in lands beyond the seas as well, a rivalry as welcome as it was productive of results.[1]

Pius XII then mentions some of the steps he has already taken to further the liturgical movement: his address to the Lenten preachers in Rome 1943, and the publishing of a new Latin translation of the psalms.[2]

Although the fact is not mentioned in the encyclical, Pius XII had received the Prefect of the Congregation of Rites, Cardinal Salotti, in an audience on May 10, 1946, and asked him to prepare a project for a general reform of the liturgy.[3] The "Historical Section" of the Congregation, established towards the end of 1930, had already been gathering material and making critical studies for the reform of the liturgical books.[4] On July 27, 1946, a special commission was established for the purpose of forming a plan for a general reform; however two years passed before the work was actually begun. Cardinal Salotti died on October 24, 1947, and was succeeded by Cardinal Micara. The following month, November 20, 1947, *Mediator Dei* was issued. It was only in May of 1948 that the members of the commission were appointed and the work began in earnest. Their plan, published as "Notes on the reform of the liturgy," was printed with the date December 30, 1948; consequently, we will examine this document in Chapter 2 of this study after we have examined the encyclical *Mediator Dei* issued in 1947.

Another aspect of the context of *Mediator Dei* is found in the events surrounding the liturgical movement in Germany in the early 1940's. The liturgical movement was not free from errors and excesses; nor was it free from opposition. When one aspect of the Christian mystery is emphasized, there is danger of neglecting other aspects.

Some of these fears and dangers were expressed in a "memorandum" circulated among the German bishops toward the end of 1942 by Archbishop Groeber of Freiburg. The letter closes with an appeal to the German bishops, and the Holy See, to do something about these excesses of the Liturgical Movement.

One immediate result of this memorandum was a letter from the Holy See to the German Bishops assembled at Fulda, January 18, 1943. More importantly, however, *Mediator Dei* addresses itself to many of the problems, fears, and excesses such as those mentioned in the memorandum of Archbishop Groeber. For this reason, we will give a summary of the document. However, in the more than thirty years that have passed since the memorandum appeared, many problems and perspectives have changed. We must not blame the Archbishop of Freiburg because he, or other contemporaries, did not have "foreknowledge" of the theological developments brought about by the Second Vatican Council twenty years later. The memorandum is presented here not to criticize the points but to give an insight into the historical context of *Mediator Dei*.

Archbishop Groeber considered the following 17 points disturbing elements in the Liturgical Movement:[5]

1. The Liturgical Movement is causing divisions in the ranks of the German clergy. The "kerygmatics" are calling the rest of us ignorant, lazy and disobedient.

2. They are causing dogmatic and systematic theology to be neglected.

3. They give a new definition to "Faith." Faith is no longer belief in revealed truths, but an experience, an emotion.

4. They neglect scholastic philosophy and theology and prefer modern systems, Hegel, etc.

5. They criticize contemporary institutions and contemporary forms of religious life because of the undue importance they place on the forms found in the primitive church.

6. They give too much attention to the Oriental Liturgies.

7. There is a growing influence of protestant dogma on the way in which we present the faith.

8. The limits of the Church are so extended as to include even the protestants. The heretical churches are sometimes considered a part of the total Church.

9. They give a new definition of the Church. The Church is no longer the "perfect society," but some type of biological organism.

10. There is a supernaturalism and a mysticism raging in theology and even in pastoral practice.

11. There is a surprising and terrifying growth of the emphasis placed on the Mystical Christ to the neglect of the Historical Christ. They affirm a mystical union between Christ and the Christian which can have disastrous consequences for the doctrine of grace and the sacraments.

12. An exaggerated importance is given to the Mystical Body of Christ.

13. The priesthood of the laity is exaggerated and emphasized at the expense of the functional priesthood. Some even say that the laity ratify the sacrifice by their "Amen." Others say that people must be present for Mass and disparaging things are being said about private Masses.

14. Some are saying that the communion of the faithful is an integral part of the Mass. Others say that Communion should not be distributed except during the sacrifice. Romano Guardini even thinks we ought to allow Communion with both bread and wine.

15. They give an exaggerated importance to the liturgy and tend to identify it with the life of the Church. In apostolic times private prayer held first place, not the liturgy, and we must be careful not to be taken in by contemporary liturgists who play down private prayers: the rosary, the way of the cross, the month of Mary. We have even heard them say "a parish which lives only by these popular devotions is religiously anemic." Nothing in history justifies this statement. After all, things weren't so bad before there ever was a Liturgical Movement.

If things are to be changed, this must be done only by the Holy See. There are those who are changing things on their own authority. Never have rubrics been treated so arbitrarily. New

forms of vestments. . . Some have even asked publicly to replace black vestments by dark green ones.

16. They would like to have the bishops declare that the community
Mass is the obligatory way of celebrating. They put too much
emphasis on the "strict right" of the laity to participate. They
say that the priest speaks in the name of the parish and that
it is the community which celebrates. They change the whole
ideal of Catholic priesthood because the Catholic priest is not
merely a servant of the word as is the protestant minister.
The true and unique priest is Christ. His priesthood is entrusted
to the ordained priest. The priest is sent to the community by
the bishop, he is not called by the parish. He celebrates Mass
for the parish, but he is not delegated by the parish to celebrate
Mass.

17. They are attempting to introduce the German language not
only into the administration of the sacraments as is already
allowed by the Congregation of Rites, but even want to use
German at Mass. A vernacular liturgy has often served the
forces of error as a weapon in the arsenal of heresy.

Mediator Dei is situated historically in this context. The Encyclical tries to give a certain theological balance to some of the above
mentioned problems, to limit excesses in the movement, and to
correct abuses, but even more to take the elements of the grass
roots liturgical movement and to bring them together into a movement which will nourish the life of the Church.[6]
The introduction to the encyclical tries to make it clear that it
wants to condemn only the abuses in the movement and certainly
not the liturgical movement itself.

It is Our prerogative to commend and approve whatever is done
properly, and to check or censure any aberration from the path
of truth and rectitude. Let not the apathetic or half-hearted imagine,
however, that We agree with them when We reprove the erring
and restrain the overbold. No more must the imprudent think that
We are commending them when We correct the faults of those
who are negligent and sluggish.[7]

Throughout the encyclical we find an attempt to bring into balance
opposing views, to correct errors, but to encourage what is good.
When we read the encyclical with an appreciation of its historical
context, this attempt to balance different aspects of theology is
seen even more clearly.

Part One of the Encyclical: The Nature, Source and Development of the Liturgy.

1. The liturgy is public worship.

The first question to be treated is the balance between public prayer and private prayer. In the brief historical introduction to this study, we saw that for several centuries the faithful were accustomed to find the principal nourishment for their spiritual life in their private prayers. Liturgy was the official prayer of the Church, but often it was separated from the devotional life of the Church. The central thrust of the Liturgical Movement was to place the liturgy at the center of Christian life. When something "peripheral" makes its way to the center of things, something will have to be displaced. We can appreciate the concern that was felt over the possible displacement of the private devotions that had nourished the lives of Christians for centuries.

Mediator Dei tries to bring a balance between private prayer and public prayer. It states that the fundamental duty of man is to orientate his person toward God.

> This duty is incumbent, first of all, on men as individuals. But it also binds the whole community of human beings, grouped together by mutual social ties: mankind, too, depends on the sovereign authority of God.[8]

The argumentation is as follows: Already in the Old Law we find that God made provision for sacred rites. He determines in exact detail the rules to be observed by his people in rendering him the worship he ordains. He establishes various kinds of sacrifice. He establishes a sacerdotal tribe. The enactments on all matters are minute and clear.

In the New Law, no sooner is the Word made flesh than he shows himself to the world vested with a priestly office and makes an act of submission to the Father: Behold I come to do your will. This submission continues throughout his life until he is lifted up in his saving sacrifice, and pours forth from his pierced heart the sacraments destined to impart redemption to men. This sacrifice is to continue forever afterwards and it is entrusted to the society he founded. This society, the Church, continues this action in the liturgy.[9]

> The sacred Liturgy is consequently the public worship which our Redeemer as Head of the Church renders to the Father as well as

the worship which the community of the faithful renders to its Founder, and through Him to the Heavenly Father. It is, in short, the worship rendered by the Mystical Body of Christ in the entirety of its Head and members.[10]

With this description of liturgy we have a great advance in reshaping the theological context of liturgical law. When we compare this perspective with that so often taught in seminaries, we find that the liturgy has become much more central to the Church. By bringing together the "Mystical Body" and "liturgy" we begin to leave the viewpoint which separates the laity from the liturgy and which considers the sacraments to be means of grace for individual members of the Church. By identifying the liturgy with the priestly activity of Christ, the liturgy begins to be seen as an "action" rather than just an "object."

However, the re-integration of liturgy and ecclesiology is not yet complete. The following paragraph of the encyclical, for example, says that the Church is forever present in the midst of her children. She gives them a second, supernatural birth, she gathers them around her altars, she purifies and consoles the hearts of sinners, she consecrates those whom God has called to the priestly ministry, and she fortifies with grace those destined to found a Christian family.[11] The liturgy is performed by the Church for the faithful. This is not yet the perspective we will find later, for example in the Constitution on the Church article 11.

Throughout the encyclical we find the underlying division "doctrine-discipline-ceremonies" or "creed-code-cult." The liturgy is subordinate to faith and morals and is seen principally as "means of grace." When speaking of the union between Christ and the Church, the encyclical says that they have the same object, office, and duty: 1.) to teach all men the truth; 2.) to govern and direct them; and 3.) to offer to God the pleasing and acceptable Sacrifice.[12] In the same paragraph we read that the society founded by Christ, whether 1.) in her doctrine, or 2.) in her government, or 3) in the Sacrifice and sacraments . . . is directed to strengthen and unify mankind.[13] Later, speaking again of the union of the members of the Mystical Body, the encyclical states: When the Church 1.) teaches us our Catholic faith, and 2.) exhorts us to obey the commandments, she is 3.) paving a way for her priestly, sanctifying action.[14]

Another factor which hinders the full re-integration of liturgy and ecclesiology is the stress given to the sacrificial aspects of the Eucharist. The encyclical speaks of the Eucharist almost exclusively as "sacrifice" and the means by which we are saved from sin.

The opening lines of the encyclical already indicate this perspective. "Mediator between God and men and High Priest who has gone before us into heaven, Jesus the Son of God had one aim in view when he undertook his mission of mercy . . . Sin had disturbed the right relationship between man and God . . . The children of Adam were wretched heirs to the infection of original sin . . . He gave Himself in sacrifice, as he hung from the cross, a victim unspotted unto God, to purify our conscience of dead works. Thanks to the shedding of the blood of the immaculate lamb, now each might set about the personal task of achieving his own sanctification, so rendering to God the glory due to him."[15]

This emphasis on sacrifice also influences the way we view priesthood and liturgy. The encyclical continues, paragraphs two and three, "Christ willed that his priestly life should continue without intermission in his Mystical Body, the Church. Therefore, he established a visible priesthood to offer the clean oblation. In obedience to this command, the Church prolongs the priestly mission of Jesus in the liturgy. This she does first of all around the altar where constantly the sacrifice of the cross is represented."[16]

This stress on the Eucharist as sacrifice hinders an appreciation of the pastoral and educative aspects of the liturgy. The liturgy of the word, the homily, the liturgical year, are all viewed from this aspect of "sacrifice" and consequently cannot receive their full importance. The priesthood is seen in relation to sacrifice and the "priesthood" of the baptized cannot receive its full importance. Active participation in the Eucharist is seen principally under the aspect of sacrifice: we are to become a victim with Christ.

While we stand before the altar, then, it is our duty so to transform our hearts that every trace of sin may be completely blotted out, while whatever promotes supernatural life through Christ, may be zealously fostered and strengthened even to the extent that, in union with the Immaculate Victim, we become a victim acceptable to the Eternal Father.

The prescriptions in fact of the sacred Liturgy aim, by every means at their disposal, at helping the Church to bring about this holy purpose in the most suitable manner possible. This is the object not only of readings, homilies and other sermons given by priests, as also the whole cycle of mysteries which are proposed for our commemoration in the course of the year, but it is also the purpose of vestments, of sacred rites and their external splendour.

All these things aim at "enhancing the majesty of this great Sacrifice, and raising the minds of the faithful by means of these visible signs of religion and piety, to the contemplation of the sublime truths contained in this Sacrifice.

All elements of the Liturgy, then, would have us reproduce in our hearts through the mystery of the Cross the likeness of the Divine Redeemer according to the words of the Apostle of the Gentiles "With Christ I am nailed to the Cross. . ." We become a victim along with Christ to increase the glory of the Eternal Father.[17]

2. The Liturgy is Exterior and Interior Worship.

The second problem of "balance" which is taken up by the encyclical is that of exterior and interior worship. We have noted earlier that the distinction "doctrine-discipline-liturgy" can lead to the identification of "liturgy" and "rites and ceremonies" and "the *external* elements of cult." For those who only saw the liturgical movement from a distance, without knowing its aims and goals, could be led to believe that it was only concerned with changing externals: altars, vestments, ceremonies. In this light, the liturgical movement would be suspected of missing the point, for the real worship must be interior, in spirit and truth. The encyclical brings these two aspects of worship into balance. "The worship rendered by the Church to God must be, in its entirety, interior as well as exterior."[18] Five reasons are listed as to why the cult must be exterior: the nature of man is composed of body and soul; we come to love the things unseen by things that are seen; every impulse of the heart expresses itself through the senses; the worship of God must be not merely individual but social, and therefore external; exterior worship reveals the unity of the Mystical Body. However, the encyclical then states: "But the chief element of divine worship must be interior."[19]

The insistence that there is no division or opposition between exterior and interior worship has several important consequences. First of all, we cannot identify liturgy with the externals or the rubrics and think of internal piety only in terms of private devotions.

It is an error consequently and a mistake to think of the sacred Liturgy as merely the outward or visible part of the divine worship or as an ornamental ceremonial. No less erroneous is the notion that it consists solely in a list of laws and prescriptions according to which the ecclesiastical hierarchy orders the sacred rites to be performed.[20]

When the liturgy is identified only with external ceremonies, the role of the liturgy can be seen as secondary to the essence of the sacraments, the matter and form. The principal consideration is given to the way in which the act is effective in itself (*ex opere operato*). The insistence of the encyclical that liturgy is not merely the ornamental ceremonies causes a re-valuation of the ceremony itself. The encyclical states that the Eucharistic sacrifice and the sacraments are effective not only from the act itself, "but if one considers the part which the immaculate spouse of Jesus Christ takes in the action, embellishing the sacrifice and sacraments with prayer and sacred ceremonies,. . . its effectiveness is due rather to the action of the Church (*ex opere operantis Ecclesiae*), inasmuch as she is holy and acts always in closest union with her Head."[21]

> In the spiritual life, consequently, there can be no opposition between the action of God, who pours forth His grace into men's hearts so that the work of the redemption may always abide, and the tireless collaboration of man, who must not render vain the gift of God. No more can the efficacy of the external administration of the sacraments, which comes from the rite itself (*ex opere operato*) be opposed to the meritorious action of their ministers or recipients, which we call the agent's action (*opus operantis*).[22]

The way is open for a more active understanding of the role of the minister; and also, if the ceremonies are so important, the work of revising them will also be seen as important.

The encyclical then takes up some of the problems that were current at that time. It discusses the "new theories on objective piety" and the relative importance of private prayer and liturgical prayer. This discussion can be seen in the light of the "memorandum" of Archbishop Groeber (especially point 15). Again there is a balance: it is an error to say that all religious exercises not directly connected with the liturgy should be omitted. Private prayer and devotional exercises are "not only highly praiseworthy but absolutely indispensable."[23] However, private prayers are "merely human acts."

> Unquestionably liturgical prayer, being the public supplication of the illustrious spouse of Jesus Christ, is superior in excellence to private prayers. But this superior worth does not at all imply contrast or incompatibility between these two kinds of prayer. . . . Both tend to the same objective: until Christ be formed in us.[24]

Consequently there is no opposition between the action of God and the action of man; no opposition between the efficacy of the liturgy which comes from the rite itself, and that which comes from the ministers or recipients; no opposition between public prayer and private prayer, between the ascetical life and the liturgy. And the encyclical adds, in the same paragraph: "Finally there is no opposition between the jurisdiction and teaching office of the Ecclesiastical Hierarchy, and the specifically priestly power exercised in the sacred ministry."[25] The encyclical does not go beyond stating that there is "no opposition" between these two aspects of liturgy, authority-ministry, and does not re-unite the two in the person of the bishop, who (as we have seen in the historical introduction to this study) was once both the one responsible for regulating the liturgy and the leader of the liturgical assembly. However, the door is open for this development later.

3. The Liturgy is under the Hierarchy of the Church.

The third question to be treated by the encyclical is directly related to the topic of our study: obedience to liturgical law. The liturgical movement, as we have seen when considering the historical background of the encyclical, not only brought a renewed interest in the liturgy and liturgical rites but also brought a desire for certain changes—which were sometimes put into practice without the consent of the Holy See. It is necessary then, to restate the fact that the Holy See alone has the right to regulate the liturgy. But here again, we see a balance of different viewpoints.

The argument begins by stating that the Church is a society, and as such requires an authority and hierarchy. Though all members of the Mystical Body partake of the same blessings and pursue the same objective, they do not all have the same powers, nor are they all qualified to perform the same acts.[26]

Only to the apostles and to those on whom their successors have imposed hands is granted the power of priesthood. This power is not given to mankind in general but only to designated persons, through the sacrament of Holy Orders, which gives a "character" conforming them to Christ the Priest and qualifying them to perform "official acts of religion," that is, the liturgy.[27]

In this line of reasoning, where the Church is seen primarily as a "society" and priesthood as a "power to offer sacrifice," and a "qualification to perform official acts of religion," we find a twofold division: those who possess the priesthood (the Apostles, their successors, and those they have ordained) and those who do not possess priesthood. The former possess authority over the liturgy; the laity, however, do not. The priest is "set apart" from the faithful who have not received this consecration.

However, this reasoning is modified by the paragraphs which follow. Now a division is made between the priest, who chiefly or ordinarily is the one who performs the Liturgy, and the Church authority. The first paragraphs of this section of the encyclical seemed to reunite the liturgical-leader and the liturgical-authority (as we have seen them united in the person of the bishop in the early Church). The encyclical stated that there is no opposition between the jurisdiction and teaching office of the hierarchy and the specifically priestly power exercised in the sacred ministry.[28] However, the encyclical makes a further distinction: the priest performs the liturgy in the name of the Church; therefore the liturgy must be regulated by the Church, that is, the Hierarchy. "Church" is identified with the "authority" and not with the "object" of the prayer.

Once again we find the viewpoint "doctrine-discipline-ceremonies," The encyclical states that the liturgy is intimately bound up with doctrinal propositions; consequently as it is the duty of the Church to safeguard doctrine, so it is the duty of the Church (hierarchy) to safeguard and regulate the liturgy.

In this context, the Pope discusses the epigram: "Lex orandi, legem credendi constituit." (The law for prayer is the law for faith). Traditionally, this epigram was a way of saying that the prayer of the Church is one of the places to which we can go to find what the Church believes. However, in a context where doctrine is prior to liturgy, the epigram loses its meaning. In fact, Pius XII turns the epigram around and states that it is perfectly correct to say: "Lex credendi legem statuat supplicandi," (Let the rule of belief determine the rule of prayer).[29] Note, however, that several paragraphs later the Pope himself uses the epigram in its original sense. When he wishes to prove that, in a sense, the faithfully *do* offer the Divine Victim at Mass, he turns to the prayers of the Eucharistic Sacrifice as proof of the doctrinal statement. He quotes the references to "My sacrifice and yours. .;" "we your servants and your whole household . . . offer to you;" . . . the plural number of the prayers of offering, "we" offer to You. . . Consequently, Pius XII uses the epigram "The rule of prayer is the rule of faith," by turning to the liturgy to show what we believe about offering the sacrifice.[30]

The encyclical then states that "from time immemorial the

ecclesiastical hierarchy has exercised this right in matters liturgical,"
(that is, to control and regulate the liturgy).[31] If "hierarchy" here
really means "the Apostolic See" then we should not say that
the right has been exercised "from time immemorial."

The encyclical states that the liturgy which has remained nearly
unchanged since the Council of Trent and which we have experienced as "unchanging" is not "unchangeable." There are
"divine elements which cannot be changed in any way," but
there are also human components which admit of modifications
"as the needs of the age, circumstance and the good of souls
may require, and as the ecclesiastical hierarchy under guidance
of the Holy Spirit, may have authorized."[32]

When stating the criteria for changing the liturgy, the encyclical
again uses the division "doctrine-discipline-ceremonies" and states
that changes are due to 1.) a more explicit formulation of doctrine,
or 2.) advances in ecclesiastical discipline (for example, receiving
Communion under a single species), or 3.) development in the fine
arts, such as painting and music, or devotional practices, such as
devotion to the Sacred Heart.[33]

These changes, however, cannot be left to the private initiative.
The encyclical states that when things are left to imprudent innovations by private individuals and particular churches many abuses
can enter the ceremonies. This is why Pope Sixtus V established
the Congregation of Rites and charged it with the defense of
the legitimate rites of the Church and the prohibition of any
spurious innovation. "This body fulfills even today the official function of supervision and legislation with regard to all matters touch-
ing the sacred Liturgy."[34]   Thus, the role of the Congregation is
seen mainly in its "restrictive" and "policing" aspects, prohibiting
changes.

The encyclical then moves from the role of the Congregation of
Rites to the role of the Sovereign Pontiff himself, and states:

> It follows from this that the Sovereign Pontiff alone enjoys the
> right to recognize and establish any practice touching the worship
> of God, to introduce and approve new rites, as also to modify
> those he judges to require modification. Bishops, for their part,
> have the duty and the right to carefully watch over the exact ob-
> servance of the prescriptions of the sacred canons respecting divine
> worship. Private individuals, therefore, even though they be clerics,
> may not be left to decide for themselves in these holy and vener-
> able matters, involving as they do the religious life of Christian
> society along with the exercise of the priesthood of Jesus Christ
> and the worship of God; concerned as they are with the honor due
> to the Blessed Trinity, the Word Incarnate and his august Mother

and the other saints, and with the salvation of souls as well. For the same reason no private person has any authority to regulate external practices of this kind, which are intimately bound up with Church discipline and with the order, unity and concord of the Mystical Body and frequently even with the integrity of Catholic faith itself.[35]

Consequently, the regulation of the Liturgy belongs to the Pope alone, because of its subordination and relation to doctrine and discipline.

The bishop has the role given him in Canon law (see Canon 1261); he is to see to it that the rubrics are exactly observed. The bishop, in the context of *Mediator Dei* seems to be separated from both of the roles which he possessed in the early Church with regard to the liturgy. The regulation of the liturgy, and the authority over the ceremonies, is no longer the right of the bishop but the right of the Holy See alone. The role of the bishop as the leader of the liturgical celebration is given to the priest. The bishop is himself a priest, of course. However, the encyclical reflects the ordinary experience of the Church at this time and the one who "chiefly performs the liturgy" is the priest.[36] Whenever the encyclical makes reference to the bishops to whom the encyclical is addressed, it is in relation to their duty to safeguard the observance of the rubrics on the part of "priests." It seems that when a priest is ordained a bishop he loses something of his liturgical role for he is no longer the one who is chiefly concerned with the sacred liturgy but now must be more concerned with the discipline of the liturgy rather than celebrating it himself. The perspective in which the bishop himself is the principal liturgist of the diocese is not explicitly presented in *Mediator Dei*. This is important for the understanding of liturgical law and the obedience due to it.

The priest has no special rights in this regard. In the paragraph quoted above we have seen mention of 1.) The Sovereign Pontiff (who alone enjoys the right to modify the liturgy), 2.) The bishop (who must see to it that the rubrics are observed), and 3.) private individuals. Priests are not seen in a relationship of assisting the bishop, but, just like any other private individuals, have no authority to regulate liturgical practices.

Following this presentation of the relation between liturgical law and the authority of the hierarchy, the encyclical balances this emphasis on "society and authority" by saying:

The Church is without question a living organism, and as an organism in respect of the sacred liturgy also, she grows, matures, develops, adapts and accommodates herself to temporal needs and circumstances.[37]

However, this view is not developed further. It is in developing this view of the Church—the Church seen as a living organism, the Mystery, the People of God, sacrament of salvation—and balancing it with the idea of Church as a society that we will find the change in the way we consider liturgical law.

The encyclical then mentions some of the abuses that can result when private individuals begin to change things. Again we are aided in understanding these warnings by recalling the memorandum of Archbishop Groeber quoted above. The memorandum warned that the vernacular liturgy has often been a weapon in the arsenal of heresy; the encyclical says that the Latin is an "effective antidote for any corruption of doctrinal truth." But the idea is balanced by saying that "in spite of this, the use of the mother tongue in connection with several of the rites may be of much advantage to the people; but the Apostolic See alone is empowered to grant this permission."[38]

The memorandum stated that the liturgical movement was giving excessive importance to the rites of the primitive Church. The encyclical warns against an exaggerated attachment to ancient usage, but balances the statement by saying that "assuredly it is a wise and most laudable thing to return in spirit and affection to the sources of the sacred Liturgy."[39] However, in returning to the sources we must not reject contemporary forms. In the reason given for this, we again see "doctrine, discipline, ceremonies." The encyclical states that "clearly no sincere Catholic can refuse to accept the formulation of Christian doctrine more recently elaborated . . . and to hark back to old formulas. No Catholic in his right senses can repudiate existing legislation . . . to return to the sources of canon law. Just as obviously, it is unwise and wrong to discard new patterns of liturgical rites and to go back to the rites and usage of antiquity."[40]

This section of the encyclical on the nature of the liturgy and and liturgical law concludes by stating:

In every measure taken, then, let proper contact with the ecclesiastical hierarchy be maintained. Let no one arrogate to himself the right to make regulations and impose them on others at will. Only the Sovereign Pontiff, as the successor of St. Peter, charged by the divine redeemer with the feeding of his entire flock, and with him, in obedience to the Apostolic See, the bishops "whom the Holy Ghost has placed to rule the Church of God," have the right and duty to govern the Christian people. Consequently, Venerable Brethren, whenever you assert your authority—even on occasion with wholesome severity—you are not merely acquitting yourselves of your duty; you are defending the very will of the founder of the Church.[41]

Part Two of the Encyclical: Eucharistic Worship.

The mystery of the Holy Eucharist is seen to be "the culmination and center of the Christian religion."[42] However, the mystery is viewed almost exclusively under its sacrificial aspects. Christ entrusted his sacrifice of the cross to the Church to remit the sins we daily commit. He established a priesthood to make this same offering. The encyclical insists that the Eucharist is a true and proper act of sacrifice and this sacrifice is "the supreme instrument whereby the merits won by the divine redeemer upon the cross are distributed to the faithful."[43] The Mass is of its very nature a public and social act because the sacrifice of the cross was a public and social act, and this is so whether the faithful are present or not.[44]

This insistence on "sacrifice" to the exclusion of other aspects of the Eucharist can be seen in the context of the liturgical movement's teaching that the Eucharist was not only a Sacrifice. but also a holy meal; a meal at which the faithful should be present, and take part, especially by receiving Holy Communion. The encyclical, again, tries to balance the positions by saying that though some things are good and desirable, it is an error to say that they are necessary.

1. The priesthood of the laity.

The first area discussed is the question of whether or not the laity are "priests." In the context of a stress on the Mass as "sacrifice" and the priest as the one "who offers sacrifice," the encyclical states that, in this sense, the laity are not priests. "The people, since they in no sense represent the divine redeemer and are not a mediator between themselves and God, can in no way possess the sacerdotal power."[45] They do not "concelebrate" with the priest, and it is an error to say that the priest should not celebrate privately when the people are absent.

However, there is a sense in which the laity do offer the divine victim. The encyclical now speaks of baptism, membership in the Mystical Body, the "character" given them in baptism conforming them to Christ the priest and by which "they are appointed to give worship to God. Thus they participate according to their condition, in the priesthood of Christ."[46]

Once these two viewpoints are placed next to one another, the encyclical mentions certain errors with regard to Eucharistic worship. First, it is an error to "disapprove altogether of those Masses which are offered privately and without a congregation."[47] At the same time the Church wants the faithful to be present. It is an error to say that priests cannot offer Masses at different altars at the same time because they would be separating the community and imperil its unity.[48] The encyclical does not state that this is good; the encyclical says that to say it is impossible is an error. But everything possible is not always preferable.

2. Means of promoting active participation.

The encyclical praises the efforts to have the faithful participate in the Eucharist. The use of the missal by the faithful allows the priest and the faithful to pray together and makes the liturgy an act in which all may share. The "dialogue Mass" is commended "when it is in complete agreement with the rubrics."[49] However, we are in a context where the liturgy is directed primarily and almost exclusively toward God. Consequently, the dialogue Mass even though it fosters participation, must not replace the high Mass, "which, though it should be offered with only the sacred ministers present, possesses its own special dignity due to the impressive character of its ritual and the magnificence of its ceremonies."[50]

The encyclical states that not everyone is capable of a dialogue Mass; for some it is too complicated. It is wrong to say that these people cannot participate in the Mass because they cannot follow the missal. "They can adopt some other method which proves easier for certain people; for instance, they can lovingly meditate on the mysteries of Jesus Christ or perform other exercises of piety or recite prayers which, though they differ from the sacred rites, are still essentially in harmony with them."[51] It is not a question here of adapting the Mass to meet the mentality of people and their capabilities, but a question of encouraging the people to participate in the Mass as best they can.

This section of the encyclical directs that a diocesan advisory committee be set up in each diocese to promote the liturgical apostolate.[52] We can only speculate on the result this would have had on pastoral liturgy if it were actually carried out in 1947. However, this will not be the last time that we see the call for diocesan liturgy committees.

3. Holy Communion.

The liturgical movement had begun to speak of the Mass as not only a sacrifice but also a meal. The encyclical now turns to errors that can follow from this statement. A meal seems to imply eating; if the Mass is a meal, perhaps the reception of Communion is necessary. The encyclical states that this is an error.

> They err from the path of truth, who do not want to have Masses celebrated unless the faithful communicate; and those are still more in error who, in holding that it is altogether necessary for the faithful to receive Holy Communion as well as the priest, put forward the captious argument that here there is question not of a sacrifice merely, but of a sacrifice and a supper of brotherly union, and consider the general Communion of all present as the culminating point of the whole celebration. It cannot be over-emphasized that the Eucharistic Sacrifice of its very nature is the unbloody immolation of the divine victim.[53]

While "it cannot be over-emphasized" that the Mass is a sacrifice, this fact must be balanced with the other aspects of the celebration. The above statement does not say that it is an error to consider the Mass under the aspects of a meal, but it is an error to say that the faithful *must* receive Communion. Once the fact is established that the Communion of the faithful is not absolutely necessary, the encyclical goes on to say how very important and desirable it is. Christ said "Take and eat. . ." The faithful should participate not only by a spiritual Communion but by a sacramental one . . . with hosts which have been consecrated at that very Mass. It is desirable that they participate every day.[54] The encyclical then takes up several other errors and tries to bring a balance between conflicting viewpoints. Again it is good to see these discussions against the background of the memorandum of Archbishop Groeber. There is no conflict between the historical Christ, the Eucharistic Christ, and the Christ in glory. There may be reasons for distributing Communion outside of Mass but it is most desirable to receive Communion during the Mass. These discussions can be seen as an effort to accept the good aspects of the liturgical movement, while not condemning former practices. With regard to receiving Holy Communion during Mass, the encyclical states that this manifests more clearly the living unity of the Mystical Body.[55] To my knowledge, this is one of the first times that the "sign value" of the rite itself is stressed. Formerly, liturgical practices were judged primarily in the light of prior doctrinal positions (Is private Mass possible?. . . . Is the

Communion of the laity absolutely necessary?. . . . Must Mass be celebrated in the vernacular?. . .). In the future, we will find increasing emphasis placed on the importance of the authentic sign value of the rite.

Part Three of the Encyclical: The Divine Office and the Liturgical Year.

The treatment of the divine office begins with the statement that the office is intended to sanctify the hours of the day—the view which we will see growing in importance, yet not implemented at this time. (Morning prayer was usually said in the evening, and evening prayer sometimes before noon.) The paragraph which treats the history of the office, speaks of the Church as the continuation of the praying Christ, and tells of how the early Christians gathered for prayer. But "thanks to the work of monks and those who practiced asceticism, these various prayers in the course of time become ever more perfected and by the authority of the Church, are gradually incorporated into the sacred liturgy."[56]

The restriction of these prayers to the monks, not only "perfected" the prayers but made them more complicated and less able to serve the needs of the faithful. By the authority of the Church, these prayers are incorporated into the liturgy, that is, made official, and thus restricted to those who are officially deputed by the Church to pray them.

> The divine office is the prayer of the Mystical Body of Jesus Christ, offered to God in the name and on behalf of all Christians, when recited by priests and other ministers of the Church and by religious who are deputed by the Church for this.[57]

Although the office is the prayer of the Mystical Body, it is not said by the whole Body but in the name of, and on behalf of them. The real implications of the encyclical in calling the liturgy the prayer of the Body of Christ are not yet fully realized.

The treatment of the liturgical year, which begins with Advent rather than Easter, gives a brief paragraph to each of the liturgical seasons.[58]   Then the encyclical turns again to "errors of modern authors" and discusses the relation of the liturgical year and the concept of "mystery." The liturgical year is not a cold and lifeless representation of past events but each feast, each mystery, brings its own special grace for salvation. The problem of the historical Christ and the glorified Christ is discussed again, and we again find heavy emphasis on sin, suffering and sacrifice.

Since his bitter sufferings constitute the principal mystery of our redemption it is only fitting that the Catholic faith should give it the greatest prominence. This mystery is the very center of divine worship since the Mass represents and renews it every day and since all the sacraments are most closely united with the cross. [59]

Part Four of the Encyclical: Pastoral Directives.

This final section of the encyclical is once again concerned with bringing different ideas into balance. As the encyclical has emphasized the liturgy, it must now encourage non-liturgical devotions. When the Mass is seen to be the center of Christian life, this does not mean that we can no longer say the rosary; and the rosary is encouraged. As the mysteries of our redemption and the life of Christ become more central in the spiritual life, this does not mean that we should neglect Mary and the saints; and their devotions are encouraged. As sacramental confession is seen more in its liturgical context, this does not mean that confessions of devotion are foreign to the spirit of Christ. On the one hand, it is an error to say that only the liturgical rites are of any real value, and on the other hand the criterion for judging pious exercises is whether or not they make the liturgy loved and spread. [60] Again it is a question of bringing ideas into balance: It would be wrong and dangerous to reduce all exercises of piety to the methods and norms of liturgical rites; however, it is necessary that the spirit (*afflatus*) of the liturgy should influence pious exercises.

It is at the end of the encyclical that we first find reference to a concept that will be mentioned more and more in the following documents: the liturgical *spirit*. In speaking of this *spirit* the encyclical says that we must strive to obey the legislation, "however, the most pressing duty of Christians is to live the liturgical life, and increase and cherish its supernatural spirit." [61] The importance of liturgical instruction in the seminaries is mentioned; and the seminarians are not only to learn the rubrics but they are to "understand the sacred ceremonies and to appreciate their beauty." [62]

The encyclical closes by stating that it is hoped that this encyclical will not only correct errors but will instill the supernatural *spirit* of the liturgy into daily life. We are to "hold fast to what is good," and preserve good order: "God is not the God of dissension but of peace" (I Cor 14:33).

CONCLUSION

The teaching of the encyclical *Mediator Dei* on liturgical law is basically that of the Code. The liturgical authority rests with the Apostolic See alone, the bishops are to see to it that the laws are properly carried out, and no private individual, even if he is a priest, may change anything in the liturgy.

However, we begin to see a change in the theological context of this legislation. The separation between "liturgy" and "church" begins to lessen by the understanding of liturgy as the prayer of the Mystical Body of Christ. Yet, the liturgy remains, by and large, in the context of "doctrine, discipline, ceremonies," and thus is seen as an action posterior to the Church. The Church is viewed primarily as the liturgical authority and the reciprocal relation of liturgy and ecclesiology is not yet clearly stated. However, as the liturgy is identified with the prayer of the Mystical Body, the laity are more closely associated with the liturgy; but here also, the association is incomplete and the liturgy is still considered as the prayer of the priests performed in the name of the Church and for the laity. However, we see an insistence on the fact that liturgy is not merely the externals, and not merely the rubrics.

The largest problem of this context is perhaps the failure to give the bishop his full liturgical role. His authority is seen to be possessed only by the Pope, and his liturgical role is exercised by the priest. There is a separation between the one leading the liturgical celebration and responsible for its accomplishment, and one who is legislating the rites and prayers of the celebration. Liturgical law remains one of the items that must be governed by Church authority. The normative role of the liturgy and its function to structure the Church will be brought out only in later documents. But first the liturgy must come out from under the excessive dominance of dogmatic theology and moral theology and canon law, and by the clear authentic expression of the sacred mysteries, and the experience of the role of the liturgical mysteries. by the hierarchy and laity, the liturgy must find its rightful place in the Church.

We are again faced with the two norms given by St. Paul in the First Letter to the Corinthians: *tradition* and *order*. However, we are now further away from the sources than was St. Paul and the Church at Corinth and it is more difficult to discover what are the most authentic elements of the tradition and what elements should be removed from the liturgy. And although the liturgical assembly itself is now highly "ordered" it must find its proper place and right order among many other devotions and practices and among the other aspects of the Christian experience and teaching. This will be the task of the documents which follow.

NOTES

¹ MD 523. NCWC 4. (The references to the encyclical are to page number as the text in the AAS does not number the paragraphs, AAS 39 (1947) 521-600. The English translation quoted in this study is the Vatican Library Translation published by the NCWC; references are to page number.)

² MD 523. NCWC 5. The new translation of the psalms was introduced by the motu proprio "In cotidianis precibus," 1945, March 24.

³ 1955 MAY 25. CSR. De instauratione liturgica Maioris Hebdomadae. S. Hist. no. 90. page 10.

⁴ Ibid. See also: A. Frutaz, *La Sezione storica della Sacra Congregazione dei Riti.* Typ. Pol. Vat., 1963.

⁵ See LMD 7 (1946) 97-114.
1. Memorandum de S.E. Mgr Groeber, 1942.
2. Lettre Circulaire aux évêques membres de la conference Episcopal de Fulda au sujet de questions Liturgiques. 1943 JAN 18.
3. Réponse de S. Em. Le Cardinal Innitzer au Memorandum De S. Exc. Mgr Groeber. 1943 FEB 24.

⁶ Dom Lambert Beauduin, "L'Encyclique 'Mediator Dei,' " LMD 13 (1948) 11.

⁷ AAS 524. NCWC 6.
Nobis igitur officium est, quod recte sit factum dilaudare ac commendare, quod vero etiusto itinere deflectat, continere vel reprobare.
Haud tamen reputent qui inertes ac segnes sunt, idcirco a Nobis comprobari, quod errantes reprehendimus audacesque refrenamus; neque imprudentes tum se a Nobis exornari laudibus existiment, cum neglegentes corrigimus atque ignavos.

⁸ AAS 525-526. NCWC 7.
Quod quidem officium si homines singillatim primo loco obligat, at humanam quoque communitatem universam, socialibus ac mutuis nexibus conformatam obstringit, cum et ipsa a summa Dei auctoritate pendeat.

⁹ AAS 528. NCWC 9.

¹⁰ AAS 528-529. NCWC 10.
Sacra igitur Liturgia cultum publicum constituit, quem Redemptor noster, Ecclesiae Caput, caelesti Patri habet; quemque christifidelium societas Conditori suo et per ipsum aeterno Patri tribuit; utque omnia breviter perstringamus, integrum constituit publicum cultum mystici Iesu Christi Corporis, Capitis nempe membrorumque eius.

¹¹ AAS 529-530. NCWC 11.

¹² AAS 528. NCWC 9.

¹³ Ibid.

[14] AAS 536. NCWC 17.
Dum catholicam fidem nos docet, nosque ad christianis obtemperandum praeceptis adhortatur, Ecclesia sternit ac munit viam ad actionem suam maxime sacerdotalem, sanctitatisque effectricem.

[15] AAS 521. NCWC 3.

[16] AAS 522. NCWC 4.

[17] AAS 558-559. NCWC 37-38.

[18] AAS 530. NCWC 11.
Universus autem, quem Ecclesia Deo adhibet, cultus, ut externus, ita internus esse debet.

[19] AAS 531. NCWC 12.
At praecipuum divini cultus elementum internum esse debet: . . .

[20] AAS 532. NCWC 13.
Quamobrem a vera ac germana sacrae Liturgiae notione ac sententia omnino ii aberrant, qui eam utpote divini cultus partem iudicent externam solumnodo ac sensibus obiectam, vel quasi decorum quemdam caerimoniarum apparatum; nec minus ii aberrant, qui eam veluti meram legum praeceptorumque summam reputent, quibus Ecclesiastica Hierarchia iubeat sacros instrui ordinarique ritus.

[21] AAS 532. NCWC 13.

[22] AAS 537. NCWC 17.
In spirituali igitur vita nulla intercedere potest discrepantia vel repugnantia inter divinam illam actionem, quae ad perpetuandam Redemptionem nostram gratiam in animos infundit, ac sociam laboriosamque hominis operam, quae donum Dei vacuum non reddat oportet; itemque inter externi Sacramentorum ritus efficacitatem, quae *ex opere operato* oritur, atque eorum bene merentem actum, qui eadem impertiunt vel suscipiunt, quem quidem actum *opus operantis* vocamus.

[23] AAS 534. NCWC 15.
. . . tum profecto eadem non modo summis laudibus digna, sed prorsus necessaria sunt.

[24] AAS 537. NCWC 18.
Procul dubio liturgica precatio, cum publica sit inclitae Iesu Christi Sponsae supplicatio, privatis precibus potiòre excellentia praestat. Quae tamen potior excellentia neutiquam significat duo haec precandi genera inter se discrepare vel repugnare. Uno enim eodemque cum sint studio animata, una simul etiam confluunt ac componuntur secundum illud "omnia et in omnibus Christus" ad idemque contendunt propositum, donec in nobis formetur Christus.

[25] AAS 537. NCWC 18.
Denique inter Ecclesiasticae Hierarchiae iurisdictionem legitimumque magisterium ac potestatem illam, quae proprie sacerdotali dicitur, quaeque in sacro exercetur ministerio.

[26] AAS 538. NCWC 18.

[27] AAS 538. NCWC 19.

[28] AAS 537. NCWC 28. Text quoted above, note 25.

[29] AAS 540. NCWC 20-21.

[30] Ibid.

[31] AAS 541. NCWC 21.
Nullo non tempre Ecclesiastica Hierarchia hoc in rebus liturgicis iure usa est, divinum instruendo ordinandoque cultum, eumque novo semper, ad Dei gloriam christianorumque profectum, spendore ac decore ditando.

[32] AAS 541-542. NCWC 22.
Sacra enim Liturgia ut humanis, ita divinis constat elementis; haec autem, ut patet, cum a Divino Redemptore constituta fuerint, nullo modo ab hominibus mutari possunt; illa vero, prout temporum, rerum animorumque necessitates postulant, varias commutationes habere possunt, quas Ecclesiastica Hierarchia, S. Spiritus auxilio innixa, comprobaverit.

[33] AAS 542-543. NCWC 22-23.

[34] AAS 543. NCWC 24.

[35] AAS 544. NCWC 24.
Quamobrem uni Summo Pontifici ius est quemlibet de divino cultu agendo morem recognoscere acstatuere, novos inducere ac probare ritus, eosque etiam immutare, quos quidem immutandos iudicaberit; Episcopis autem ius et officium est vigilare diligenter ut sacrorum canonum praescripta de divino cultu seduluo observentur. Haud igitur fas est privatorum arbitrio, etsi iidem ex Cleri ordine sint, sacras atque venerandas res illas permittere, quae ad religiosam christianae societatis vitam pertineant, itemque ad Iesu Christi sacerdotii exercitium divinumque cultum, ad debitum sanctissimae Trinitati, Incarnato Verbo, eius Genitrici augustae ceterisque caelitibus honorem reddendum, et ad hominum salutem procurandam attineant; aedemque ratione privato nemini ulla facultas est externas hoc in genere actiones moderari, quae cum Ecclesiastica disciplina et cum Mystici Corporis ordine, unitate ac concordia, immo haud raro cum catholicae etiam fidel integritate coniunguntur quam maxime.

[36] AAS 539. NCWC 20.
Quoniam igitur sacra Liturgia imprimis a sacerdotibus Ecclesiae nomine absolvitur, . . .

[37] AAS 544. NCWC 24.
Ecclesia procul dubio vivens membrorum compages est, atque adeo in iis etiam rebus, quae ad sacram respiciunt Liturgiam, succrescit, explicantur atque evolvitur, et ad necessitates rerumque adiuncta, quae temporum decursu habeantur, sese accommodat atque conformat, sarta tamen tectaque servata suae doctrinae integritate.

[38] AAS 545. NCWC 25.

[39] Ibid.
Ad sacrae Liturgiae fontes mente animoque redire sapiens profecto ac laudabilissima res est, . . .

[40] AAS 546. NCWC 26.

41 AAS 546. NCWC 26-27.
Omnia igitur ita fiant ut debita servetur cum Ecclesiastica Hierarchia con-
iunctio. Nemo sibi arbitrium sumat normas sibimet ipsi decernendi eas-
demque ex voluntate sua ceteris imperandi. Summus dumtaxat Pontifex,
ut beati Petri successor est, cui divinus Redemptor curam concredidit universum pascendi gregem, unaque simul Episcopi, quos Apostolicae ob-
temperantes Sedi, "Spiritus Sanctus posuit . . . regere Ecclesiam Dei"
iure officioque pollent christianum gubernandi populum. Quamobrem, Ven-
erabiles Fratres, quotiescumque—salutari etiam, si oporteat, adhibita sever-
itate—auctoritatem tuemini vestram, non modo officium vestrum adimple-
mini, sed ipsam Ecclesiae Conditoris in tuto ponitis voluntatem.

42 AAS 547. NCWC 27.
Christianae religionis caput ac veluti centrum sanctissimae Eucharistiae
Mysterium est, . . .

43 AAS 551. NCWC 31.
Augustum autem altaris Sacrificium eximium est veluti instrumentum, quo
promerita e divini Redemptoris Cruce orta credentibus distribuuntur.

44 AAS 557. NCWC 36.

45 AAS 553-554. NCWC 33.
Populum contra, quippe qui nulla ratione Divini Redemptoris personam
sustineat, neque conciliator sit inter se ipsum et Deum, nullo modo iure
sacerdotali frui posse.

46 AAS 555. NCWC 34.
Baptismatis enim lavacro, generali titulo christiani in Mystico Corpore
membra efficiuntur Christi sacerdotis, et "charactere" qui eorum in animo
quasi insculpitur, ad cultum divinum deputantur; atque adeo ipsius Christi
sacerdotium pro sua condicione participant.

47 AAS 556. NCWC 35.

48 AAS 556. NCWC 36.

49 AAS 561. NCWC 39.

50 Ibid.

51 AAS 561. NCWC 40.
At ii alia ratione utique possunt, quae facilior nonnullis evadit; ut, verbi
gratia, Iesu Christi mysteria pie meditando, vel alia peragendo pietatis
exercitia aliasque fundendo preces, quae, etsi forma a sacris ritibus different, natura tamen sua cum iisdem congruunt.

52 AAS 561-562. NCWC 40.

53 AAS 563. NCWC 41.
Ex veritatis igitur itinere ii aberrant, qui sacris operari nolint, nisi si christiana plebs ad divinam mensam accedat; ac magis etiam ii aberrant, qui ut
contendant necessarium omnino esse christifideles una cum sacerdote Eucharistica pasci dape, captiose asseverent heic agi non de Sacrificio solummodo,
sed de Sacrificio ac caena fraternae communitatis, atque sacram synaxim
ponant, communiter actam, quasi totius celebrationis culmen.

54 AAS 564. NCWC 42.

[55] AAS 566. NCWC 44.
. . . quibus vivens Mystici Corporis unitas clarius ad altare patescat.

[56] AAS 572-573. NCWC 49-50.

[57] AAS 573. NCWC 50.
Est igitur "Divinum Officium" quod vocamus, Mystici Iesu Christi Corporis precatio, quae christianorum omnium nomine eorumque in beneficium adhibetur Deo, cum a sacerdotibus aliisque Ecclesiae ministris et a religiosis sodalibus fiat, in hac rem ipsius Ecclesiae instituto delegatis.

[58] AAS 577-579. NCWC 54-56.

[59] AAS 580. NCWC 56.
Quoniam vero acerbi eius cruciatus praecipuum constituunt mysterium, ex quo salus nostra oritur, catholicae fidei consentaneum est in maxima illud sua luce poni; est siquidem divini cultus veluti centrum, cum Eucharisticum Sacrificium cotidie illud repraesentet et innovet, et cum Sacramenta omnia arctissimo vinculo Cruci coniungantur.

[60] AAS 584-586. NCWC 60-62.

[61] AAS 591. NCWC 66.
Quidquid ad externum religionis cultum attinet suam profecto habet gravitatem; attamen pernecesse potissimum est christianos Liturgiae vitam vivere, eiusque supernum alere ac refovere afflatum.

Note: The word "spiritus" is not used in the encyclical for "liturgical spirit." Each time that the NCWC speaks of "spirit of the liturgy" the Latin word is "afflatus."

In this regard, see: Romano Guardini, *Geist der Liturgie*. English Translation: *The Spirit of the Liturgy* (New York, 1954). French Translation: *L'esprit de la liturgie*, (Paris, 1929).

[62] AAS 594. NCWC 69.

II.

A Study Of The Documents Influencing The Theological Context Of Liturgical Law 1947 To 1960

At the same time that *Mediator Dei* warned against unauthorized changes in the liturgy, the Holy See itself was preparing an official reform of the liturgy. We noted above that already in 1946 Pius XII had asked Cardinal Salotti to begin preparing a general reform of the liturgy. However, the work did not really get underway until 1948.

On May 28, 1948, the members for the commission to form the project for a general liturgical reform were appointed. Rev. Ferdinando Antonelli, O.F.M., the general director (*relatore generale*) of the historical section of the Congregation of Rites, was appointed general director of the commission. Rev. Joseph Löw, C.Ss.R., was appointed assistant. Rev. Annibale Bugnini, C.M., editor of the *Ephemerides Liturgicae,* was made secretary of the commission.

The commission held its first meeting on June 22. Present were Cardinal Micara, who had succeeded Cardinal Salotti as prefect of the Congregation of Rites; Msgr. Alfonso Carinci, secretary of the Congregation; Fr. Antonelli and Fr. Löw; Rev. Anselmo Albareda, O.S.B., prefect of the Vatican Library; and Rev. Agostino Bea, S.J., rector of the Pontifical Biblical Institute. The discussions of the commission led to the printing of the *Memoria sulla Riforma Liturgica* which was given to the members of the commission.

1948 DEC 30 The Memoria: Notes for a Liturgical Reform

The *Memoria* was printed with the date of December 30, 1948. However, it was not actually completed until June of 1949. It was presented by Fr. Antonelli, director of the commission, who stated that it was principally the work of Fr. Löw.[1] The *Memoria* is divided into four chapters; we will look at each of them in turn.

Chapter 1. The necessity of a liturgical reform.

This first chapter mentions in a general way some of the factors that made a reform of the liturgy necessary; for example, the increase in the number of feast days of saints, the introduction of new octaves, and the increasing complexity of the rubrics of the breviary. Mention is then made of the great progress which has been made in liturgical research. The critical editions of many liturgical texts have appeared; there has been progress in Christian archaeology, patristic studies, the history of art and sacred chant. These studies will permit the liturgical reform to be scientifically based on historical principles.

The *Memoria* then stated that the liturgical movement has met with great success and has sensitized clergy and laity alike to appreciate the beauty of the liturgy. But at the same time, the movement has made us more aware of the need for reforms in the rites so that they can be even more fruitful. Furthermore, the pastoral situation of the clergy also calls for a revision of the liturgy. With priests responsible for ever increasing apostolic duties, many do not have the time to really pray the divine office. If the office were shorter, if it were less complicated, it would better serve its purpose.

Chapter 2. Fundamental Principles.

The mention of "fundamental principles" (or general principles, higher principles) will become increasingly important in this study of the context of liturgical law. We saw in the introduction that liturgical law was formerly considered primarily under the aspect of the individual rubrics rather than rubrics which are the application of "higher principles." The *Memoria* stated three principles upon which the reform of the liturgy is to be based.[2]

Principle: "There must be a balance between the tendency to conserve the old and desire to be innovative." *Mediator Dei* warned against an exaggerated attachment to ancient rites.[3] The ancient usage must not be esteemed more suitable and proper simply on the ground that is it old. The liturgy is not a museum. But we must also resist the errors of those who wish to make the liturgy such an expression of modern life that they want only modern vestments, modern languages, modern music, prayers and gestures. With the help of recent critical liturgical studies, we must preserve the valuable aspects of the tradition and avoid the danger of useless innovations.[4]

Principle: "Given the fact that the liturgy is by its very nature primarily directed to the worship of God, the cult of the saints must be subordinated to the divine cult. Consequently, in the revision of the liturgical calendar, the temporal and weekday cycle must take precedence over the sanctoral cycle." This will imply giving more importance to the Sunday liturgies and especially to the Easter liturgy.

In this connection a description of the liturgy is given: "The liturgy is by its very nature the external expression of the worship which the Church offers for the whole of humanity to God the Creator and Lord of the Universe, and to Christ the Redeemer of the human race; this cult is pre-eminently that called *latria* (adoration in its proper sense)."[5] The liturgy is seen as something which the Church *does;* it is not yet considered as a self-expression of the Church itself. Also the liturgy is considered to be directed to God; there is no mention of its educative dimension. There is also a tendency to identify liturgy with externals.

Principle: "Given the fact that the liturgy forms an organically interrelated unity, the reform will have to consider all the aspects of the liturgy." A change in the relative importance of saints' feasts and Sunday celebrations implies a new classification of feasts and a modification of the liturgical calendar. A change in texts implies a change in the chants. The office must be coordinated with the missal. Consequently, nine areas of reform were projected:

1. The Classification of Feasts and the Liturgical Calendar
2. The Roman Breviary
3. The Roman Missal
4. The Roman Martyrology
5. The Books of Chant
6. The Roman Ritual
7. The Ceremonial for Bishops
8. The Roman Pontifical
9. The "Codex Iuris Liturgici"—A Code of Liturgical Law.[6]

Chapter 3. An integrated plan for the reform of the liturgy.

The *Memoria* then considers each of these in turn. However the largest portion of the book (pages 20 to 304) is devoted to the first two of these reforms. The classification of feasts, treated both here and in the first supplement to the *Memoria,*[7] involves not only a simplification of the existing system, but also the search for the theological and historical principles upon which the simplification can be based.[8]

Suggestions for the reform of the office fill over a hundred pages of the *Memoria.* Because of the difficulty that priests in the active ministry find in reciting the office due to its length, there was proposed the possibility of having two different obligations to recite the Office. The "Contemplative Church" would celebrate the entire Office. The "Active Church" would be bound only to a morning prayer of Matins-Lauds and an evening prayer of Vespers-Compline, with an optional mid-day prayer.[9]

The remaining seven items on the above list are treated only summarily in the *Memoria*. Concerning the missal, however, there is mention of the fact that the liturgical movement has made us aware of the pastoral dimensions of the Mass and the importance of the active participation of the faithful. This poses the very delicate problem of celebrating the Mass in the vernacular languages. Another problem will be the revision of the internal "structure" of the Mass.[10]

The final item on the list was the "Code of Liturgical Law." The *Memoria* stated that such a code was necessary because the clergy need to be able to find the rubrics all in one place. At that time, the rubrics were scattered throughout the several liturgical books and their revisions, various papal documents, and the over four thousand official decisions of the Congregation of Rites. This multitude of sources, with its frequent contradictions, was seen to be one of the reasons that some clerics were becoming indifferent toward liturgical law and why the rubrics were sometimes considered of little importance. Such a code would also serve to stabilize and perpetuate the reform. The fundamental principles for this code of rubrics should be "simplicity" and "clarity." These would be achieved if the code adopted the style of the present Code of Canon Law and presented the rubrics in simple, concise articles.[11]

Chapter 4. The practical implementation of the reform.

The final pages of the *Memoria* outline the stages of implementing this reform. The first phase will be a discussion of the *Memoria*. Then the reform will pass to sub-commissions for the various aspects of the work: biblical, historical, poetic, musical, rubrical, stylistic. The reform will start with the breviary in which will be brought together many of the different elements of the reform, for example, the classification of feasts and the calendar. The reform will then continue with the missal and the martyrology. The crowning achievement will be the code of liturgical law.[12]

The *Memoria* was printed and given to the members of the commission on June 25, 1949 and was presented to Pius XII the following month. Cardinal Micara thought it would be good to have an even larger base of consultation and, on November 3, 1949, with the express consent of Pius XII, the *Memoria* was given *sub secreto* to Dom Bernardo Capelle, O.S.B., abbot of Mont Cesar, Rev. Josef A. Jungmann, S.J., professor at the University of Innsbruck, and to Msgr. Mario Righetti. It was felt that Dom Capelle could bring a French viewpoint to the work; Jungmann, the German mentality; and Msgr. Righetti, a pastoral perspective. Their comments on the *Memoria* were co-ordinated by Fr. Bugnini and published in a second supplement to the *Memoria,* dated April 21, 1950.[13] A third supplement, containing historical and critical material for the reform of the calendar, was printed in 1951.[14]

1951 FEB 09 The Restoration of the Solemn Paschal Vigil.

On November 22, 1950, Cardinal Lienart, president of the assembly of the cardinals and archbishops of France, formally petitioned the Holy See for permission to celebrate the Easter Vigil in the evening rather than in the morning of Holy Saturday. The German bishops sent a similar request to the Holy See. Cardinal Lienart states that an evening celebration would allow many of the faithful to be present at the liturgy, whereas modern working conditions do not permit most people to be free to attend church early Saturday morning.[15] Pius gave this request to the commission for the liturgical reform and the result was the "Rite for the Restoration of the Solemn Paschal Vigil."

The decree which introduces the rite states that the primary reason for the reform is the fact that the "inner sense" of the vigil implies that it takes place at night rather than in the morning. The rite, originally accomplished during the night which preceded the Resurrection of the Lord, during the course of time was moved back, first to the early evening, then to the afternoon, and finally to the morning of Holy Saturday. This change was accompanied by various other changes in the rites to the detriment of the original symbolism.[16] Thus, the primary motive for the restoration given in the decree is the principle of "authenticity." In order for the rite to be a true vigil, in order that the symbolism of the light ceremony express its full meaning, in order that the praises sung anouncing "This is the night when. . ." be an authentic expression of the actual time of day, the rite is to be celebrated in the evening or at night and not in the morning.

The decree then mentions the role that recent liturgical studies have played in the restoration: Our times have seen the birth of the growing desire, fostered by investigations into the history of the liturgy, to restore especially the Paschal Vigil to its original splendor and its original place as a vigil, namely the night preceding the Resurrection.[17]

Then mention is made of the petition of the bishops: "Another reason in favor of this restoration is pastoral—that the faithful might attend in larger numbers. Holy Saturday is no longer a non-work day as it once was and consequently many of the faithful cannot be present for the rites when they are held early in the morning."[18]

The restored rite is approved facultatively for one year. The local ordinary is to report back to the Congregation of Rites concerning the attendance and devotion of the faithful.

Turning to the rite itself, perhaps one of the most important innovations was the renewal of the Baptismal promises, in the vernacular, during the litany of the saints. Although this innovation, introduced after a certain amount of discussion and hesitancy,[19] is very important in the restored rite, we will mention here only a minor detail of the rubrics, but a detail which is very important for our understanding of liturgical law.

At the beginning of the rite, the blessing of the new fire, rubric 3 reads "the ministers with the cross and holy water and incense stand either at the entrance or in front of the church or in the vestibule, wherever *the people* can best follow the rite."[20] This is the first time that I have found the rubrics explicitly take account of the fact that there are people present. For the reading of the lessons the rubric reads: "The lessons are read by a reader, in the middle of the choir, before the Paschal candle so that he has the altar at his right and the body of the church on his left. The Celebrant and ministers, clerics *and people,* sit and listen attentively." Commenting on this "listen attentively" *sedentes auscultant,* Martimort writes that the formulation of the rubric is remarkable. Finally we are reminded that the readings are to be listened to and everyone has a right to hear them. The usual, unintelligible way in which the lessons are chanted contributed to the rubric which we find in the ceremonial, namely: the celebrant is always to read privately whatever the lector is singing. Now, however, the rubric states that the celebrant, the ministers, the people and the clergy are to *listen* (rather than reciting their breviary). Martimort takes exception with the fact that the rubric indicates that the reader is not facing the people but facing the wall and the paschal candle, with his back to the celebrant—thus making the "listening attentively" more difficult. However, he goes even further in his interpretation of the rubric:

If the faithful are to sit and listen attentively, their books closed, they should be able to hear not only with their ears but with their intelligence. This is impossible unless the four prophecies are to be read in the vernacular. Note that this interpretation was instinctively adopted in nearly all the parishes from the very first year the vigil was celebrated. The entire structure of the new rite is so clearly pastoral that such an interpretation seems altogether natural. . . . It seems to me that there are very serious reasons to consider the formulation of this new rubric *sedentes auscultant* to be able to be legitimately interpreted as a discreet but certain invitation to draw such a pastoral conclusion.[21]

Whether or not we agree with the interpretation of the rubric given by Martimort, one thing is clear: once the rubrics themselves begin to take into account the fact that the laity are present at the rites and that they have an active part in the liturgy, something new has entered into our study of liturgical law.

1955 MAR 23 On the reduction of the rubrics to a simpler form.

With this decree of the Congregation of Rites, the first steps toward a reform of the calendar and the classification of feasts are taken. The committee for the general liturgical reform treated this question first in the "notes for a liturgical reform" and they present here those modifications which can be implemented without reprinting the liturgical books.

The decree states the reason for this simplification:

In our present times, priests—especially those with the care of souls—are often burdened with new and increasing apostolic duties, even to the extent that often they do not find it possible to have that peace of mind necessary for the recitation of the divine office. Therefore, some of the local ordinaries have petitioned the Holy See that this difficulty be removed and that the complicated system of rubrics might be simplified.[22]

Reading this simplification of rubrics twenty years later, one can receive the impression that this simplification left the rubrics still very complicated; however such a judgment only emphasizes the extent of the reforms following the Council.

With regard to the calendar: the degree and rite of semi-double is suppressed. Liturgical days which up to now were celebrated as semi-doubles will be celebrated with the rite of simplex. However, the Sundays which were formerly semi-doubles now become doubles. What this means in practice is that the Sunday liturgy

will be replaced by a saint's feast much less frequently, in accord
with the general principle stated in the *Memoria:* The liturgy is by
its very nature directed primarily to the worship of God, and the
cult of the saints must be subordinated to the Divine Cult.

The number of "facultative" or optional rubrics is increased.
The priest is given the freedom to choose which Mass text he will
use on certain days, but these options are still very few. Also,
the celebrant can choose to celebrate the ferial office or the feast
of the saint of double rank on the weekdays of Lent. Up to this
time the rubrics did not give the slightest liberty of choice with
regard to the office. However, this option is given only for "private
recitation" and for the first time a distinction is introduced between
the public and private recitation of the office.

However, we should not put too much importance on the options
given by the rubrics at this time. Most priests did not study the
rubrics themselves to determine what office or Mass they would
say, but daily consulted the *Ordo*—a book which listed in detail
the rubrics to be followed on that particular day. In a commentary
on this decree of the Congregation of Rites Martimort writes:

> The new rubrics go into effect January 1, 1956. This is a convenient
> date because the diocesan *Ordos,* edited according to the new prin-
> ciples, will give all the priests the daily presciptions which will
> dispense them from any personal effort to interpret the new rubrics.[23]

In this same commentary by Martimort, it is interesting to compare
the language used to describe certain parts of the liturgy with the
language of *Mediator Dei.* We have seen the liturgy described as
the priestly prayer of Jesus Christ, the center of the Christian
spirit. . . However, when examining certain concrete aspects of
the rites, Martimort speaks of the preces at Sunday prime as a
"nightmare"[24] and calls the lectionary used during octaves "a
drudgery."[25] One can love the liturgy and see, at the same time,
the need for reform.

1955 NOV 16 The restoration of the liturgy of Holy Week.

The decree of February 9, 1951, which introduced the restored
rite for the Pashcal Vigil, indicated that the local ordinary was to
report to the Congregation of Rites concerning the attendance and
devotion of the faithful.

Nearly all of these reports from the bishops were positive and
enthusiastic. We might expect this from the French and German
bishops who had petitioned for the new rite, but the same response

was received from around the world. Cardinal Gilroy of Australia
wrote:

> The experiment was an unqualified success. The Cathedral was half-
> filled when the ceremonies began at 10:45 p.m. At midnight when
> Mass began there was a full congregation. Three priests assisted me
> in the distribution of Holy Communion. With profound reverence
> a very large number of people communicated. It is safe to say there
> were very few in the congregation who did not receive Holy Com-
> munion. All who participated in the ceremonies were profoundly
> impressed by them.[26]

Cardinal Gilroy's letter is typical of many of the letters received.
Archbishop Alter from Cincinnati reported that 1.) there was a
substantial increase in the number of people participating in the rite;
2.) the new rite allowed for a greater understanding and appreciation
of the liturgy; 3.) There was a genuine and deep expression of faith
and devotion during the renewal of baptismal vows; and 4.) a
consoling number of adults received Holy Communion.[27]

The only difficulties reported by the bishops seem to be with
certain "extra-liturgical" elements which were the custom in Italy
or in Europe but with which we were not familiar in the United
States: the traditional ringing of the bells of Rome on Saturday
morning; the blessing of the homes on Holy Saturday with the new
Easter Water blessed that morning. . . Another objection concerned the fact that many priests were exhausted after a long day
of hearing confessions of those who wished to make their Easter
Duty. It was better to have the liturgy in the morning when the
priests were not so tired.

The majority of the letters from the bishops were not only
positive, but more than that, many of the bishops felt that the
restoration of the Vigil was such a pastoral success that the reform
ought to be extended to the whole of Holy Week.

In view of this request, the committee for the reform of the
liturgy printed a book entitled, "The Restoration of the Liturgy
of Holy Week." This book contained a history of this development,
a selection of the letters from the bishops, the request for the
extension of the reform, and the general lines that this reform
would take. This report was presented to the Congregation of
Rites, which was now under Cardinal Caietano Cicognani, who had
become prefect on December 7, 1953. The report is signed by
Fr. Antonelli and bears the date of May 25, 1955. In view of these
developments, the Congregation of Rites issued the decree for the
reform of Holy Week, November 16, 1955.

The decree introducing these reforms is similar to that for the restoration of the Vigil. The new rites are inspired by the desire that *1) the rite be authentic*—that is, that the rite express more clearly the holy things which it is meant to signify; and *2) the rite be pastorally fruitful*—that is, allow the Christian people, as far as possible, to attend, understand, and take an active part in the rites so that the liturgy may be, in a real sense, the center of their Christian life.

The decree begins by stating the importance of the Holy Week liturgies. It tells how, during the Middle Ages, the rites were gradually celebrated earlier in the day—not without harm to the sense of the rites and not without confusion between the Gospel narratives and their liturgical representations.[28] In 1642, Urban VIII changed the last days of Holy Week from holidays to work days because of the social conditions of the time. However, this has resulted in the fact that the liturgy for these days has become an affair of the clergy, and it takes place in churches that are practically empty.

> Clearly this situation is regretable. The liturgy of Holy Week, not only because of its special dignity, but also because of its special sacramental force and efficacy, should nourish the Christian life. The pious devotions, which should be called extra-liturgical, which now take place during the afternoons on these sacred days, cannot compensate for this liturgical efficacy.[29]

The decree of the Congregation of Rites is followed by an instruction which has as its purpose to facilitate the transition to the new rites and to aid the full and fruitful participation of the faithful. The first article of this instruction states a principle which is important for our study of liturgical law:

> Local ordinaries should carefully make provisions that the priests, especially those who are entrusted with the care of souls, are well informed not only about the celebration of the restored rites for Holy Week, but also well informed as to their liturgical meaning and pastoral implications.[30]

This is the first time I have found the rubrics themselves and the official texts insisting that the rubrics must be not only obeyed but also *understood.* An obedience which springs from an understanding of the law is more likely able to communicate that meaning to the faithful.

The changes in the rites themselves we will not consider in detail here. We will note only the fact that the underlying principles of authenticity and pastoral effectiveness can be seen throughout the new rites. They are to be celebrated at times which correspond more closely to the biblical narratives and times which will enable more of the faithful to be present and participate.[31] We also find in these rubrics an alternate, simplified set of directives for churches which do not have deacon and subdeacon.[32] We noted the first appearance of the "people" in the rubrics; this practice is now extended to all the rites. The rubrics mention the people in the responses and hymns. The beginnings of role differentiation are seen in the rubrics; as noted above, the priest celebrant need not read privately what is being read or sung by another minister—even if he is a layman.

A very important change is found in the rubrics for Holy Thursday. The rubric following the Gospel reads:

13. After the Gospel, it is very fitting to give a short homily which illustrates the most important mystery recalled in this Mass: namely, the institution of the Holy Eucharist and the sacerdotal order, and also the commandment of the Lord regarding brotherly love.[33]

Here we have a double restoration. This is the first time that the *homily* is indicated in the rubrics, and it is the first time that the word "homily" is used. Msgr. Jounel, commentating on this double restoration, says:

Preaching as a liturgical act and as mystery, is an integral part of the liturgy of the word. However, it was practically unknown under these essential aspects since the end of the patristic period.[34]

The reform for the liturgy of Holy Week is another step in restoring the liturgy to the center of the devotional life of the faithful. In the course of history a devotional vacuum was experienced by Christians in the place which should have been occupied by the Holy Week liturgy once these rites became inaccessible to them. This vacuum was often filled by developing popular devotions to take the place of the liturgy. The present instruction invites us to reconsider these devotions.

23. In various localities and with various peoples, many popular customs have arisen in connection with the celebration of Holy Week. Let the local Ordinaries and the priests who have the care of souls see to it that these customs, of whatever sort, which seem to foster solid piety, he brought into harmony with the restored rite for Holy Week. Furthermore, they should instruct the faithful with regard to the superior value of the sacred liturgy which has always and continues today to far exceed, by its very nature, other

kinds of devotions and customs, no matter how praiseworthy they may be.[35]

1957 JUL 29 Consultation of the Episcopate concerning a reform of the Roman Breviary.

The first projected area of the reform presented in the *Memoria* was "the classification of feasts and the Liturgical Calendar." After the decrees concerning the simplification of the rubrics, a change in the classification of feasts, a revaluation of the Sunday, a revision in the Paschal Vigil and Holy Week, we might expect a reform pertaining to point two of the projected reform: The Roman Breviary.

This reform was being prepared by the commission; however, in their meeting of November 25, 1955, Cardinal Cicognani proposed the idea of asking the episcopate for their advice concerning this reform. The proposal met with the approval of the commission and after being presented to Pius XII in an audience on January 31, 1956, a letter was sent to the metropolitans under the date of May 17, 1956.[36]

This letter first spoke of the importance of the divine office, and cited *Mediator Dei* in this regard. Then the letter states: "as this matter concerns not only personal piety, but the life and activity of the entire Church"[37] the Holy Father has asked for the opinion and suggestions of the metropolitans, archbishops and bishops concerning the reform of the Breviary.

The letter of May 17 stated that the replies were to arrive in Rome within six months; however, it was soon realized that this time was too short and was extended to a year. Towards the end of May, 1957, most of the letters had arrived and the suggestions placed on 1800 cards and coordinated by Fr. Bugnini, secretary of the commission, together with Fr. Carlo Braga. The results were analyzed by Fr. Löw, reviewed by Fr. Antonelli, and presented in a Fourth Supplement to the *Memoria,* July 29, 1957.

The consultation of the bishops concerning a reform of such importance points toward an ecclesiology in which the bishops have a larger liturgical role than merely to safeguard the observance of the rubrics; however, the consultation had a negative aspect of slowing down the work of the commission while the consultation was in process. Consequently, the practical results of the reform are only first seen in the Code of Rubrics of 1960.

About 85% of the metropolitans responded (341 of 400). And because the bishops were not asked for their opinion on any specific proposals but were left perfectly free to give any type of comment they wanted, the responses touch upon many different aspects of the Breviary.

The replies are co-ordinated by the number of times a specific item was mentioned in the letters. The item mentioned most often was "simplify the hymns." This suggestion was found 79 times, that is in about 23% of the replies. The next most frequently mentioned item concerns the vernacular languages; 61 letters or 17.9% of the response asked for permission to use the vernacular in at least some form or part of the office. This percentage is not large, especially when placed in the context of the number of bishops who explicitly ask that the Latin be retained.[38]

The ten letters received from the United States are about equally divided on the issue. Nine of the letters mention the language of the office. About half strongly favor the retention of the Latin: "The sentiment here is overwhelmingly opposed to the introduction of the vernacular." "All the bishops here are for the retention of Latin, even in private recitation." "Some have asked to say the Breviary in English, but I am not for it; it would not be good for the Church or for priests." Others ask for some degree of the vernacular, either in private recitation, or a part of the private recitation. One suggested the readings in English and the psalms and orations in Latin. Or, permit the English on alternate years or certain seasons. Or, shorten the office and say it twice each day, once in English and once in Latin.

One of the strongest statements for the vernacular is found in the letter from Archbishop Alter of Cincinnati.

The use of the vernacular:

1. That Latin be retained for all choir recitations of the Divine Office.

2. That the vernacular language be made at least optional for private recitation. It is the predominant option of our bishops and priests of this Province that the recitation of the Breviary in the vernacular will promote personal piety and more effective preaching of God's holy word.

3. That our minimum request is to have Vespers and Compline in the vernacular for all parish churches and oratories. At present the Office of Vespers has been universally replaced by popular devotions because of the inability to understand Latin and profit by its recitation.[39]

This letter is interesting for several reasons; not only because of the relation made between the prayer life of the priest and his effectiveness as a preacher of God's word, but also because of the fact that the letter mentions office celebrated with the people. Throughout the letters from the bishops the office is considered primarily, or even exclusively, the prayer of the priest. "The recitation of the breviary, after the Holy Sacrifice of the Mass, is the priestly prayer par excellence."[40] From the context we see that this implies not the prayer of the priestly people of God, but the prayer of the ordained priest. The *Supplement* discusses at what point in the day the priest should interrupt his apostolic work to say his breviary. The letter of Archbishop Alter also reminds us of the fact that has often been repeated in history: when the Liturgy no longer serves the needs of the people, this need is filled by non-liturgical prayers and popular devotions.

Commenting on the letters received, Fr. Löw states that there are several reasons for the present crisis with regard to the divine office. First of all, there is the fact that the apostolic activity of priests is such that the office cannot be given the time necessary to be prayed properly. Second, the hours have been detached from their chronological time and the "obligation" to recite the office has become attached to the whole block of the office so that the office is considered something which must be said during the space of 24 hours, rather· than a prayer which should be said morning and evening according to the sense of the hour. Third, the sense of "obligation" has become so strong as to outweigh the sense of "prayer."[41] Fr. Löw states that what is needed, first and foremost, is to create a change in the mentality of the priests and in the way they consider the divine office.[42]

One of the most important changes in the office, then, is to rediscover the relation between the hours and their chronological time. The office should really serve as a morning prayer and an evening prayer. However, the bishops are very hesitant in this regard. Whereas 21 bishops ask that the office be reduced to these two times, and another 7 bishops asked for some modification in the structure of the office (about 8% of the bishops), over 52% ask that the traditional structure be preserved.[43] And some bishops asked that there be no changes at all.

One bishop quotes Saint Thomas (Summa I-II q. 97, art. 2) where he states that the modification of any positive law will naturally bring with it a certain lessening of discipline. Consequently, if there is to be a change, it must be not just for something "a little better" but for something "much better" in order to compensate for this falling off of discipline which necessarily accompanies any change in legislation. Therefore, the bishop states, we must be very cautious in this matter. It is not easy to say "no" to requests for change, but that is the proper action here. The bishop concludes by stating that he is among that large number who are not only satisfied with the liturgy as it is, but who consider any change not only undesirable but dangerous to the Church.[44]

1958 SEP 03 Instruction on Sacred Music and the Liturgy

The final document of the liturgical reform during the pontificate of Pius XII bears the date of what was then the feast of St. Pius X, September 3. It is titled: "The Sacred Music and the Sacred Liturgy according to the norms of the encyclical letters of Pope Pius XII 'The Art of Sacred Music' and 'The Mediator between God and Man.' "[45] Martimort and Picard, in their commentary on the instruction, state that we can see in the document something of a spiritual testament of the deceased pope and the summary of the immense work which he had accomplished in the area of pastoral liturgy.[46]

The instruction was prepared by the commission for the liturgical reform working together with experts in Sacred Music.[47] The document covers 33 pages in the *Acta;* this is the first time that the Congregation of Rites issued an instruction of such a general nature. It treats not only of music but of the nature of the liturgy, liturgical language, and the active participation of the faithful.

The structure of the Instruction is similar to the structure of the Code of Canon Law in that the Code begins with a section of General Norms which define terms and give the general principles of interpretation for the Code (canons 1 to 86) and then the longer section of more specific legislation (canons 87 to 2414). The Instruction first defines its terms (Articles 1 to 10: "liturgy," "pious exercise," "high Mass," "sacred music"). The next section treats of General Norms (articles 11 to 21) followed by a longer section of specific legislation or Special Norms (articles 22 to 118).

1. Definitions and General Norms.

Liturgical actions and Non-liturgical actions. The first term to be defined by the instruction is "liturgy." We find the first article of the instruction places side by side the description of the liturgy given in *Mediator Dei* and the definition given in the Code. We have noted above that the former follows upon an ecclesiology which sees the Church in terms of the Mystical Body; the latter sees the Church in its institutional role.

The sacred liturgy consists in the totality of the public worship of the Mystical Body of Jesus Christ, that is of the Head and his members. Therefore, "liturgical actions" are those sacred actions which, whether instituted by Jesus Christ or instituted by the Church, are performed in their name according to the liturgical books approved by the Holy See, by persons legitimately deputed for this, and which offer the cult which is due to God, the saints and the blessed. Other sacred actions are called "pious exercises" whether or not they are performed in a church, with or without the presence of a priest.[48]

The last part of this article attemps to draw a clear line between liturgical actions and non-liturgical acts. A clear, juridical distinction will be useful for the legislation which follows. For example, with regard to the language of the liturgy the instruction states that the liturgical language is Latin (with certain exceptions indicated in the liturgical books) whereas pious devotions may be in any language useful to the people.[49] The music defined as "religious music" according to article 10 of the instruction, may be used during "pious exercises" but is excluded from liturgical actions.[50] We recall that in canon law the bishop can exercise a certain control over pious exercises, whereas the liturgy is under the exclusive control of the Holy See.[51] The definition of the liturgy presented by the instruction is perhaps the most juridical understanding of the liturgy that we will meet in this study.

Despite the usefulness of this distinction, the liturgy itself sometimes seems unwilling to submit to a strictly juridical definition of what is liturgical and what is not. For example, is the homily liturgical or not? It is not a text found in a liturgical book approved by the Holy See; it is also permitted in the vernacular. It escapes the juridical control of the Holy See over other liturgical texts. These facts might indicate that the homily is a "pious devotion." However, the homily is given (in last place) in the list of liturgical acts in *Mediator Dei.*[52] We saw above that the rubrics for Holy Thursday call for a homily to be given. Is the homily on Holy Thursday more liturgical because it is called for by the rubrics than the homily on Easter Sunday? Evidently the distinction between liturgical and non-liturgical acts is not intended to be used in this way. If the homily were considered a "pious exercise" it would not be allowed at Mass by the instruction, for article 12 directs that liturgical acts are not to be mixed with non-liturgical acts.[53]

Strictly speaking the instruction indicates that the first hymn at Benediction is a pious exercise whereas the second hymn is a liturgical devotion.[54] This distinction may be useful, for example as to the choice of the language for the hymn. Such a distinction, although legitimate in itself, must not be given an importance it does not deserve.[55]

Public prayer—Private prayer. Article 2 of the instruction states:

> The most holy sacrifice of the Mass is an act of public cult offered to God in the name of Christ and of the Church, no matter where or how it is celebrated. Therefore the term "private Mass" should be avoided.[56]

The meaning of the word "public" in connection with the liturgy can be understood in several different ways. We will only note here the fact that the instruction stresses an ontological perspective: The liturgy is *in itself* a public act. The sacrifice of the cross was a public act, in itself and by its very nature it has a public dimension. The Mass is always a public act. Whenever the priest offers the Sacrifice it is of its very nature a public act in as much as he who offers it acts in the name of Christ and the Church, as was stated in *Mediator Dei.*[57]

After the Council there is stress on the fact that the liturgy is a sign. And because the liturgy is necessarily a sign, it must therefore be public. The Constitution on the Liturgy states that the liturgy should be celebrated in a way which makes provision for a communal celebration with the presence and active participation of the faithful. This way of celebrating the liturgy is to be preferred to a celebration that is individual and quasi-private (SC 28).

These two perspectives are complementary and in no way contradict one another. However, to emphasize the fact that the liturgy is public "in itself" and to neglect the importance of the liturgy as "sign" is to elevate the public nature of the liturgy to an ontological level that was never intended. For example, the following quotation from John Miller appeared in *Theological Studies* in 1957:

> The quality *public* means that, regardless of the external appearance of any particular act of worship of the Church, each and every member of the Church prays and offers on one hand, and is affected for the better, on the other.

He continues by saying that even if the priest would say Mass entirely alone

> every Catholic throughout the world would be praying and offering through him. Whether you advert to it or not, you are acting

in and affected by every single liturgical act performed no matter where in God's great world![58]

The difficulty with such a statement is that it needs the balance of a semiological perspective; the phrase "regardless of the external appearance of any particular act" cannot be dismissed as unimportant to the question.

The same distinction is made in article 40 concerning the divine office. The office is always the public prayer of the Church whether it is said "in choir," "in common," or "by one person alone"— the text uses "a solo" in place of "private recitation." However, this change of vocabulary was often ignored and people continued to speak of private recitation of the breviary, as well as private Masses.

Sung Mass—Read Mass. Article 3 of the instruction distinguishes between "sung Mass" (in cantu) and "read Mass" (lecta). In English the terms high Mass and low Mass were ordinarily used, perhaps because singing was not restricted to a "sung Mass" but "read Masses" could have singing also. In actual practice, the read Mass sometimes had more singing than the sung Mass because at the read Mass the entire congregation could sing English hymns. On the other hand, many high Masses were sung by only the priest celebrating at the altar and the organist and choir (often reduced to one and the same person playing the organ and singing) with the congregation not singing at all. Perhaps this practice was not universal; however, the present author recalls playing the organ and singing "solo" high Masses, (often several times a day, during this period and not feeling in any way that the practice was limited to his particular seminary.)

Once again, the distinction is made in view of the legislation to follow. For example, article 18 states that popular religious chants can be used at low Mass but cannot be sung at high Masses. While this type of legislation preserved the purity of the high Mass, it also hindered "liturgical" singing during low Mass. During a low Mass one could sing only hymns. The legislation concerning high and low, sung and read Masses is modified in the rubrics of the instruction on music in 1967. The distinction itself is no longer found in the missal of 1970.

The following articles of the opening section of the instruction give definitions to specific kinds of sacred music: Gregorian chant, sacred polyphony, modern sacred music, sacred organ music, popular religious chants, and religious music. Some of these distinctions are more clear than others. Again, they are destined to facilitate the legislation which follows; however, liturgically and musically the distinctions were not always easy to apply. The distinction between "popular religious chants" and "religious music" was not always clear, nor was it always easy to tell the difference between sacred organ music and non-sacred organ music.

Each of the definitions and distinctions of this introductory section of the instruction serves a purpose in the legislation which followed. If the rubrics are to be formed into a "Code of Rubrics" we must begin by definition of terms and general norms. However in this instruction we have a indication that the liturgy is not entirely adaptable to the same type of juridical precision as is usually found in the Code of Canon Law.

2. Specific Norms.

Degrees of Participation. If the first part of the instruction leaves something to be desired, the specific norms mark a great advance in the liturgical legislation. The instruction goes far beyond merely encouraging some form of active participation and states clearly that "the Mass, by its very nature, requires that everyone present participate in the action according to his proper role."[59] Furthermore, the instruction gives "degrees" of participation.

This is the first time that I have found this type of rubric. Formerly the rubrics indicated what was permitted and what was forbidden. Here we have rubrics which state that some things are good, and others are even better. The question of liturgical obedience in this context cannot be answered simply yes or no—it is right or wrong. The instruction presents ideals and goals to be achieved.

At a high Mass, the people can begin by singing the responses; the second degree would have them sing the ordinary, and the third degree would include the propers.[60] At a low Mass the people can follow the priest, perhaps using a missal, or even sing or recite prayers in common. Even better, they can respond "liturgically" to the prayers of the Mass "saying out loud their proper parts."[61] (This is, to my knowledge, the first time these prayers are referred to as being proper to the *people;* they were sometimes considered the proper prayers of the ministers.) The first degree would include "Amen," and "Et cum spiritu tuo." The second degree includes the "Confiteor," and the "Domine, non sum dignus," and the third degree includes the ordinary; the final degree would include even the propers.[62]

While this type of legislation is an advance in giving the laity their proper role in the liturgical action, and consequently, reflecting their proper role in the Church, at the same time there is, perhaps, a certain hesitancy in the instruction. There seems to be an unresolved problem between a liturgy which is truly worthy of God (in so far as any can be worthy), and a liturgy which is "pastorally adapted." A pastoral liturgy seems to require a liturgy which is less "magnificent" and sacred. *Mediator Dei* stated that a "dialogue" Mass cannot replace the high Mass, which, though it should be offered with only the sacred ministers present, possesses its own special dignity due to the impressive character of its ritual and the magnificence of its ceremonies.[63] The instruction states that the most noble form of the celebration is the solemn high Mass because of its solemnity, ceremonies, music, ministers—all of which point to the magnificence of the mystery. The higher forms of participation indicated in the instruction seem to indicate that the best liturgies are those performed by clerics: the third degree of the high Mass is for "religious Communities and seminaries."[64]   And the highest degree of low Mass "cannot be realized worthily except with special groups who have received   a certain training and formation."[65] When we begin to see the liturgy as a sign of the Church, a liturgy reserved for priests and religious will indicate similar reservations on "real" membership in the Church.

Although there may be a certain hesitancy with regard to the pastoral adaptation of the rite, when viewed in its historical perspective, the instruction shows a marked advance over previous legislation. For example, this is the first time that the Congregation of Rites has recommended a "dialogue Mass." Martimort and Picard point out in their commentary that formerly the attitude of the Congregation was that of a response of August 4, 1922 (decree 4375) which stated that the bishop was allowed to permit a dialogue Mass; but the Congregation does not hide its fears that all this noise of people talking out loud will be a distraction to the other priests saying Mass at the other altars of the church.[66] The instruction brings the discipline of the Congregation into harmony with the "approval and commendation" of the dialogue Mass given by *Mediator Dei*.[67]

Liturgical Roles. The instruction also marks an advance over previous legislation in the way it speaks of the various liturgical roles. (Section 5: The Persons who have the Principal Roles in the Sacred Music and the Liturgy. Articles 93 to 103.) If the former legislation could give the impression that the liturgy was primarily the concern of the clergy, the present instruction clearly states that each member of the Church participates in the liturgical action according to the manner proper to him.

The celebrating priest presides at every liturgical action. However, everyone else participates according to their proper mode.[68]

The laity participate actively in virtue of their baptismal character. The ministers and servers at the altar exercise a direct, but delegated, ministerial service.[69]

Article 96 of the instruction states that the participation of the faithful can be aided by a "commentator" and the instruction gives his principal duties and outlines his ministry. The instruction, in this same section on liturgical roles, mentions the organist, choir director, singers and musicians.

The priest not only presides at every liturgical action; he is to do so *well*. When the rubrics indicate that prayers are to be said aloud, the prayers are to be said not only "aloud," but "in such a way that the faithful can hear and easily follow the sacred action."[70] The parts indicated by the rubrics to be sung, are not only to be "sung" but "sung well, correctly and beautifully."[71] We see here the beginnings of rubrics which demand more of the celebrant than mere mechanical obedience.

When the instruction speaks of "liturgical roles" no mention is made of the bishop. The following list is a summary of the references to the liturgical role of the bishop in the instruction:

45. He is to see to it that sung vespers do not disappear from the parishes.

52. He is to watch over the composition of popular religious chants.

55. He is to regulate musical concerts given in churches.

64. He is to give permission for electric organs when he judges it necessary.

75. He is to watch over the broadcasting of the Mass on radio or television.

84. He can make rules for when the organ is to remain silent.

88. He can permit the ringing of church bells for secular purposes.

100. He is to provide for the education of church musicians.

102. He is to regulate the salaries for church musicians.

(The adaptation of sacred music to the conditions of mission countries, mentioned in article 112 of the instruction, gives this responsibility not to the bishop but to the missionary.)

The instruction recognizes that in the present circumstances due to the many other duties of administration for which he is responsible, the bishop cannot personally control every aspect of the government of his diocese and consequently he is to be aided by a commission of priests and laymen.

In each diocese there should be a *Commission for Sacred Music* since the time of St. Pius X. The members of this commission, whether priests or laymen, are nominated by the Ordinary of the place, who will choose men who are qualified by learning and by experience in the various kinds of sacred music. . . Because sacred music is so closely tied to the liturgy and to sacred art, each diocese should also have a Commission for Sacred Art, and a Commission for Sacred Liturgy.[72]

The liturgical commission was mentioned in *Mediator Dei.*[73] The commission for sacred art is called for by the letter of the Secretary of State, September 1, 1924.[74] The commission for sacred music was prescribed by *Tra le sollecitudine.*[75] Perhaps the continual mention of the importance of these commissions indicates that they were not functioning in all the dioceses. The present instruction gives the commission for sacred music such tasks as the following: judging the suitability of sacred polyphony (48); regulating concerts given in sacred places (55c); deciding which instruments can be used in churches (69); and regulating the salaries of church musicians (102).

The Council: Announcement and Preparatory work

Pope Pius XII died on October 9, 1958. Pope John XXIII was elected on October 28. Three months later, January 25, 1959, Pope John announced his intention to call a general Council.

He named the members of the General Preparatory Commission on May 17, and asked them to consult the bishops of the world to determine what topics might be discussed at the Council. Cardinal Tardini was president of this commission and Archbishop Felici was secretary. On June 18, 1959, Cardinal Tardini sent a letter to the cardinals, bishops, heads of religious orders and certain other communities, and asked for their suggestions for the Council. This correspondence has been published in the "Acts and Documents of the Council, Series one: the pre-preparatory period."[76]

The following year, in June of 1960, Pope John established the preparatory commissions and secretariats for the Council. The activities of these commissions are published in the "Acts and Documents of the Council, Series two: prepa ory period.'

Among these preparatory commissions is that for the liturgy.

There is a relation between this commission and the Congregation of Rites. The prefects of the Congregations (in this case, Cardinal Cicognani) became the presidents of the corresponding preparatory commissions. However, in order that these commissions might have a certain freedom in preparing for the Council, other members of the Roman Congregations were not appointed members of the preparatory commissions. Fr. Bugnini, who was serving as secretary to the commission for the general liturgical reform of Pius XII, was appointed to serve also as secretary of the Preparatory Liturgical Commission for the Council.[78]

At the same time that this Preparatory Liturgical Commission for the Council began to gather the suggestions of the episcopate into a schema for the liturgy, the commission for the reform of the liturgy, begun under Pius XII, continued its work:

1960	JUL 25	Code of rubrics for the breviary and missal
1961	FEB 14	Norms for the revision of local calendars
1961	APR 05	A new typical edition of the breviary
1961	APR 13	A partial revision of the pontifical
1961	APR 16	A modified rite for the baptism of adults
1961	JUN 23	A new typical edition of the missal[79]

Perhaps this committee wanted to influence the reform to be enacted by the Council; perhaps the Congregation of Rites wanted to make the more important liturgical reforms before the Council met and consequently the Council Fathers would find the reform less urgent and would be less tempted to go too far in their reform of the liturgy. On the other hand, the responses of the bishops given to the consultation for the reform of the breviary[80] and again to the consultation for the Council would not imply that the bishops would necessarily go too far in their reform.[81] We might even infer from the supplement to the *Memoria*[82] that the Congregation would have gone further in their reform of the Breviary had they not consulted the bishops and acted on their suggestions. From the documents available to this author, we cannot attribute any particular motive for the commission of Pius XII continuing their work while the preparatory commission for the Council was already considering many of the same reforms. Perhaps the explanation lies in the fact that when men have been working hard on a project for five years and are coming to the end of their mandate, it is natural to publish the results of the work accomplished during that time, even if it is not as complete as it might otherwise be.

We will look briefly at the first of the reforms listed above, the *Code of Rubrics for the Breviary and Missal.* These were the rubrics in force during the time of the Council.

1960 JUL 25 Code of Rubrics of the Roman Breviary and Missal

The motu proprio introducing the new *Code of Rubrics*[83] reminds us of what was said in the *Memoria*[84] regarding the final item of the projected reform, the *"Codex Iuris Liturgici."* This code would be helpful to the clergy by making it possible for them to find all the rubrics together in one place. The code would express the rubrics simply and clearly in short, concise articles as found in the Code of Canon Law. Such a code would also serve to stabilize and perpetuate the reform and inspire respect for the liturgical legislation.

The motu proprio states that the aim of the present Code is to present the rubrics with clarity and simplicity.[85] "The structure of the rubrics of the breviary and missal is reduced to a better form, distributed in a clearer order and brought together into a single text."[86] These regulations are to be "firmly established."[87]

Pope John states the relation between the reforms started with the *Memoria* and the reforms of the forthcoming Council:

> After we had decided, under the inspiration of God, to convene an ecumenical council, we turned over in our mind what was to be done about this project begun by our predecessor. After mature reflection, we came to the conclusion that the more important principles (Latin: altiora principia) governing a general liturgical reform should be laid before the members of the hierarchy at the forthcoming ecumenical council, but that the above-mentioned improvement of the rubrics of the breviary and missal should no longer be put off.[88]

The "fundamental principles" which formed the second chapter of the *Memoria* are to be the subject of the schema for the liturgy presented to the Council Fathers.

The motu proprio closes with the mention of another problem which we have seen mentioned before: the relation between the length of the office and the pastoral duties of priests.

> Some special modifications have been introduced by which the divine office is somewhat shortened. This shortening was petitioned by very many of the bishops, in view especially of the constantly increasing burden of pastoral cares laid upon many priests. In a fatherly spirit we urge these and all who are bound to the recitation of the divine office to make up for any shortening of that office

by greater attentiveness and devotion.[89]

The *Code of Rubrics* is divided into three parts:

1. General Rubrics (the liturgical day in general, feasts, and calendar)
2. The Roman Breviary
3. The Roman Missal.

The *Code of Rubrics* reminds us again of the *Memoria,* where the first three areas for the projected reform were to be:

1. The classification of feasts and the liturgical calendar
2. The Roman Breviary
3. The Roman Missal.[90]

The Code was to present the rubrics simply and clearly. The articles show much progress in this direction; however, in general, the system remains relatively complex, especially when compared with the post-Conciliar rubrics. The classification of liturgical days is as follows:

Article:
10. Sundays are of the first or second class
22. Ferial days are of the first, second, third, or fourth class
28. Vigils are of the first, second, or third class
36. Feasts are of the first, second, or third class
65. Octaves are of the first or second class
107. Commemorations are either privileged or ordinary.

The post-Conciliar calendar of 1969 treats of:

1. The liturgical day in general
2. Sunday
3. Solemnities, feasts, and memorials
4. Week days.

With regard to the style of the rubrics, the Code of 1960 presents the legislation in short, direct statements of fact:[91]

1. The following rubrics pertain to the Roman Rite.

2. The term "calendar" means both the calendar of the universal Church and particular calendars.

7. The precedence among the various liturgical days is determined solely by the special table, N° 91.

However, the Code starts to change from the strictly juridical style of rubrics to a style in which the articles are generally longer, in paragraph form, giving the rubric and the reasons for the rubric and an explanation of the law. For example:[92]

> 270. The Mass, together with the divine office, constitutes the summit of the entire Christian cult. Therefore, the Mass should normally correspond to the office of the day. Nevertheless, there are Masses different from the office of the day; namely, votive Mass and those for the dead.

The articles which treat of the relation of the parts of the Divine Office to the time of day at which they should be said are interesting for two reasons. Not only do they mark a change in the legislation and break away from the overly juridical concept of obligation in which the Hours are something which had to be said during the space of 24 hours; but also these articles mark a change in the style of legislation. We see here an example of the style which will be adopted by the post-Conciliar rubrics.[93]

> 142. By their very nature the canonical hours of the divine office are oriented to the sanctification of the various hours of the natural day. Therefore, it is fitting, both for truly sanctifying the day, and so that the hours produce their spiritual fruit, that each canonical hour be said at the time nearest to the true time for each canonical hour.

> 145. Lauds, as it is the morning prayer, is said early in the morning in choir and in common. It is fitting to observe this rule also in the recitation performed by one alone.

> 147. Compline is most appropriately said as the last prayer at the end of the day, by all those who are bound to the recitation of the Divine Office, but especially by those living in religious communities, even if for just cause Matins of the following day have already been anticipated.[94]

We find here the beginnings of a new type of rubrical vocabulary:

> 142. it is better that. . .
> 143. it is sufficient to. . .
> 144. . . . may be anticipated.
> 145. . . . which it is fitting to observe.
> 147. It is most fitting that. . .
>   for a just cause. . . .
>   for a reasonable length of time. . . .[95]

Another aspect of the Code of Rubrics which is related to our study of obedience to liturgical law is the fact that they begin to make provision for local adaptations. Local ordinaries have the faculty, for example, of transferring the Rogation Days to three other successive days which may be found more suitable according to the customs or needs of different regions.[96]

Article 117 is the first rubric where I have found direct reference to the liturgical authority of the Episcopal Conference of a region.

> In missionary regions, when by reason of an ancient and long established tradition of a people, it happens that the meaning of one or another liturgical color of the Roman Church does not agree with the meaning those people are accustomed to, then the Episcopal Conference of the same region, or of a larger territory if that is more expedient, has the faculty to substitute a more suitable color for the one that is unsuitable. This is not to be done, however, without consulting the Sacred Congregation of Rites.[97]

To some readers, the color of vestments may not seem a very important topic for discussion during a meeting of the National Conference of Bishops, but here again we are perhaps influenced by the developments which have taken place since 1960 and the role of the Episcopal Conferences found in the post-Conciliar liturgy.

Certain options are also given to the celebrant; for example, regarding votive Masses and the choice of orations. In a strictly juridical framework, it is difficult to give such a permission because choices presume that there is a higher level of principles upon which the choice can be based. Without these guiding principles, the choices possible within the system must be clearly explained and limited. Over half of the articles relating to the *Roman Missal* in the Code of 1960 are concerned with regulating this type of choice: 84 articles for votive Masses, 34 articles for Masses for the dead, 33 articles on choosing an oration. (The oration, at this period, was seen to be more important than the readings in giving the liturgy of the word its distinctive character. In circumstances when a wedding Mass cannot be celebrated, there are times when the orations from the wedding Mass can be added to the Mass of the day. For a Mass of thanksgiving on the anniversary of the wedding, you can say the Mass of the Trinity, or the Mass of the Blessed Virgin, and add the orations for thanksgiving.)[98]

One of the positive features of the Code was to have all the rubrics gathered together into one book. However, the Code of

1960 does not intend to contain all existing legislation. For example, article 272, speaking of the active participation of the faithful, states that "this active participation of the faithful has been amply explained in the instruction on Sacred Music and Liturgy of September 3, 1958." As is the case with any "code" of law, the Code does not dispense us from knowing the *sources* of the law which enable us to determine the spirit and purpose of the legislation.

The Code of 1960 is written in a context where the active participation of the faithful is of the utmost importance. For example:

> 474. After the Gospel, especially on Sundays and Holy Days of obligation, there is to be given, according to the occasion, a short homily for the people.
>
> This homily, however, if it is given by a priest other than the celebrant, is not to be superimposed on the Mass and impede the participation of the faithful. In this case, consequently, the Mass must be interrupted and only taken up again after the homily is over.[99]

The Mass is not to be continued while the homily is going on for this would "impede the participation of the faithful." We note also that the homily is spoken of as "interrupting the Mass." The Mass is viewed primarily as an act of worship offering to God the Sacrifice of Christ. The liturgy of the word, and especially the homily which is "given for the people" has difficulty finding its proper place in a cult directed toward the divine worship.

NOTES

1948 DEC 30 The Memoria. Notes for a Liturgical Reform.

[1] See Bibliography 1948 DEC 30. Memoria sulla Riforma Liturgica. The historical background of the document is given on pages 317-318.

[2] Memoria 14.
  1°. Si devono equilibrare le opposte pretese della tendenza conservatrice e della tendenza innovatrice.

2° Dato che la liturgia è per natura sua eminentemente latreutica, il culto di dulia dev'essere subordinato a quello di latria; consequentamente, nel Calendario liturgico, il *Temporale* et il *Feriale* devono predominare súl Santorale.

3° Dato che la liturgia e un complesso unitario e organico, conviene che la riforma sia anche unitaria ed organica.

3 MD. AAS 545. NCWC 25.

4 Memoria 15.

5 Memoria 16.
La liturgia è, per natura sua, l'espressione esterna del culto che la Chiesa rende per tutta l'umanita a Dio Creatore e Signore dell'Universo, e a Christo Redentore del genere umano, culto quindi eminentemente latreutico.

6 Memoria 19-20.

7 See Bibliography 1950 MAR 25.

8 The details of this reform are not treated here as they form the subject of Chapter V of the thesis of Hans-Eric Jung, "Le renouveau de l'annee liturgique dans son enracinement historique," Institut Catholique: Paris, 1975.

9 Memoria 287-291.

10 Memoria 305.

11 Memoria 314.
Il requisito principale per le nouove rubriche dovra essere semplicità e chiarezza, facilitate dalla forma piu concisa di singoli articoli, alla guisa dei canoni del Codice di Diritto Canonico.

12 Memoria 317.

13 See Bibliography 1950 APR 21, pages 3-7.

14 See Bibliography 1951 JUN 19.

1951   FEB   09   The Restoration of the Solemn Paschal Vigil.

15 See Bibliography 1955 MAY 25, page 11.

16 AAS 43 (1951) 129.

17 AAS 129.

18 Ibid.

19 See Bibliography 1950 APR 21. Supplement II. pages 20-22.

20 De Vigilia Paschali. 15. . . . Leguntur vero a Lectore, in medio chori, ante Cereum benedictum, ita quidem ut Lector habeat a dextris altare, a sinistris aulam ecclesiae. Celebrans et Ministri, clerus et populus, sedentes auscultant.

21 Martimort, "Sedentes Auscultant," LMD 31 (1952) 150-151.
Si les fidèles sedentes auscultant, leur livre livre fermé, c'est qu'on leur dit des choses qu'ils entendent, non seulement de leurs oreilles, mais de

de leur intelligence. Ils ne le pourront faire que si la lecture des quatre pro-
pheties a lieu dans leur langue maternelle. Reconnaissons que cette interpretation a ete instinctivement adoptée dans la presque unanimité des
paroisses òu la Vigile pascale a été célébrée, et des la premiere année.
Le nouveau rite étant tout entier d'une structure si franchement pastorale,
la chose a semblé toute naturelle . . . Il me semble donc qu'on a des
raisons très sérieuses d'estimer que la formule des nouvelles rubriques
sedentes auscultant peut s'interpreter légitimement comme une discrète mais
sûre invitation dont nous pouvons tirer un parti pastoral. (Martimort probably goes beyond the intention of the rubric.)

1955 MAR 23 On the reduction of the rubrics to a simpler form.

[22] AAS 47 (1955) 218.
Cum nostra hac aetate sacerdotes, praesertim illi qui curam animarum
gerunt, variis novisque in dies apostolatus officiis onerentur, ita ut divini
offici recitationi ea qua oportet animi tranquillitate vix attendere possint,
nonnulli locorum Ordinarii enixas preces S. Sedi detulerunt, ut huiusmodi
difficultati amovendae benigne provideret, ac saltem rubricarum copiosum
instructum ad simpliciorem redigeretur formam.

[23] Martimort, LMD 42 (1955) 15.

[24] Ibid. 19.

[25] Ibid. 20.

1955 NOV 16 The restoration of the liturgy of Holy Week.

[26] See Bibliography 1955 MAY 25, page 28.

[27] Ibid. 66.

[28] AAS 47 (1955) 838.

[29] Ibid. 839.

[30] Ibid. 842.

[31] It is interesting to note that after 20 years these most basic principles
of authenticity and pastoral fruitfulness are not universally understood or
applied. The list of Holy Week services for the center of the Catholic Traditionalist Movement for 1975 lists:

Holy Thursday, March 27
11:00 A.M. High Mass and Procession—Gregorian Chant
12:00 noon to 8:00 P.M. adoration at the repository
8:00 P.M. Low Mass

Holy Saturday, March 29
10:00 A.M. Blessings: Fire, Paschal Candle, Holy Water, Baptismal Water.
11:00 A.M. High Mass—Gregorian Chant

When the "vigil" is held in the morning the meaning of the light ceremony
is lost and the rite is reduced to a "blessing."

[32] AAS. 844. Article 4.

33 De Missa Solemni Vespertina in Cena Domini. 13. Valde convenit ut post Evangelium habeatur brevis HOMILIA ad illustranda mysteria potissima, quae hac Missa recoluntur, institutio scilicet sacrae Eucharistiae et Ordinis sacerdotalis, necnon et mandatum Domini de caritate fraterna.

34 Jounel. LMD 45 (1956) 27.

35 AAS 847.

1957 JUL 29 Consultation of the Episcopate—reform of Breviary

36 See Bibliography 1957 JUL 29. Memoria, supplement IV. page 5. The other references in this section are all taken from the above source.

37 page 6. "Agitur proinde de re magni momenti, quae non solum personalem pietatem, sed vitam quoque atque operositatem totius Ecclesiae respicit."

38 page 13.

39 page 122.

40 page 70.

41 pages 32-33.

42 page 38.

43 page 36.

44 pages 101-102.

1958 SEP 03 Instruction on Sacred Music and the Liturgy

45 See Bibliography 1958 SEP 03. Instruction . . . AAS 50 (1958) 630-663.

46 A.-G. Martimort et F. Picard, *Liturgie et Musique* (Paris: Cerf, 1959), p. 9.

47 AAS 50 (1958) 631.

48 Article 1.

1. "Sacra Liturgia integrum constituit publicum cultum mystici Iesu Christi Corporis, Capitis nempe membrorumque eius." (Mediator Dei 528) Propterea sunt "actiones liturgicae" illae actiones sacrae, quae, ex institutione Iesu Christi vel Ecclesiae eorumque nomine, secundum libros liturgicos a Sanctá Sede approbatos, a personis ad hoc legitime deputatis peraguntur, ad debitum cultum Deo, Sanctis ac Beatis deferedum (cfr. can. 1256); ceterae actiones sacrae quae, sive in ecclesia sive extra, sacerdote quoque praesente vel praeeunte, peraguntur, "pia exercitia" appellantur.

49 Article 13.

Lingua actionum liturgicarum est latina, . . . In piis exercitiis quaevis lingua adhiberi potest fidelibus magis conveniens.

50 Article 20.

51 Canon 1257; canon 1259.

52 MD. AAS 529.

53 Article 12.

12. Actiones liturgicae peragi debent ad normam librorum liturgicorum rite ab apostolica Sede approbatorum, sive pro universa Ecclesia, sive pro aliqua ecclesia particulari aut familia religiosa (can. 1257); pia autem exercitia fiunt secundum consuetudines et traditiones locorum aut coetuum, a competente auctoritate ecclesiastica approbatas (can. 1259).

Actiones liturgicas et pia exercitia inter se commisceri non licet; sed, si causas ferat, pia exercitia actiones liturgicas aut praecedant aut sequantur.

54 Article 47.

55 In this regard,.see the comment by Fr. Gy, LMD 124 (1975) 11.

56 Article 2.

Sacrosanctum Missae sacrificium est actus cultus publici, nomine Christi et Ecclesiae Deo redditi, quovis loco vel modo celebretur. Denominatio proinde "Missae privatae" vitetur.

57 MD. AAS 557. Concerning prayer celebrated in the name of Christ and of the Church, see: Bernard Dominique Marliangeas, "In persona Christi, in persona ecclesiae: Etude de vocabulaire théologique." Thése, Institut Catholique de Paris. 1966.

58 John H. Miller, "The Nature and Definition of the Liturgy," *Theological Studies* 18 (1957) 334.

59 Article 22.

Missa natura sua postulat, ut omnes adstantes, secundum modum sibi proprium, eidem participent.

60 Article 25.

61 Article 31 . . . et partes sibi proprias clara voce dicendo.

62 Ibid.

63 MD. AAS 561. NCWC 39.

64 Article 25.

65 Article 31d.

Hic ultimus gradus a selectis tantum cultioribus coetibus bene institutis, digne, prouti decet, adhiberi potest.

66 Martimort et Picard, page 91.

67 MD. AAS 561. NCWC 39.

68 Article 93.

Sacerdos celebrans toti actioni liturgicae praeest. Ceteri omnes actioni liturgicae modo sibi proprio participant.

69 Ibid.

70 Article 34.

71 Article 94.

72 Article 118.

73 MD. AAS 561-562. NCWC 40.

74 AAS 44 (1952) 542-546.

75 AAS 36 (1903-4) 329-330, article 24.

The Council: Announcement and Preparatory work.

76 See Bibliography 1959 JUN 18.

77 1960 JUN 05.

78 1960 JUN 06 and 1960 JUL 11.

79 For complete references, see the dates listed in Bibliography, pages 81-20

80 1957 JUL 29.

81 1959 JUN 18.

82 1957 JUL 29.

1960 JUL 25 Code of Rubrics of the Roman Breviary and Missal

83 1960 JUL 25, AAS 52 (1960) 593-595.

84 1948 DEC 30, pages 313-314.

85 AAS 593. NCWC 10.

86 AAS 595. NCWC 12.

87 Ibid.

88 AAS 594. NCWC 10-11.

Nos autem, postquam, adspirante Deo, Concilium Oecumenicum coadunandum esse decrevimus, quid circa huiusmodi Praedecessoris Nostri inceptum agendum foret, haud semel recogitavimus. Re itaque diu ac mature examinata, in sententiam devenimus, altiora principia, generalem liturgicam instaurationem respicientia, in proximo Concilio Oecumenico Patribus esse proponenda; memoratam vero rubricarum Breviarii ac Missalis emendationem diutius non esse protrahendam.

89 AAS 595. NCWC 12.

90 1948 DEC 30, pages 19-20.

91 Articles 1, 2, and 7.

92 Article 270.

93 Compare, for example, the style and vocabulary of the three articles quoted here with article 88 of the Constitution on the Liturgy.

[94] Articles 142, 145, and 147.

142. Horae canonicae Officii divine ordinantur, ex earum constitutione, ad sanctificationem diversarum horarum diei naturalis. Praestat, proinde, sive ad diem revera sanctificandum sive ad ipsas Horas cum fructu spirituali recitandas, ut in earum absolutione, tempus servetur quod proxime accedat ad tempus verum uniuscuiusque Horae canonicae.

145. Laudes, cum sint precatio matutina, in choro et in communi primo mane dicuntur: quod convenienter servatur etiam in recitatione a solo facta.

147. Completorium, ab omnibus qui ad recitatione, divini Officii obligantur, praesertim autem in familiis religiosis, valde opportune dicitur tamquam ultima precatio in fine diei, etiam si, ob iustam causam, Matutinum diei sequentis anticipatum fuerit.

[95] Articles:

142. Praestat ut. . .

143. Sufficit ut. . .

144. Anticipare licet. . .

145. . . .quod convenienter servatur.

147. . . .valde opportune . . . ob iustam causam . . . per rationabile tempus protractum. . .

[96] See articles 82-87.

[97] Article 117.

Siubi vero in regionibus Missionum, ex probata et originali traditione gentis indigenae, significatio unius vel alterius coloris liturgici Ecclesiae Romanae cum significatione quae illis populis congenita est non congruit, Conferentiae episcopali eiusdem regionis, vel maioris territorii, si ita magis conveniat, facultas datur, ut in locum coloris inepti alium colorem magis aptum substituant; hoc tamen non fiat inconsulta S. Rituum Congregatione.

[98] Articles 380 and 382.

[99] Article 474.

Post Evangelium, praesertim in dominicis et diebus festis de praecepto habeatur, iuxta opportunitatem, brevis homilia ad populum.

Homilia vero, si fiat ab alio sacerdote ac celebrante, non superimponatur Missae celebrationi impendiendo fidelium participationem; proinde, hoc in casu, Missae celebratio suspendatur, et tantummodo expleta homilia resumatur.

III.

The Theological Context
Of Liturgical Law At The Time
Of The Second Vatican Council

Even while the Code of Rubrics was being published by the Congregation of Rites, the liturgical reform of the Second Vatican Council was beginning. As we noted earlier, Cardinal Tardini had asked the episcopate for their suggestions as to what topics should be discussed at the forthcoming Council.[1] In an interview on French television, January 24, 1960,[2] the Cardinal stated that he had already received nearly 2,000 replies from the bishops and their suggestions touched on almost everything imaginable.[3] He also stated that from the way things were developing, it was clear that the Council would treat problems which were of the practical order rather than primarily doctrinal problems.[4]

As we study the development of the document treating the liturgy, however, we will see that the "practical order" cannot be separated from the "doctrinal order." The liturgical and pastoral decisions of the Council are best understood by seeing them in relation to their theological context.

The development from individual suggestions to a unified document

On July 9, 1960, Cardinal Tardini gave Cardinal Cicognani, the president of the preparatory liturgical commission, the report listing the themes to be treated by the Council with regard to the liturgy: that is, those suggestions from the bishops which pertained to the preparatory commission for the liturgy. The suggestions are arranged under seven headings:

1. The reform of the calendar. Criteria proposed.
2. The Mass. Principles for reforming text and rubrics.
3. Sacred Rites. Simplification of the Pontifical. Rite for consecration of a church. Blessing of bells, etc.
4. Sacraments. The reform of the rites of baptism, confirmation,

61

extreme unction, and matrimony so that they better signify what
they effect.
5. The Breviary. Adapting the breviary to the spiritual needs of
   clerics and the ministry.
6. Liturgical language. Carefully consider whether it is wise to permit
   the vernacular languages in certain parts of the Mass and the administration of the sacraments.
7. The simplification of liturgical vestments.[5]

The invitation to offer suggestions for the Council was given not
only to the bishops but also to the cardinals and to the Sacred
Congregations of the Curia. Many of these suggestions touch the
liturgy and our theme of liturgical law.

We mentioned earlier (see above, page xxiii) the tendency to associate "church" with "the hierarchy" and the resulting separation
of "church" and "laity." In this context it is interesting to find
among the suggestions of the Holy Office:

To be discussed at the Council; concerning the laity: —The concept
of the "laity" and their place in the Church. The laity not merely
as an *object,* but also as *subject* and indeed, an *active* subject, in the
Church.

—The "priesthood of the faithful." The dignity of the laity due to
the character received in Baptism and Confirmation. Their position
and responsibility in the Mystical Body.

—The juridical position of the laity in the Church in relation to the
hierarchy. The apostolic of the laity.

—The insertion into the Code of Canon Law of a chapter giving
integral treatment of the laity.[6]

With regard to the liturgy, the Holy Office suggests for discussion:

The importance of the liturgy both as the worship of God and the
sanctification of the faithful. The Liturgy as a theological source.
(Lex precandi, lex credendi.)

The Church has complete authority in liturgical matters, especially
with regard to the arrangement of the rites and the language to be
used. What power can be given to the bishops in this regard?[7]

The Congregation for the Propagation of the Faith (Missions)
asked that the liturgical books be reformed to take into account
missionary conditions—the climate, for example, or the fact that
there are very few priests. They also asked that the rites be simplified. The rubrics are scattered throughout several books and these

books are not always available in the missions. They also asked whether it might not be good to allow the vernacular languages to be used more extensively in the liturgy, especially in the administration of the sacraments and sacramentals. In conclusion, they asked that: "the liturgical books be reformed and adapted to contemporary conditions in the missions and that the rubrics be gathered together into a Code of Liturgical Law."[8]

As we would expect, the two Congregations directly concerned with the liturgy have extensive suggestions for the preparatory commission for the Council. The remarks of the Congregation for the Discipline of the Sacraments are directed principally toward the sacraments of Holy Orders and Matrimony. However they also mention the other sacraments: Baptism (the sponsors, the place for Baptism); Confirmation (the minister, the proper age to be confirmed); Eucharist (the composition of the bread, additives in the wine, reasons for saying two or three Masses a day, the time of day at which Mass is permitted).[9]

The suggestions of the Congregation of Rites are given under 8 headings; however they first state that two areas ought not be treated by the Council: 1) the details of application of the general reform, which is more the work for a Commission than a task for the Council; and 2) the entire area of beatification and canonization, which is a reform which should be given to experts.[10] The following pages speak of:

1. Concelebration
2. The Divine Office
3. Liturgical Language
4. Local Adaptations of the Liturgy
5. Liturgical Formation
6. The Participation of the Faithful
7. The Vestments and Insignia for Bishops
8. The Calendar [11]

In the light of what was said above about the relation of the laity and the liturgy, the remark of the Congregation of Rites with regard to liturgical language is interesting. After giving the history of the question and devoting a full ten pages to the principal arguments in favor of permitting the vernacular they state their conclusions:

1. Having considered and studied carefully each and all of the above arguments, this Sacred Congregation of Rites has arrived at the following general consensus: We wish to state as clearly as possible that the use of the Latin language in the liturgy of the Latin Church

is to be preserved as it is.

2. However, it is our desire to ask the Council to find efficacious means by which in the future clerics throughout the world may be so instructed in the Latin language that they will be truly capable of using it properly in all liturgical rites and offices, and will fully understand it, so that in this regard there will be removed all just reason for the requests against preserving Latin in the liturgy.[12]

But what of the laity? The way in which the request is phrased could lead to the impression that only the clergy need be concerned with understanding the liturgy.

In August of 1960 the names of those who will serve on the preparatory liturgical commission are announced. Originally there were 18 members and 29 consultants (periti);[13] however, during the course of the following year, other names were added and in September 1961 there are 26 members and 37 consultants. It is the task of these men to take the suggestions of the bishops, the congregations, the universities, and to form them into a unified document. They performed their task so well that when we now read the Constitution on the Liturgy, we are more likely to think that the document grew organically from an original plan or idea, rather than to think of it as the arrangement of several hundred file cards.

The first schema is formed during the second general meeting of the commission in the Spring of 1961, April 12 to 22.[14] With this schema serving as a basis for discussion, the members and consultants made their observations and corrections and sent them to Fr. Bugnini. It was his task as secretary to take these suggestions and to emend the text accordingly.

It soon became apparent that many things had been repeated and other items left out. The items of a more general or theological nature were taken from their various chapters and placed together into a new preliminary chapter. The secretary remimeographed the schema and sent it to the commission under the date of August 10, 1961.[15]

The project plan for reform given in the *Memoria*[16] was to follow the division of liturgical books; the present plan is organized by topics—topics under which can be grouped the various suggestions which have been received:

1. Promotion and restoration of the liturgy in general
2. The most holy Sacrifice of the Mass
3. The divine office
4. The sacraments and sacramentals
5. The liturgical year

6. Sacred furnishings, vestments, and liturgical ornaments
-7. Sacred music
8. Sacred art[17]

The same process was repeated once again. The commission examined the text and sent their suggestions, listed on file cards according to topic, to the secretary. They were assembled; the schema corrected, mimeographed again and sent to the Commission under the date of November 15, 1961.[18] This schema is similar to the former. However, the articles are arranged in better order and the document is more unified. The schema appears to be more an organic document than a juxtaposition of individual suggestions.

The chapter on "The Most Holy Sacrifice of the Mass" becomes the chapter on "The Most Sacred Mystery of the Eucharist." The sacraments become chapter 3, moved ahead of the Divine Office which is now chapter 4. Articles are added in chapter 3 so that all of the sacraments are mentioned. (The former document had no mention of Penance.) The sixth chapter on Sacred Vestments is reduced from an original 12 articles to an introduction and only 3 articles. (In the final text of the Constitution this chapter disappears as a separate chapter and is joined with Sacred Art becoming the third paragraph of article 122, the second half of article 128, and article 130.)

As some items are placed ahead of others and as some articles grow in length and others diminish or disappear, it becomes evident that not everything in the liturgy is of the same importance. We saw in the introduction to this study that it had been taught that "there is nothing of little importance in the liturgy" and that the Mass was to be discontinued for want of a candle. The members of the commission are aware that, even if there is nothing of little importance in the liturgy, there are things that are of greater importance and things that are of less importance.

The commission held its third plenary session January 11 to 13, 1962, at which time they discussed the schema of November, revised it, and this revised schema was unanimously approved and given to the president of the commission. Cardinal Cicognani, now 80 years old, signed the document on February 1; he died four days later, February 5, 1962.

The schema was sent to the General Secretary for the preparation of the Council and was studied by the central preparatory commission March 23 to April 3, 1962. It is printed in the first volume of the "Schemata of the Constitutions and Decrees to be discussed in the Council sessions," dated July 13, 1962, and sent to the entire episcopate.[19] Thus the suggestions given in response to the letter of Cardinal Tardini, June 18, 1959, have become a schema for the Constitution on the Liturgy.

Vatican II and the nature of the liturgy

From the very beginning of the Constitution on the Liturgy[20] we note a new relationship between the liturgy and the Church.

> The liturgy is thus the outstanding means by which the faithful can express in their lives, and manifest to others, the mystery of Christ and the real nature of the true Church.[21]

The liturgy is not only something that the Church does, the liturgy is also an expression of the Church. And the Church is understood not only as the Church as institution, but the Church as mystery. The article quoted above continues: "It is of the essence of the Church that she is both human and divine, visible and yet invisibly endowed, eager to act and yet devoted to contemplation, present in this world and yet not at home in it."[22]

We noted above that with the schema of August 10, 1961, the general liturgical principles and the specifically theological items of the schema were brought together in an introductory chapter. In the final text this chapter begins:

> God, who wishes all men to be saved and come to know the truth, in many and various ways . . . spoke of old to our fathers by the prophets. When the fulness of time had come he sent his son, the Word made flesh, anointed by the Holy Spirit, to preach the gospel to the poor, to heal the contrite of heart, to be a "bodily and spiritual medicine," the Mediator between God and man. . . .

> He achieved his task principally by the paschal mystery of his blessed passion, resurrection from the dead, and glorious ascension, whereby dying, he destroyed our death, and, rising, he restored our life. For it was from the side of Christ as he slept the sleep of death upon the cross that there came forth the wondrous sacrament which is the whole Church.[23]

When studying *Mediator Dei* we noted that the encyclical began with a perspective in which Jesus the Mediator comes to save man from sin. Sin had disturbed the right relation between man and God. The children of Adam were wretched heirs to the infection of original sin. Jesus gave Himself in sacrifice to save man. He instituted the Church to continue this sacrifice, to prolong the priestly mission of Jesus in the liturgy.

Here, in the Constitution on the Liturgy, we find that the document begins with a God who wishes to reveal his love and in the fullness of time he reveals himself in Jesus. The climax of this revelation is the paschal mystery. Here the mission of Jesus to save us from sin is balanced by his mission to reveal the Father. The cross is not only sacrifice but revelation. The Church is not only an institution which continues the sacrifice, but the Church itself is spoken of as "sacrament." "By her relation with Christ, the Church is a kind of sacrament or sign of intimate union with God and of the unity of all mankind."[24]

The theological perspective of the Constitution on the Liturgy is different from that of *Mediator Dei*. This can also be seen in the way they use Scripture. Both documents are very scriptural—the passage quoted above is a mosaic of scripture texts. I have counted approximately 91 quotations from Scripture in *Mediator Dei* and about 50 in the Constitution, and given the length of the two documents the proportion is about the same. However, of these 141 citations, only 6, to my knowledge, are common to both documents. *Mediator Dei* makes reference to the sacrifices of the Old Testament and stresses the sacrifice of Christ with reference to the Epistle to the Hebrews. The quotations from Scripture found in the Constitution are predominantly references to the work of Christ as the revelation of the love of the Father.

The Constitution then speaks of the relation between the liturgy and the Church (article 6). "Christ is always present in His Church, especially in her liturgical celebrations" (article 7).[25] The relation between liturgy and the Church presented in the Constitution is further developed in the Constitution on the Church. The Constitution on the Liturgy was the first document to be studied by the Council. The Constitution on the Church, promulgated a year later was able to profit from the discussions on the former Constitution.

We have only to compare the Chapter titles of the final text of the Constitution on the Church and the schema prepared by the preparatory commission and given to the Fathers of the Council on November 10, 1962, to see the change in the way the "Church" was viewed. The schema presented to the bishops for discussion contained 11 chapters:

SCHEMA OF THE DOGMATIC CONSTITUTION ON THE CHURCH[26]

Chapter:
1. The nature of the Church militant
2. The members of the Church militant and the necessity of the

Church for salvation
3. The episcopate as the supreme degree of the sacrament of Orders and the priesthood
4. Residential bishops
5. The states of evangelical perfection (Religious)
6. The laity
7. The teaching authority of the Church
8. Authority and obedience in the Church
9. Church-State relations
10. The need for the Church to announce the Gospel to all nations
11. Ecumenism

The bishops did not react favorably to this schema—we see their remarks in the "Acts of the discussions during the Council" (Acta Synodalia Sacrosancti Concilii Oecumenici Vaticani II). They found it was composed in terms which were too "juridical" and which did not correspond to the purpose of the Council. The chapter titles of the document approved by the Council Fathers two years later, November 21, 1964, are as follows:

DOGMATIC CONSTITUTION ON THE CHURCH[27]

Chapter:
1. The Mystery of the Church
2. The People of God
3. The Hierarchical structure of the Church, with special reference to the episcopate
4. The Laity
5. The call of the whole Church to holiness
6. Religious
7. The eschatological nature of the pilgrim Church and her union with the heavenly Church
8. The role of the Blessed Virgin Mary, Mother of God, in the mystery of Christ and the Church

This final version of the Constitution begins with the Church seen as a mystery and sacrament of union with God. It does not, of course, deny that the Church is also an "institution," however the Constitution creates a balance between "institution" and "mystery."

The Constitution then speaks immediately of the People of God, before speaking of the hierarchy, emphasizing the fact that the laity are not "second class members" of the Church. Commenting on the development from the schema to the Constitution, Fr. Avery Dulles writes:

Among all the documents of Vatican II probably none underwent more drastic revision between the first schema and the finally approved text. The successive drafts of the Constitution, compared with one another, strikingly reveal the tremendous development of the Church's self-understanding which resulted from the dialogue within the Council. The original schema, prepared by the Theological Commission before the first session in 1962, resembled the standard treatise on the Church as found, for example, in most of the theological manuals published between the two world wars. Influenced by centuries of anti-Protestant polemics, the writers of this period placed heavy emphasis on the hierarchical and juridical aspects of the Church, including the supremacy of the Pope.

[The revised document] . . . instead of beginning with a discussion of the structures and government of the Church—as was the tendency at Vatican I—the Constitution starts with the notion of the Church as a people to whom God communicates Himself in love. This provides an excellent foundation for a new and creative approach to the role of the laity in the Church.[28]

The second chapter of the Constitution on the Church presents the Church as the "People of God" formed into a people by the sacraments:

It is through the sacraments and the exercise of the virtues that the sacred nature and organic structure of the priestly community is brought into operation. Incorporated into the Church through baptism, the faithful are consecrated by the baptismal character to the exercise of the cult of the Christian religion. . . . Bound more intimately to the Church by the sacrament of confirmation, they are endowed by the Holy Spirit with special strength. . . . Taking part in the Eucharistic Sacrifice,. . . they manifest in a practical way that unity of God's People which is suitably signified and wondrously brought about by this most awesome sacrament.[29]

In this view of the Church, the relation between the Church and the liturgy is different than in the perspective of *Mediator Dei*. The Church as institution makes laws which regulate the liturgy. The Church, formed by the sacraments, finds in the liturgy a *source* of Church Law. K. Barth states that Church law is liturgical in its origin, that it creates order based upon the cult and is renewed in the cult at the same time that it assures liturgical order.[30] Congar states that it is the sacraments which constitute and structure the Church, and consequently the liturgy constitutes one of the sources of Church law. In this regard, Congar quotes St. Thomas: "The source of all law is found in the sacraments."[31]

This perspective allows us to see the liturgical authority and responsibility of the bishop as something central to his Order.

The Church, called together by the proclamation of faith, is constituted the "assembly of the faithful"—the "Church"—by Baptism (the sacrament of Faith); assembled by its Head and given life by the Eucharist; presided over by a sacramental and apostolic minister. It is the sacraments which structure the Church.

This fact is fundamental for liturgical law—both in itself, and in its consequences for the responsiblity of the bishop. The sacraments—and the fundamental principles of pastoral theology relative to the sacraments—pertain to the very structure of the Church in so far as the Church comes from God and constitutes the Sacrament of God.

The bishops of the Church of the first eleven centuries were aware of this fact and they gave it a large portion of their collegial activity. Documents concerning the liturgy together with papal consultations form the law of the Church during this period.[32]

Concerning the liturgical role of the bishops, the Constitution on the Church states:

In the bishops, therefore, for whom priests are assistants, our Lord Jesus Christ, the supreme High Priest, is present in the midst of those who believe. For sitting at the right hand of God the Father, he is not absent from the gathering of his high priests, but above all through their excellent service he is preaching the Word of God to all nations, and constantly administering the sacraments of faith to those who believe.[33]

The role of the bishop is not merely to see to it that the laws concerning the liturgy are properly carried out; the bishop's role itself is sacramental—the bishop is a sacrament of Christ.[34]

In the Constitution on the Liturgy, the role of the bishop is expressed in article 41:

The bishop is to be considered the high priest of his flock. In a certain sense it is from him that the faithful who are under his care derive and maintain their life in Christ.

Therefore all should hold in very high esteem the liturgical life of the diocese which centers around the bishop, especially in his cathedral church.

The principal manifestation of the Church is the full and active participation of the entire holy people of God, united in the same liturgical celebration, especially in the same Eucharist, in one prayer, at one altar, presided over by the bishop, surrounded by his presbyterium and ministers.[35]

This sacramental role of the bishop might seem foreign to those who are familiar only with a church in which the bishop is occupied primarily with administration, for those who rarely if ever celebrate the liturgy in the cathedral church with the bishop, and for those who have never seen a bishop except at their confirmation. However, this is not an ideal situation and it is not the model of the Church to which the Constitution makes reference. As we noted in the introduction to this study, the early Church had a very special relation to its bishop. The Constitution on the Liturgy gives three references to St. Ignatius of Antioch to situate the sacramental role of the bishop. As some readers of this study are perhaps unfamiliar with these passages, perhaps it is useful to quote them here:

Letter to the Church at Magnesia-on-the-Meander, Chapter 7.

In the same way as the Lord was wholly one with the Father, and never acted independently of Him, either in person or through the Apostles, so you must never act independently of your bishop and clergy. On no account persuade yourselves that it is right and proper to follow your own private judgement; have a single service of prayer which everybody attends; one united supplication, one mind, one hope, in love and innocent joyfulness. All of you together, as though you were approaching the only existing temple of God and the only altar, speed to the one and only Jesus Christ—who came down from the one and only Father, is eternally with that One, and to that One is now returned.

Letter to the Church at Philadelphia, Chapter 4.

Make certain, therefore, that you all observe one common Eucharist; for there is but one Body of our Lord Jesus Christ and but one cup of union with His Blood, and one single altar of sacrifice—even as also there is but one bishop, with his clergy and my own fellow-servitors, the deacons. This will ensure that all your doings are in full accord with the will of God.

Letter to the Church at Smyrna, Chapter 8.

Abjure all factions, for they are the beginning of evils. Follow your bishop, every one of you, as obediently as Jesus Christ followed the Father. Obey your clergy too, as you would the Apostles; give your deacons the same reverence that you would to a command from God. Make sure that no step affecting the Church is ever taken by anyone without the bishop's sanction. The sole Eucharist you should consider valid is one that is celebrated by the bishop himself, or by some person authorized by him. Where the bishop is to be seen, there let all his people be; just as wherever Jesus Christ is present, we have the world-wide Church. Nor is it permissible to conduct baptisms or love-feasts without the bishop. On the other hand, whatever does have his sanction can be sure of God's approval too. This is the way to make certain of the soundness and validity of anything you do.[36]

It is evident, however, that the situation of the Church today is somewhat different than that of St. Ignatius of Antioch. It is no longer possible for the bishop to preside at each and every Eucharist celebrated in his Church. Consequently, he must share his liturgical role with his priests.

The Constitution, after speaking of the role of the bishop in article 41 (quoted above), continues:

42. But because it is impossible for the bishop always and everywhere to preside over the whole flock in his Church, he cannot do other than establish lesser groupings of the faithful. Among these the most important are the parishes set up locally under a pastor, who takes the place of the bishop.[37]

The priest is called "one who takes the place of the bishop." Eariler we saw him called "the assistant of the bishop" in the Constitution on the Church.[38] The priest is no longer merely one who is charged with the responsibility of confecting the sacraments.

When the role of the priest is seen only in the limited perspective of "one who brings together the matter and form of the sacraments" so that the sacraments, of themselves, can produce their saving effects, harm is done to the role of the priest. Such a perspective brings with it four dangers: 1.) The priest can be isolated from the laity if we stress only the fact that the priest is different—he has powers they do not have. 2.) The priest can be seen in isolation from his bishop, for once ordained, the priest has the powers necessary to confect the sacraments. 3.) The priest can be seen in isolation from his fellow priests—he does not need them to exercise his office. 4.) The priest can be viewed as a merely passive instrument in the confecting of the sacraments and the real value of his active role overlooked.

The documents promulgated by the Council do not allow us to take such a restricted view of the priest's role. They stress his fellowship with the laity, the bishop, and his fellow priests. They also show the importance of the priest's active and sacramental role in the liturgy.

The *Decree on the Ministry and Life of Priests* begins its presentation of the priesthood by stating that in Christ, "all the faithful are made a holy and royal priesthood."[39] It is "among the faithful" that the Lord has established certain ministers "to join them together into one body where, although one body, not all have the same function."[40] While the priest is anointed by the Holy Spirit and marked with a special character so that he can act in the person of Christ[41] he is not to be isolated from the laity by that fact. He is to "deal with other men as with brothers."[42] The priest "cannot be of service to men if they remain strangers to the life and conditions of men."[43]

The priest must be able to "apply the perennial truth of the Gospel to the concrete circumstances of life."[44] The basis for this unity of priest and people is to be found in their common baptism, confirmation, and especially in their Eucharistic unity.[45]

The priest is responsible for the formation of the community in the Eucharist. He is to cooperate and work together with the laity; the decree states: "The priest is to foster with diligence the various humble and exalted charisms of the laity. . . He should confidently entrust to them duties in the service of the Church, allowing them freedom and room for action."[46]

Christ sent the apostles as he had been sent by the Father. Through these same apostles He made their successors, the bishops, sharers in His consecration and mission:

> Their ministerial role has been handed down to priests in a limited degree. Thus established in the order of the priesthood, they are co-workers of the episcopal order in the proper fulfillment of the apostolic mission entrusted to the latter order by Christ.
>
> Inasmuch as it is connected with the episcopal order, the priestly office shares in the authority by which Christ himself builds up, sanctifies, and rules his Body.[47]

The *Constitution on the Church* spoke of the relation of bishop and priest by using the words "helpers" (. . . with their helpers, the priests and deacons,[48] bishops have therefore taken up the service of the community . . .[49]); "assistants," (in the bishops, for whom priests are assistants . . .[50]); and the *Decree on the Pastoral Office of Bishops* speaks of the priests as "cooperators" or "co-workers."

> All priests, both diocesan and religious, participate in and exercise with the bishop the one priesthood of Christ and are thereby meant to be prudent cooperators of the episcopal order.[51]

The *Constitution on the Liturgy* spoke of the priest as "taking the place of the bishop" at the liturgy[52] and the *Decree on Priests* states that the priest is so united with the bishop, as we have seen above in the citations from St. Ignatius, that "in a certain way the priest makes the bishop present in every gathering of the faithful."[53]

The documents of the Council also state that the priest, at one with the faithful and with the bishop, must also be in fellowship with the other priests. "No priest can accomplish his mission satisfactorily in isolation. . . All priests are united among themselves in an intimate sacramental brotherhood. . . They form one presbytery in a diocese to whose service they are committed under their bishop."[54]

This sharing of ministry and priesthood by priest and bishop has important implications for our study of obedience to liturgical law. The vision of the Council calls for a close cooperation between the bishop and his priests. "On account of this communion in the same ministry and priesthood, the bishop should regard priests as his brothers and friends."[55] Priests on their part must stand by their bishop in sincere charity and obedience.

> This priestly obedience animated with a spirit of cooperation is based on the very sharing in the episcopal ministry which is conferred on priests both through the sacrament of orders and the canonical mission.[56]

This an obedience which "leads to mature freedom of the people of God; of its nature it demands that in the fulfillment of their work priests lovingly and prudently look for new avenues for the greater good of the Church."[57] "Where there is need, they are ready to undertake new pastoral approaches under the lead of the loving Spirit who breathes where he will."[58] However all this "requires that a priest always work in the bond of communion with the bishop and with his brother priests, lest his efforts be in vain."[59]

The *Declaration on Religious Freedom* begins with the words:

> A sense of the dignity of the human person has been impressing itself more and more deeply on the consciousness of contemporary man. And the demand is increasingly made that men and women should act on their own judgment, enjoying and making use of a responsible freedom, not driven by coercion but motivated by a sense of duty.[60]

What is said here in regard to religious freedom in general applies, in a certain sense, to the relation of the priest to liturgical law.

More and more priests must be motivated not merely by the external laws and rubrics, but also by a sense of duty to their mission as priests, to the meaning of the liturgical rite, and to the harmony which must exist within the Church and the diocese.

> In order that the liturgy may produce its full effect, it is necessary that the faithful come to it with proper dispositions, that their thoughts match their words, and that they cooperate with divine grace lest they receive it in vain. Pastors of souls must realize that, when the liturgy is celebrated, more is required than the mere observance of the laws governing valid and licit celebration. It is their duty also to ensure that the faithful take part knowingly, actively, and fruitfully.[61]

Norms for the reform of the liturgy

The first chapter of the Constitution on the liturgy, after treating 1.) The Nature of the Sacred Liturgy and its importance in the Church's life, and 2.) The Promotion of Liturgical Instruction and Active Participation, then turns to the problem of the reform of the liturgy.

The section begins with an introductory paragraph (article 21). After stating that the liturgy is composed of unchangeable elements and changeable elements, it gives the basic principle guiding the reform. Again we see the importance of the liturgy as "sign." We noted that the chapter began with a statement of the sign value of the liturgy: "the liturgy is the outstanding means by which the faithful can express in their lives and manifest to others the mystery of Christ and the real nature of the Church."[62] Here, the role of the liturgy as sign is again emphasized:

> In this restoration, both texts and rites should be drawn up so that they express more clearly the holy things which they signify. Christian people, as far as possible, should be able to understand them with ease and to take part in them fully, actively, and as befits a community.[63]

From the very beginning of the reform, the liturgy is considered in its relation to the "Christian people," the "community."

A. General norms.

The constitution then states three "general norms" (articles 22, 23, and 24).

Article 22 states that the "regulation of the sacred liturgy depends solely on the authority of the Church, that is, on the Apostolic See, and as laws may determine, on the bishop."[64] This norm is the same as we have found above in *Mediator Dei;* however, we must now "re-read" the phrase in the light of the new theological context. We have seen that there has been a change in the way the Council speaks of "Church" and in the way in which the office of the bishop is related to the liturgy.

The second paragraph of the article 22 is not found in the schemata but was added during the Council:

22   2. In virtue of power conceded by the law, the regulation of the liturgy within certain defined limits belongs also to various kinds of competent territorial bodies of bishops legitimately established.[65]

In the introduction to the emendations in which this paragraph is added to the text, we read:

In this article (once 28, now 22) between the first and second sentence, it seems best to insert a new paragraph which treats of the Episcopal Conferences in such a way that this body can be referred to when needed in subsequent articles.

This is a very difficult and at the same time a very important addition. Our entire Constitution on the Sacred Liturgy hinges upon the fact that a large part of the liturgical reform will be given to the bishops for implementation according to the different regions and conditions.[66]

This paragraph is important for an understanding of the liturgical role of the bishop, for its implications for the way in which the bishops are related as a body, and for its decentralization of the liturgical authority.[67]

The third paragraph of article 22 is a quotation from *Mediator Dei:* "Therefore, absolutely no other person, not even a priest, may add, remove, or change anything in the liturgy on his own authority." This paragraph, like the first paragraph of the article, must now be read in the light of the change in its context.

Article 23 states another "general norm"—that there is room for progress but we must retain the tradition. New forms should grow organically from the forms already existing. Here we are reminded of the principles given in the *Memoria:* that the liturgy should retain the good of the tradition and refuse to accept the unworthy elements of the new.

Article 24 gives the principle: "The Sacred Scriptures are of paramount importance in the celebration of the Liturgy." In a context in which we are concerned with the sign value of the liturgy, and in which the liturgy continues the work of Christ revealing the love of the Father, the Scriptures, the homily, and the totality of the sign-value of the rite take on new importance. The emphasis has changed from "matter and form" to the totality of the sacramental sign.

B. Norms drawn from the Hierarchic and Communal nature of the Liturgy.

In the following section (Articles 26 to 32) we see some of the further results of the new relationship between liturgy and Church. If the liturgy is a sign which makes the Church visible to men, the liturgy must be both hierarchic and communal even as is the Church. We stated above that the liturgy was "public" both because it is public "in itself" (ontological perspective) and because it is a "sign" of something public (semiological perspective). Here, in article 26, the two are united in one paragraph: "liturgical services pertain to the whole body of the Church; they manifest it and have effects upon it."

There is no longer any question as to whether or not the liturgy is the concern of only the clergy: the liturgy belongs to the Church, the People of God. However, "it concerns individual members of the Church in different ways, according to the diversity of holy orders, functions, and degrees of participation."[68]

Consequently, as a general principle, (article 27) the rites should make provision for communal celebration and a celebration that involves the presence and active participation of the faithful is to be preferred to a celebration that is "quasi-private." Everyone should perform his role but only his role (article 28). Servers, lectors, commentators, choir—all have a "genuine liturgical ministry" (article 29). The rubrics themselves should make clear the fact that the liturgy pertains to the whole people of God and take the role of the people into account (article 31).

C. Norms based upon the Educative and Pastoral nature of the Liturgy.

Although the sacred liturgy is above all things the worship of the divine Majesty, it likewise contains abundant instruction for the faithful.[69]

The explanation of this article, given in the schema of August 10,

1961 (which included not only the articles but also much explanatory material and historical references) reads:

> Not only the seven sacraments, but in its own fashion, the entire liturgy by its very nature is made up of sensible signs: words and things perceptible by the senses. And "signs are oriented to instruction."
>
> Therefore, even though the liturgy is primarily directed to the worship of God, nevertheless, the entire liturgy, by its very essence, is also directed to a pastoral and didactic end. This is true whether we consider the sensible objects and actions used in the rite, or whether we consider the words and texts. It is true even more so in the case of vocal prayers and songs, especially those which are said by the people, but it is also true even of those things which are said to God by the minister in the name of the people.[70]

After the general introduction stated in article 33 as quoted above, the article gives another reason for the educative and pastoral nature of the liturgy: "In the liturgy God speaks to His people through Christ in still proclaiming his Gospel. The people reply to God both by songs and by prayer." The liturgy continues the work of Christ revealing the Father for in the liturgy God continues to speak to us through Christ.[71]

The three articles which follow (Articles 34, 35, 36) state general norms which will allow the educative and pastoral nature of the liturgy to be more fully realized:

Article 34 states that the rites should be simple and noble; clear, short, unencumbered by useless repetitions; they must be understandable.

Article 35 again emphasizes the importance of the liturgy of the Word: there is to be more reading from holy Scripture, the sermon is to be included in the rubrics as an integral part of the liturgy, the ministry of preaching is to be fulfilled with exactitude and fidelity.

Article 36 treats of one of the major factors in the educative and pastoral dimension of the liturgy: the question of liturgical language.

D. Norms for adapting the Liturgy to the Genius and Traditions of Peoples.

The Church transcends all limits of time and race and is destined to extend to all regions of the earth and to enter into the history of mankind.[72] If the Church is destined to extend to all cultures and peoples, the liturgy as a manifestation of the Church must also be so destined. The introduction to this section of the Constitution states:

> Even in the liturgy, the Church has no wish to impose a rigid uniformity in matters which do not involve the faith or the good of the whole community. Rather she respects and fosters the spiritual adornments and gifts of the various races and peoples.[73]

Three principles are given for this adaptation: Article 38 states that the revised books should allow for legitimate variations. Article 39 states that within the limits set by the typical editions of the liturgical books, the Conferences of Bishops are to adapt the liturgy to their regions. Article 40 speaks of places and circumstances in which an even more radical adaption of the liturgy is needed. In actual practice, and as the new liturgical books are published, we will see that these last two articles are not always distinguished but merge into one: the authority of the Episcopal Conferences.

Conclusion: The change in the theological context of liturgical law.

At the beginning of this study we noted some of the deficiencies in the presentation of the theological context of liturgical law. We have seen how some of these deficiencies were remedied by *Mediator Dei.* However, with the teachings of the Council, many of these problems now disappear.

First of all, the liturgy is reunited to the Church—the liturgy is a manifestation of the nature of the Church—the Church is formed and structured by the liturgy. The liturgy, and the sacraments therefore, are essentially public expressions of cult and not only "personal means of grace."

The emphasis is no longer merely on the "matter and form" of the sacrament but upon its entire liturgical expression. The role of the minister takes on a new importance in assuring that the rite truly signifies the holy things that it effects.

The Church itself is seen as sacrament and mystery. The laity take their rightful place in the Church, and consequently, in the liturgy.

The bishop is not only the liturgical "authority" but the liturgical leader. His role is not only juridical but symbolic and sacramental. The liturgical role of the priest is seen as common with that of the bishop of the diocese.

Liturgical law takes on a new importance: liturgical law is not only the regulation of something the Church *does*; liturgical law is important in relation to what the Church *is*. It is in the liturgy that we can see the true nature of the Church.

NOTES

[1] 1959 JUN 18.

[2] Ibid. ADVatII. Series I. Vol. I. pp. 159-163.

[3] Ibid. p. 162.

[4] Ibid. p. 159.

Ce sera, comme on peut le criore aujourd'hui, un Concile, je dirais d'ordre réel, pratique, plutôt qu'un Concile vraiment d'ordre doctrinal.

[5] For the Latin text, see *1960 JUL 09* of the Bibliography.

[6] ADVat II. Series I. Vol. III. Proposita et Monita SS. Congregationum Curiae.Romanae, p. 11.

7. De Laicis

Notio et locus Laici in Ecclesia. Laicus non merum *obiectum* sed etiam *subiectum,* et quidem *activum,* in Ecclesia.

Quid de *Sacerdotio fidelium.* Laicorum dignitas ex *charactere baptismi* et *confirmationis:* eorum positio ac responsabilitas in Corpore Mystico.

Laicorum *conditio iuridica* in Ecclesia, relate ad Hierarchiam; eorum apostolatus.

De Laicis integrum caput esset in C.I.C. inserendum.

[7] Ibid. p. 13.

Magnum momentum Liturgiae quoad cultum Dei et fidelium sanctificationem. Liturgia, connexa cum Praedicatione et Regimine, neutri surrogari potest.—Liturgia ut locus theologicus (*Lex precandi, lex credendi*).

De plena auctoritate Ecclesiae in materia liturgica, praesertim quoad ordinationem rituum et linguam adhibendam. Quid circa hoc Episcopis tribui possit.

[8] ADVatII. Series I. Vol III. p. 249.

Reformentur libri liturgici adaptando eosdem ad conditiones hodiernas praesertim in Missionibus et conficiatur Codex liturgicus.

Utrum et quousque liceat quod omnino expedire videtur, ut longua "vernacula" amplius adhibeatur in actionibus liturgicis, maxime quidem in administratione sacramentorum et sacramentalium.

[9] ADVatII. Series I. Vol III. pp. 80-94.

[10] Ibid. p. 255.

[11] Ibid. pp. 251-296.

[12] Ibid. pp. 274-275.

1. Votum generale.—Omnibus et singulis supra expositis ponderatis et per-pensis, haec S. Rituum Congregatio ad hanc sententiam generalem pervenit, adnitendum esse quam maxime, ut usus linguae latinae in Liturgia Ecclesiae latinae in suo statu servetur.

2. Rogandum vero est Concilium, ut inveniat modos efficaces quibus procuretur, ubique terrarum, talis futuri cleri in lingua latina institutio, ut reapse capax sit ad hanc linguam in omnibus ritibus et officiis liturgicis recte adhibendam et plane intelligendam, ita ut ex hoc capite removeatur omnis iusta contra linguam latinam liturgicam quaerimonia.

[13] In Latin, the text uses three words: the members (sodales) of the commission are either members (membra) or consultants (periti). In this study *members* translates *soldales* or *membra,* the sense will be determined by the context.

[14] see Bibliography 1961 APR 12 to 22. (Note also that it is not until after this meeting that the results of the consultation of the bishops of 1956-1957 are published.)

[15] 1961 AUG 10.

[16] 1949 DEC 30, pages 19-20.

[17] 1961 AUG 10, page IV.

[18] 1961 NOV 15.

[19] 1962 JUL 13.

[20] All references to the Constitution on the Liturgy are to the final text as promulgated by the Council, see Bibliography 1963 DEC 04. If the reference is to an earlier schema, this fact will be noted and the date of the schema given. Full reference can then be found from the Bibliography.

[21] SC 2.

Liturgia enim, per quam, maxime in divino Eucharistiae Sacrificio, "opus nostrae Redemptionis exercetur" somme eo confert ut fideles vivendo exprimant et aliis manifestent mysterium Christi et genuinam verae Ecclesiae naturam, . . .

[22] previous quotation continues:

. . . cuius proprium est esse humanam simul ac divinam, visibilem invisibilibus praeditam, actione ferventem et contemplationi vacantem, in mundo praesentem et tamen peregrinam.

[23] SC 5. passim.

[24] LG 1.

Cum autem Ecclesia sit in Christo veluit sacramentum seu signum et instrumentum intimae cum Deo unionis totiusque generis humani unitatis.

[25] SC 7.

Ad tantum vero opus perficiendum, Christus Ecclesiae suae semper adest, praesertim in actionibus liturgicis.

[26] See Bibliography 1962 NOV 10. The Latin titles:

Schema constitutionis dogmaticae de Ecclesia

Caput
1. De Ecclesiae militantis natura
2. De membris Ecclesiae militantis eiusdemque necessitate ad salutem
3. De Episcopatu ut supremo gradu Sacramenti Ordinis et de Sacerdotio
4. De Episcopis residentialibus
5. De statibus evangelicae acquirendae perfectionis
6. De laicis
7. De Ecclesiae magisterio
8. De auctoritate et obedientia in Ecclesia
9. De relationibus inter Ecclesiam et Statum
10. De necessitate Ecclesiae annuntiandi Evangelium omnibus gentibus et ubique terrarum
11. De oecumenismo

Schema constitutionis dogmaticae de Beata Maria Virgine Mater Dei et Mater Hominum

De Beata Maria Virgine Mater Dei et Mater Hominum.

²⁷ LG. Latin titles:

Constitutio Dogmatica de Ecclesia

Caput
1. De Ecclesiae Mysterio
2. De Populo Dei
3. De Constitutione Hierarchica Ecclesiae et in Specie de Episcopatu
4. De Laicis
5. De Universali Vocatione ad Sanctitatem in Ecclesia
6. De Religiosis
7. De Indole Eschatologica Ecclesiae Peregrinantis Eiusque unione cum Ecclesia Caelesti
8. De Beata Maria Virgine Deipara in Mysterio Christi et Ecclesiae

²⁸ Avery Dulles, S.J. "The Church," in Abbott, *Documents* . . . pp. 10-12.

²⁹ LG 11. passim.

³⁰ K. Barth. *Kirchliche Dogmatik* IV/2. Zollikon-Zurich, 1955, p. 791. Cited by Gy, LMD 112 (1972) 21.

³¹ Congar. "Rudolf Sohm nous interroge encore," RSPT 57 (1973) 263-294. We quote here Congar's conclusions on page 286. The reference to St Thomas, Fundamentum cuiuslibet legis in sacramentis consistit, is from IV Sent. D.7, 9. q. a 1; ad Im.

³² Gy. LMD 112 (1972) 20.

L'Eglise, convoquée par l'annonce de la foi, est constitutuée comme *congregatio fidelium* par le baptême, sacrement de la foi, assemblée a son Chef et vivifiée par lui dans L'Eucharistie, dirigée par le ministère apostolique sacramentel. Ce sont les sacrements qui la structurent. Là est le plus important du droit liturgique, en soi et par conséquent dans la responsabilité de l'évêque. Les sacrements et les données de base de la pastorale sacramentelle appartiennent à la structure de L'Eglise, à ce qui en elle vient de Dieu et la constitue sacrement de Dieu. Les évêques de l'Eglise ancienne en ont conscience et y donnent une grande part de leur activité collégiale, dont les documents forment avec les consultations papales le droit ancien de L'Eglise.

33 LG 21.

34 In relation to the "bishop as sacrament" we refer the reader once again to the article of Fr. John E. Rotelle, "Liturgy and Authority," *Worship* 47 (1973) 514-526.

35 SC 41. English translation by the Author.

Episcopus ut sacerdos magnus sui gregis habendus est, a quo vita suorum fidelium in Christo quodammodo derivatur et pendet.

Quare omnes vitam liturgicam dioeceseos circa Episcopum, praesertim in ecclesia cathedrali, maximi faciant oportet: sibi persuasum habentes praecipuam manifestationem Ecclesiae haberi in plenaria et actuosa participatione totius plebis sanctae Dei in iisdem celebrationibus liturgicis, praesertim in eadem Eucharistia, in una oratione, ad unum altare cui praeest Episcopus a suo presbyterio et ministris circumdatus.

36 M. Staniforth, *Early Christian Writings* (Penguin Books, 1968), pp. 88-89; 112; 121-122.

37 SC 42.

Cum Episcopus in Ecclesia sua ipsemet nec semper nec ubique universo gregi praeesse possit, necessario constituere debet fidelium coetus, inter quos paroeciate, localiter sub pastore vices gerente Episcopi ordinatae, eminent: nam quodammodo repraesentat Ecclesiam visibilem per orbem terrarum constitutam.

38 See above, page 108, LG 21, Latin note 33.

39 PO 2.

40 Ibid.

41 Ibid.

42 PO 3. ". . . cum ceteris hominibus tamquam cum fratribus conversantur."

43 PO 3.

Ministri Christi esse non possent nisi alius vitae quam terrenae testes essent et dispensatores, sed neque hominibus inservire valerent si ab eorum vita condicionibusque alieni remanerent.

44 PO 4.

Sacerdotalis vero praedicatio, in hodiernis mundi adiunctis haud raro perdifficilis, ut auditorum mentes aprius moveat, verbum Dei non modo generali et abstracto tantum exponere debet, sed concretis applicando vitae circumstantiis veritatem Evangelii perennem.

45 PO 5.

46 PO 9.

Probantes spiritus si ex Deo sint, charismata laicorum multiformia, tam humilia quam altiora, cum sensu fidei detegant, cum gaudio agnoscant, cum diligentia foveant.

. . . Presbyteri sincere laicorum dignitatem atque propriam, quam laici in missione Ecclesiae habent partem, agnoscant et promoveant. Iustam etiam libertatem, quae omnibus in civitate terrestri competit, sedulo in honore habeant.

[47] PO 2.

Itaque, missis Apostolis sicut Ipse missus erat a Patre, Christus per ipsos Apostolos consecrationis missionisque suae participes effecit eorum successores, Episcopos, quorum munus ministerii, subordinato gradu, Presbyteris traditum est, ut in Ordine presbyteratus constituti, ad rite explendem missionem apostolicam a Christo concreditam, Ordinis episcopalis essent cooperatores.

Officium Presbyterorum, utpote Ordini episcopali coniunctum, participat auctoritatem qua Christus Ipse suum exstruit, sanctificat et regit.

[48] The liturgical ministry of the deacon does not figure predominantly in the discussions of the Council as the restoration of the permanent deaconate is still a relatively "new" factor in the liturgical experience of the Latin Church. Perhaps with the development of the deaconate and as the deacons begin to exercise their proper liturgical functions—and perhaps also serve as the liturgical focus in those communities without priests—what is said here with regard to the obedience to liturgical law with regard to priests can be applied, with the necessary adaptations, to deacons also.

[49] LG 20.

[50] LG 21.

[51] CD 28.

Omnes quidem presbyteri sive dioecesani sive religiosi, unum sacerdotium Christi cum Episcopo participant et exercent, ideoque episcopalis providi cooperatores constituuntur.

[52] SC 42. Latin text, see above note 37.

[53] PO 5.

In omnibus autem Sacramentis conficiendis, ut iam primaevae Ecclesiae temporibus testatus est beatus Ignatius Martyr, Presbyteri diversis rationibus cum Episcopo hierarchice colligantur, et sic eum in singulis fidelium · congregationibus quodammodo praesentem reddunt.

[54] PO 7 and 8.

[55] PO7.

. . . Episcopi ut fratres et amicos suos habeant Presbyteros, . . .

[56] PO 7.

Quae sacerdotalis oboedientia, cooperationis spiritu perfusa, fundatur in ipsa participatione ministerii episcopalis, quae Presbyteris per Sacramentum Ordinis et missionem canonicam confertur.

[57] PO 15.

Haec oboedientia, quae ad maturiorem libertatem filiorum Dei adducit, natura sua exigit ut, dum, in suo munere adimplendo, caritate moti, vias novas ad maius Ecclesiae bonum prudenter exquirunt, Presbyteri incepta sua fidenter proponant, et necessitudines gregis sibi commissi instanter exponant, parati semper ad illorum se subiiciendos iudicio, qui princeps in Ecclesia Dei regenda munus exercent.

[58] PO 13.

. . . et, ubi opus sit, ad novas vias pastorales ingrediendas parati, sub ductu Spiritus amoris, qui ubi spirat.

[59] PO 14.

Pastoralis ergo caritas postulat ut Presbyteri, ne in vacuum currant, in vinculo communionis cum Episcopis et cum aliis in sacerdotio fratribus semper laborent.

[60] *Dignitatis Humanae. Declaratio de Libertate Religiosa.*

1. Dignitatis humanae personae homines hac nostra aetate magis in dies conscii fiunt, atque numerus eorum crescit qui exigunt, ut in agendo homines proprio suo consilio et libertate responsabili fruantur et etantur, non coercitione commoti, sed officii conscientia ducti.

[61] SC 11.

Ut haec tamen plena efficacitas habeatur, necessarium est ut fideles cum recti animi dispositionibus ad sacram Liturgiam accedant, mentem suam voci accommodent, et supernae gratiae cooperentur, ne eam in vacuum recipiant. Ideo sacris pastoribus advigilandum est ut in actione liturgica non solum observentur leges ad validam et licitam celebrationem, sed ut fideles scienter, actuose et fructuose eandem participent.

[62] SC 2. Latin text, see above, note 21.

[63] SC 21.

Qua quidem instauratione, textus et ritus ita ordinari oportet, ut sancta, quae significant, clarius exprimant, eaque populus christianus, in quantum fieri potest, facile percipere atque plena, actuosa et communitatis propria celebratione participare possit.

[64] SC 22 1.

Sacrae Liturgiae moderatio ab Ecclesiae auctoritate unice pendet: quae quidem est apud Apostolicam Sedem et, ad normam iuris, apud Episcopum.

[65] SC 22 2.

Ex potestate a iure concessa, rei liturgicae moderatio inter limites statutos pertinet quoque ad competentes varii generis territoriales Episcoporum coetus legitime constitutos.

[66] See 1962 OCT 22, page 7.

Olim 28 nunc 22: In hoc articulo, inter primam et secundam sententiam, censuimus inserendam paragraphum novam quae ita tractet de conferentiis episcopalibus, ut deinceps ad illam referatur quoties de hac materia in subsequentibus articulis agendum sit.

Res quam difficillima erat, et simul maximi momenti, Tota enim nostra constitutio de Sacra Liturgia eum cardinem habet ut liturgica instauratio pro magna parte ab Episcopis, varie secundum varias regionum conditiones, executioni mandetur.

[67] For example, see the commentary by Josef Andreas Jungmann in *Lexikon Für Theologie and Kirche,* Das. Zweite Vatikanische Konzil, Konstitutionen, Dekrete und Erklarungen, 1966, pp. 32-33.

Mit Artikel 22 wird das Recht der Liturgischen Gesetzgebung auf eine neue Grundlage gestellt. Die strenge Zentralisierung, mit der die Liturgie der abendländischen Kirche nach dem Konzil von Trient aus dem Zerfall der liturgischen Formem am Ausgang des Mittelalters herausgefuhrt und wieder zu einer festen Ordnung zurückgeführt worden war und die sich im CIC formuliert fand, wird darin ac 400 Jahren zum erstenmal wesentlich gelockert.

[68] SC 26.

Quare ad universum Corpus Ecclesiae pertinent, illudque manifestant et afficiunt; singula vero membra ipsius diverso modo, pro diversitate ordinum, munerum et actualis participationis attingunt.

[69] SC 33.

Etsi sacra Liturgia est praecipue cultus divinae maiestatis, magnam etiam continet populi fidelis eruditionem. In Liturgia enim Deus ad populum suum loquitur; Christus adhuc Evangelium annuntiat. Populus vero Deo respondet tum cantibus tum oratione.

[70] See Bibliography 1961 AUG 10. Note on what is now SC 33 reads:

Generales normae instaurationis ex natura didactica et pastorali liturgiae:

Non solum septem sacramenta, sed suo modo, tota liturgia, ex essentia sui, etiam signis sensibilibus constat: verbis et rebus, quibus etiam actus sensibiles pertinent. "Signa vero ad instructionem pertinent."

Quare, quamvis liturgia praeprimis intendat cultum Deo debite reddendum, tamen tota ex essentia sui etiam aliquem finem pastoralem et instructionis prosequitur, tum in rebus et actibus sensibilibus cum in verbis quibus utitur. Et hoc summo gradu in actibus directe didacticis: in gradu vero adhuc magno in orationibus vocalibus et cantibus: primarie in illis quae ab ipso populo dici debent, secundarie vero etiam in eis quae a pinistro, nomine populi, ad Deum diriguntur.

[71] SC 33. Latin text, see above, Note 69.

[72] LG·9.

Ad universas regiones extendenda, in historiam intrat, dum tamen simul tempora et fines populorum transcendit.

[73] SC 37.

Ecclesia, in iis quae fidem aut bonum totius communitatis non tangunt,

rigidam unius tenoris formam ne in Liturgia quidem imponere cupit, quin-
immo, variarum gentium populorumque animi ornamenta ac dotes colit
et provehit.

IV.

The Theological Context Of Liturgical Law Found In The Documents Implementing The Reform Of The Council

The change in theológical perspective brought about by the Council has progessively found expression in the liturgical rites. In this chapter of our study we will examine the documents which have been promulgated after the Council with regard to liturgy and liturgical law and trace the stages of the incorporation of the change in theological context into the expression of the liturgical laws. This chapter is not a commentary on each of the texts nor is it a history of the liturgy after the Council. We want only to show the way in which the liturgical laws have changed after the council and the implications with regard to the obedience due to the new liturgical laws.

1964 JAN 25 The motu proprio "Sacram Liturgiam"

The implementation of the Constitution on the Liturgy began soon after its promulgation on December 4, 1963, at the close of the second session of the Council. The following month Pope Paul made an ecumenical journey to the Holy Land (January 4 to 6, 1964) and later that same month (January 25) issued the motu proprio "Sacram Liturgiam" on implementing the Constitution.

> Since among the norms of the constitution there are some which can be made effective now, we desire that they enter immediately into force, so that the souls of the faithful may not be further deprived of the fruits of the grace which are hoped for from them.[1]

The introduction to the document also states that a special commission is being established to revise the rites and prepare the new liturgical books. This is the origin of the "Commission for the implementation of the Constitution on the Liturgy," which we will refer to as the "Consilium." The Consilium begins its work without delay and we will see the first of their documents appear the following September.

The motu proprio exhorts bishops and priests to "hasten to act in order that the faithful entrusted to their care may understand the strength and inner value of the liturgy."[2] The date set for the first of the changes implementing the Constitution was the First Sunday of Lent, February 16, 1964.

Pope Paul then lists in 11 articles those aspects of the Constitution which will go into effect on that date. The first of the articles of the Constitution which are to be applied quickly are articles 15-17 concerning the teaching of liturgy in seminaries. The introduction to these articles states that "there is no hope of realizing a liturgical reform unless the pastors themselves become thoroughly penetrated with the spirit and power of the liturgy and become masters of it."[3] When the motu proprio speaks of teaching liturgy in the seminaries, evidently the reference is not directed primarily toward teaching the new rubrics for they have not yet been published; rather these articles concern the teaching of the principles of the liturgy and the integration of this instruction with the entire course of theology. The liturgy course is to be a "theology course" and not merely a course in the externals of the rites. It is not just a question of teaching new laws and rubrics but of allowing the seminarians to become "masters of the liturgical spirit."

Section II of the document calls for the rapid establishment of liturgical commissions. The reform cannot take place properly unless those bodies which will be responsible for the preparation and implementation of the reform are established and functioning.

Section III calls for the homily to be given on Sundays and Holy Days. During this time of change, the faithful will need to know the underlying reasons for the reform and the "general principles" which make the reform necessary and desirable. If this instruction is lacking, the reform will not be understood or perhaps not even accepted. And in many cases, the only time when this instruction can be given is during the homily on Sundays and Holy Days. And if there is to be more reading from Scripture (SC 24, 35, 51) so that "richer fare may be provided for the faithful at the table of God's Word," these texts will often have to be made understandable and relevant to the congregation—especially for those with little or no formation in biblical studies.

Sections V through XI allow certain changes in confirmation, matrimony, and the divine office which do not require the liturgical books to be revised. The relation between the sacraments as an act of faith in response to the call of the Gospel is demonstrated by placing the sacramental rites after the proclamation of the Gospel and homily at Eucharistic celebrations.

Section X speaks of the National Conferences of Bishops mentioned in SC 22 § 2. This body will be of key importance for the adaptation of the liturgy to the different countries.

Section XI restates 1 and 3 of this same article: the regulation of the liturgy comes under the authority of the Church, and consequently no one else, not even a priest, can on his own initiative add or subtract or change anything in liturgical matters.[4]

1964 SEP 26 The First Instruction (Inter Oecumenici) for the proper implementation of the Constitution.

The third session of the Council opened on September 14, and in the opening address, Pope Paul stated that the central objective of this session would be to investigate and clarify the doctrine of the nature of the Church. We have already studied the results of this session of the Council and the description of the Church in terms of "mystery" and "sacrament."

In relation of the growing recognition of the place of the laity in the Church and the liturgy, we might note that there were women observers at this session of the Council. In his address Pope Paul stated that "We are delighted to welcome among the auditors our beloved daughters in Christ, the first women in history to participate in a conciliar assembly."[5]

While the Council Fathers were debating and voting on the Constitution on the Church (September 16 to November 21) the Consilium and the Congregation of Rites published their *First Instruction* on the implementation of the *Constitution on the Liturgy.*

Before treating of any specific changes in the liturgy the instruction first speaks of the "spirit" of the liturgy. We noted earlier that liturgical law before the Council was primarily the statement of individual, specific directives. The final paragraphs of *Mediator Dei* begin to speak of the "spirit" of the liturgy and the *Constitution on the Liturgy* often speaks of the importance of this "spirit."[6] From the very first paragraph of this Instruction we find mention of the importance of this "spirit" if the reform is to be fruitful: "it will bear more abundant fruit the more profoundly the pastors and the faithful of Christ perceive its genuine spirit and put it into practice with good will."[7]

Article 5 states that the primary intention of the Council was not just to change the rubrics and the texts but was directed toward the theological context of the rites:

5. Nevertheless, it is necessary first that all be persuaded of the in-

tention of the Constitution on the Sacred Liturgy of the Second Vatican Council: not only to change liturgical forms and texts, but rather to stir up that formation of the faithful and pastoral activity which has the sacred liturgy as summit and font. The changes thus far introduced and to be introduced into the sacred liturgy in the future are directed toward this end.[8]

If the Church is structured and constituted liturgically, then the liturgy must be central to the mission of the Church and the pastoral activity of its ministers. The instruction states that the pastoral and liturgical action of priests must be closely joined. "It is especially necessary that there be a close union between the liturgy and catechesis, religious formation, and preaching."[9]

The Instruction then turns to the application of some of the "general liturgical principles" of the Council which can be applied without waiting for the reform of the liturgical books. For example, we saw that one of the general principles was: "The rites should be distinguished by a noble simplicity; they should be short, clear, and unencumbered by useless repetitions" (SC 34). The Instruction then indicates some of the applications of this principle: simplification of the salutations to the choir, the incensation of the clergy, the elimination of the kisses of the hand and of objects being presented or received (Art. 36).

This is an example of the law presenting a general principle and then giving examples of when it is to be applied. But what is to keep the individual bishop, pastor or priest from applying the principle to other, similar cases? Formerly, when the laws listed only specific directives, this type of dilemma did not often arise with regard to obedience to liturgical law. Once the law gives "principles" and "applications" there is the possibility of conflict between the obedience demanded on each of these levels.

The Instruction states that no one is to try to apply the principles himself:

20. Regulation of the sacred liturgy pertains to the authority of the Church; therefore, no other person shall proceed in this matter on his own authority to the detriment, as may often happen, of the liturgy itself and of its restoration by the competent authority.[10]

Receiving Communion twice on the same day.—Article 60 of the Instruction states that the faithful who communicate in the Mass of the Easter Vigil or in the midnight Mass of Christmas may also receive communion again in the second Mass of Easter and in one of the Masses which are celebrated on Christmas in the daytime.

The Constitution does not mention the reception of Communion more than once a day, but it does state the importance of receiving Communion as a sign of the participation in the Eucharistic celebration (SC 48, 55). The Instruction permits this participation by sacramental Communion twice at Christmas and Easter.

In *Notitiae* the question is asked: why are there only two days when this principle can be applied? The reply states that on these two days there are two distinct liturgies and it is not a question of mere repetition of Communion. The reply concludes: "Briefly, when one liturgy is celebrated, even if it is repeated, we may go to Communion only once; when two offices are celebrated, we may go to Communion twice."[11] But what of other days when two offices are celebrated? Little by little, the legislation takes note of these situations. In the ten years which follow, at least six different documents expand the applications of this principle.[12]

1965	MAR 07	Rite for concelebration, number 15
1967	MAY 04	Second instruction, number 14
1967	MAY 25	Instruction on Eucharistic Worship, number 28
1969	APR 06	Order of Mass, numbers 76 and 158
1972	AUG 07	Declaration on Concelebration, numbers 1 and 3
1973	JAN 29	Instruction facilitating Communion

Neither the clergy nor the laity were accustomed to a liturgical law which involved the application of general principles, and the continual changing of the specific legislation applying the principles no doubt contributed to the difficulties with obedience to liturgical law at this time. This legislation can also indicate a certain lack of co-ordination between the various congregations and commissions issuing the legislation.

After the Instruction went into effect on March 7, 1965, the Consilium asked the presidents of the various Episcopal Conferences to give a report on the reception of the Instruction.[13] Reading these reports we find that the bishops mention certain difficulties with regard to obedience which the new rubrics present to the priests. They sometimes have to make decisions concerning the pastoral applications of liturgical principles, and formerly these decisions were the responsibility of the bishop or the Holy See. Priests have not been trained to make this type of liturgical decision.

Also mentioned was the difficulty found in allowing each member of the liturgical assembly to perform his or her proper liturgical role; formerly the priest was trained to accept the total responsibility for the liturgical action.

As an example of these replies from the bishops, we cite the report of the French bishops, which states, in part:

> Much more than new rubrics, priests want a solid explanation of the principles of the reform; they expect this. Many of them have received only a rubrical training in liturgy and have studied little regarding the content and the expression of the liturgical mysteries.

> Dialogue with the laity, in this matter, is elementary, although there is a real beginning. The diversity of ministeries in the liturgical action is not always understood: up to this time the priest has always done everything.[14]

1965 JAN 27 The Order of Mass.

The decree "Nuper edita" which introduces this new order of Mass states that the document is necessary because of the many changes that have taken place in the rite. This new "Ordo" is to be printed in new editions of the missal so that there is no need to continue printing rubrics which are already "out of date."

The document represents the last stages of the missal of St. Pius V and also one of the last examples of the pre-Conciliar style of liturgical law. The rubrics are simple and direct statements. No general principles are given; nor does the "Ritus" give footnotes referring to the Constitution on the Liturgy stating where the general principles may be found. The rubrics determine each detail of the celebration: "Arriving at the altar the celebrant makes the sign of the cross: with the palm of his right hand turned toward himself and all the fingers joined and extended, he forms the sign of the cross, beginning from his forehead. . ." Although this degree of detail may seem exaggerated to those familiar only with the more recent rubrics, they did assure that the rite would have a certain dignity and elegance—principles which are to be understood as general principles of the new rubrics even when they are not explicitly stated. Also, the degree of detail regulated by the rubrics is not to be confused with the sometimes minutely detailed instruction given in some liturgy manuals. We must not reproach the official text for things found only in the commentaries.

The new rubrics take into account the possibility of Mass facing the people, the priest going to the chair for the liturgy of the word, and for the prayer of the faithful "according to local custom." However, we do not yet find the wide possibility of options and possibility for adaptation which have become so characteristic of the new rubrics.

The "Ordo" gives only the directions as to what is to be done; the *spirit* of the rubrics must be found elsewhere. For example, we have mentioned several times above the growing importance of the homily and the role it plays as an integral part of the liturgical action.[15] The "Ordo" states merely: "After the Gospel, the celebrant gives the homily, if there is to be one, from his seat, from the altar, or in the pulpit or at the Communion rail."[16] However, for the spirit of the rubric and the importance of the homily the priest must read the documents giving the spirit of the liturgical laws.

Although the Council stressed the importance of the sacramental role of the bishop in the liturgical assembly, the "Ordo" does not give any particular importance to a celebration led by the bishop. The rite explains how the bishop is to mention himself in the canon (even as direction is given for how the Supreme Pontiff is to name himself in the canon), but the more general position for the bishop seems to be that he "presides" from his throne and the priest celebrates "before" or "in the presence" of the bishop. Although the rite for concelebration was not published until a month and a half later, the rite was already approved along with the rite for Communion under both Kinds, by the Consilium on June 20, 1964, and sent to the Pope on June 26, 1964—six months before the publication of the new "Ordo" for Mass.[17] Yet the "Ordo" does not mention either rite. If the publication of the "Ordo" were delayed a month, it would have been possible to include many more of the changes then under consideration.

This is the last example that I have found of rubrics which explicitly mention that the laws bind under grave sin. For example in the section "De defectibus" we read that if the bread is not wheat bread, the sacrament is not confected. If the bread has has begun to go stale or if the bread is leavened, the sacrament is confected, but the one confecting sins gravely (graviter peccat, article 5). If one should omit or add anything to the formula for consecration, he sins most gravely (gravissime peccaret, article 20).

1965 MAR 07 Rite for Concelebration of Mass.

The Rite for Concelebration and the Rite for Communion under both species were approved by the Consilium June 20, 1964 (at the same time as the "First Instruction") and they were promulgated the following year on March 7. They were to go into effect for the celebration of Holy Thursday, April 15, 1965. The English translation received the imprimatur on April 6, leaving only *nine days* to be printed, distributed to the bishops and priests of the United States, and explained to the faithful as directed by number 11 of the rite: "Pastors of souls are to see to it that the faithful who are to be present for the concelebration are given the proper instruction regarding the significance of this rite."[18] At this time in the history of liturgical law, the priests of the United States were not often informed of the documents under consideration in Rome, but were only presented the documents in their final form, often leaving little time for the priests to absorb the spirit of the new rites so as to be able to explain them to others and to celebrate them with the obedience called for by the spirit of the document.

The Council stated that "in the restoration of the liturgy both the texts and rites should be drawn up so that they express more clearly the holy things which they signify" (SC 21). The decree introducing the new rite begins:

It has always been the concern of the Church, where establishing and restoring the celebrations of the Sacred Mysteries, that these rites be true signs of the inexhaustible riches of Christ, which they contain and which they communicate to those who are well disposed, and in this way more easily enrich the souls and the lives of the faithful who participate in them.[19]

Again we see the importance of the liturgy as a "sign." The Constitution on the Liturgy called for the restoration of the rite of concelebration "by which the unity of the priesthood is appropriately manifested" (SC 57). The introduction to the new rite very carefully explains that it is because of the sign value of the rite, much more than for reasons of the merely practical order, that concelebration has been restored to the Roman rite.[20]

After this theological and liturgical introduction the rite lists the times when the rite may be employed. As in the case of "receiving Communion more than once," the practical application of the principles undergoes many changes—the applications become larger and larger with each new document. The progressive nature and continual change of this type of legislation leads us to conclude that while the legislation is important from the viewpoint of liturgical discipline, the more important values are the theological values.

1965 MAR 07 Rite for the Distribution of Communion under Both Kinds

The Constitution on the Liturgy (SC 55) stated:

The dogmatic principles which were laid down by the Council of Trent remaining intact, Communion under both kinds may be granted when the bishops think fit, not only to the clerics and religious, but also to the laity, in cases to be determined by the Apostolic See, as, for instance, to the newly ordained in the Mass of their sacred ordination, to the newly professed in the Mass of their religious profession, and to the newly baptized in a Mass following their baptism.[21]

The dogmatic principles of Trent referred to (XXI 1-9) state that Christ is present whole and entire even under the bread (or wine) alone; no grace necessary for salvation is denied to those who receive only the bread; the Church has power to regulate, not the substance of the sacraments, but those things which are for the welfare of those who receive them.

The new rite for Communion under both species is, as was the case with concelebration, directed primarily toward the sign value of the rite. The introduction states that "pastors should urge the faithful to exert themselves most eagerly to participate in this sacred rite by which the sign of the Eucharistic banquet is more clearly seen."[22] The Order for Mass of 1969 will state the principle clearly:

240. The sign of communion is more complete when given with both bread and wine since the sign of the Eucharistic meal appears more clearly. The intention of Christ that the new and eternal covenant be ratified in his blood is better expressed, as is the relation of the Eucharistic banquet to the heavenly banquet.[23]

If the sign of Communion under both kinds is "better" or "more complete" than Communion with bread alone, we might ask why this form of Communion is not always permitted. From the legislation, the answer to this question seems to depend on two factors: the new rites are usually introduced gradually, beginning with a few examples and then being extended to other cases. Secondly, there seem to be reservations on the part of the Holy See because of the technical difficulties involved and because of the danger of irreverence to the sacrament.

As we have seen above with reference to Communion more than once a day and concelebration, the practical applications of the principle with regard to Communion under both kinds has undergone many changes in the past ten years. The more important documents are listed in the alphabetical listing of the official documents found in the Bibliography, under the heading "Communion under the forms of both bread and wine." At least twelve changes have been made in the application of the principle in ten years.

1965 JUN 30 Letter of Cardinal Lercaro (president of the Consilium) to the presidents of the Episcopal Conferences.

The response to the First Instruction (Inter Oecumenici) was very positive and Cardinal Lercaro writes that "it is with emotion and admiration that we witness a new movement of the Holy Spirit in the Church . . . . From all over the world we have received evidence of an unexpected springtime for the liturgy."[24] In order that this development might continue and grow, the Consilium asked him to give this letter to the bishops and the clergy offering them guidelines in making the liturgy even more fruitful.

The letter is important for our study of liturgical law for here we have perhaps the first explicit statement of what has come to be one of the characteristics of the new legislation: flexibility within limits.

> The new liturgical norms have been formulated with a certain flexibility which permits adaptation and consequently allows for a higher degree of pastoral effectiveness. This, however, does not mean that each priest can act with complete liberty and reconstruct the sacred rites of the Church according to his own whim. He must first consider to whom the Church has given the faculty to make such adaptations; second, he must take into account the intention of the lawgiver and determine to what extent adaption is envisioned.[25]

Several points in this quotation are important to the interpretation of liturgical law: first, the lawgiver intends the law to have a "certain flexibility"; second, the purpose of this flexibility is the "pastoral effectiveness" of the rite; third, some adaptations are for the Episcopal Conferences, some are for the local Ordinary, and some are for the celebrating community—the flexibility is within limits; fourth, the priest is to take into account the "intention of the lawgiver."

The second article of the letter speaks of another aspect of the revised liturgy: community. The revised rites have increased this sense of community at worship, and the letter states it should continue to do so. However, the letter states that the growth in this sense of community must not diminish the sense of hierarchy in the liturgy. As communities discover their own identity, they must not lose their relation to the bishop and the whole Church. The title of articles 26 to 32 of the Constitution reads: "Norms drawn from the hierarchic and communal nature of the liturgy."

The third article of the letter is an appeal for obedience and patience. The Cardinal states that the Consilium is moving ahead as rapidly as possible. He asks all priests not to go beyond the specific directives and try to apply the principles on their own. He calls for an obedient, trusting attitude on the part of priests with regard to the judgment of the Holy See in this matter. He then tells the bishops:

> I would have you emphasize this to the clergy in order that there be an end to these personal, premature, and harmful initiatives which God does not bless and which consequently are not capable of producing lasting fruit; indeed, on the contrary, they do harm to the faithful people and to the renewal happily begun.[26]

This statement is perhaps a disservice to the respect demanded by liturgical law because of the way in which it is phrased. Several times the Council addressed itself to the meaning of religious obedience and the type of obedience which should exist between the laity and the hierarchy (LG 37), between priest and bishop (PO 7) and between religious and their superiors (PC 14). In each of these places the obedience is in a context of service and charity, dialogue and a sense of personal responsibility.

The appeal for obedience in this letter of the Concilium to the bishops is difficult to harmonize with the spirit of the Council when it passes beyond this type of obedience and calls for an obedience based only on authority, and an authority which claims to know which actions God will bless and which he will not. Karl Rahner in his book *The Shape of the Church to Come* writes:

> No damage is done to office or office-holders if the latter honestly admit uncertainties, doubts, and the need of experiment and further reflection, without knowing the outcome, and don't behave as if they had a direct hot line to heaven to obtain an answer to each and every question in the Church. The formal authority of an office. even when the office-holder exercises it legitimately, does not relieve him of the duty, in the light of the question before him and within really contemporary horizons of understanding, of effectively winning a genuine assent on the part of those affected by his decision. It seems to me that Roman decrees in particular do not sufficiently take account of this principle, and therefore in such enactments too much weight is laid on Rome's formal authority.[27]

The fourth article of the letter of Cardinal Lercaro speaks of those who are not moving ahead and implementing the directives of the Consilium and the Council. During this period we begin to find two different kinds of "disobedience" referred to in the official documents. First there are those who want to go beyond the decrees and make changes on their own; second, there are those who do not want to change the liturgy, or who do not want to change it as quickly as called for by the Consilium.

The reasons for this hesitancy are often a mixture of theological, psychological, sociological reasons. There is always a certain difficulty and uncertainly in change. Cardinal Lercaro quotes the address of Paul VI of January 13, 1965, in which he said: "No doubt the reforms touch upon habits which we love and which are worthy of our respect; no doubt the reforms will depend on an effort which at the beginning will not be easy. But we must be docile and have confidence."[28]

Perhaps the speed with which the new rites were implemented played a role in this movement which we have come to call "traditionalist." Perhaps there were those who tried very hard to accept the changes, but when the changes were so frequent and so far-reaching they were no longer able to keep up. Perhaps the fact that the teaching on liturgical law, as seen above in the introduction to this study, had not prepared us for the possibility of such rapid and radical changes contributed to the traditionalists. Often the members of these groups make an appeal to the relation of the liturgy and orthodoxy of belief. In the period after the Council the first effort was to preserve the Latin as a means of preserving unity and orthodoxy; however after the publication of the *Rite of Mass* in 1970 the emphasis changed from the language to the rite. One of the leaders of the traditionalist movement in the United States writes:

Much as we had previously concentrated our fight on the retention of Latin in the Mass as a sign of our Church's universality, a safeguard of doctrinal orthodoxy, and a symbol of our link with the nineteen hundred years old Church of Rome, the liturgical language was no longer a principle issue now. Come March 22, 1970, America's Catholics would no longer have the "old Mass" in English, but would have to swallow a truly "new Mass" (?) as essentially different from the Catholic sacrifice as any other Protestant communion service ever was.[29]

The letter of Cardinal Lercaro sees both of these tendencies—that of going too fast and that of going too slow—as equally harmful to the renewal of the liturgy:

If on one hand, it is necessary to invite some to stay within the limits indicated by the authentic legislation of Holy Church, it is necessary on the other hand to make a new appeal to everyone to put into effect the totality of the new norms, those contained in the Conciliar documents themselves and those added for the application of the former. In fact, the two attitudes are equally harmful to the renewal undertaken by the Church: the intemperate action on the part of some, and the inaction of others, whether it be due to incomprehension or to simple inertia.[30]

1965 SEP 03 Encyclical Letter on The Holy Eucharist

One of the reasons this encyclical was written was to refute certain errors concerning Masses celebrated privately, the dogma of transubstantiation, and devotion to the Eucharist.[31] However, the document was prepared by theologians and not presented to the Consilium; and this fact resulted in certain deficiencies in the document. For example when treating the problem of private Masses, the encyclical makes no reference to the rite of concelebration. Moreover, the theological context is more that of *Mediator Dei* than that of the Vatican Council in reference to some of the arguments given.

The Encyclical states that it is not allowable to put such emphasis on what is called the "communal" Mass as to disparage Masses celebrated in private.[32] The reasons for this are as follows:

> Every Mass, even though a priest should offer it in private, is not something private; it is an act of Christ and of the Church. In offering this sacrifice, the Church learns to offer herself as a sacrifice for all and applies the single, boundless, redemptive power of the Sacrifice of the Cross for the salvation of the entire world. For every Mass which is celebrated is offered not for the salvation of ourselves alone, but also for that of the whole world. Hence, it follows that although the very nature of the action renders most appropriate the active participation of many of the faithful in the celebration of the Mass, nevertheless, that Mass is not to be disparaged but is to be fully approved which, in conformity with the prescriptions and lawful traditions of the Church, a priest for a sufficient reason offers in private, that is, in the presence of no one except his server. From such a Mass an abundant treasure of special salutary graces enriches the celebrant, the faithful, the whole Church, and the entire world—graces which are not imparted in the same abundance by the mere reception of Holy Communion.[33]

When speaking of the Instruction on Sacred Music and Liturgy of September 3, 1958 we saw that "public" can be viewed ontologically (in itself) or semiologically (as a sign). We have seen that the Council placed a new value on the liturgy as a public sign, and tried to balance this view with the liturgy as public "in itself." The argument here can be seen as a warning not to go too far in the other direction; when we say that the liturgy should appear as something "public" we must not deny that it is public "in itself." Also, we note that the discussion is in terms of "sacrifice" and that the Mass is viewed primarily under this aspect, as we have seen above in *Mediator Dei.*

The encyclical refers to the Constitution on the Liturgy in this regard and quotes the second paragraph of article 27. However, an examination of the schemata of the Constitution shows that this paragraph was added in the "Modi" where the reference for the statement is "Pius XII, Encyclical *Mediator Dei,* AAS 39, p. 557."[34] Perhaps the emphasis would have been different had the encyclical been reviewed by the Consilium before its promulgation. This fact is mentioned here because it has been the experience of this author that there are American Catholics who imagine that each Roman document comes from one, consistent and unified source. A study of the Roman documents reveals that there are sometimes inconsistencies in the documents depending on the source from which they originate.

1966 APR 17 The Prayer of the Faithful

The complete title of this work reads: "The Common Prayer, or Prayer of the Faithful: Its nature, importance, and structure. Criteria and examples offered to the National Bishops' Conferences." The book is not merely a list of rubrics and texts but rather presents the meaning, importance, and history of this prayer. The introduction gives references to the documents which preceded it and refers to the general principles which it implements. This is a characteristic of the new legislation; the new rites state the sources of the law and the documents where the spirit of the law may be found.

We note also that the schemata proposed here are not obligatory but are intended to explain and illustrate the directives of the Council, and to give the competent territorial authorities norms to properly prepare formulas for their territories. This is, perhaps, the first legislation presented in this manner for the implementation of the Constitution.[35]

The document gives several paragraphs on the "Nature and Pastoral Importance" of the prayer. This too will be a characteristic of nearly all the rites which follow.

Because of the nature of the prayer, there is also a section on the "liberty" to be maintained in this prayer. Article 17 speaks of the "principles and norms" given by the Consilium; article 18 speaks of the role of the Episcopal Conference; then we read of the liberty given to the rectors of Churches, article 19.

The document also includes a history of the Prayer of the Faithful.

This type of presentation gives not only the spirit of the law but also gives material that will allow the document to be used as a text for the presentation of this material in courses of liturgical formation in accord with article 16 of the Constitution.

1967 MAR 05 Instruction on Music in the Liturgy

When we compare this document with the instructions on music which go before it and come after it, we find this document to be a "transition" statement. For example, the instruction of 1958 made a distinction between "high" Mass and "low" Mass (sung/read). The present instruction states: "The distinction between solemn, sung, and read Mass sanctioned by the Instruction of 1958, article 3, is retained, according to the traditional liturgical laws at present in force." But the instruction of 1967 then modifies the legislation so that one might ask why the distinctions were retained. Rev. Frederick McManus (who at that time was director of the Secretariat of the Bishops' Committee on the Liturgy), in the presentation of the document to the Catholics of the United States stated: "Perhaps it would have been easier to suppress all distinctions between sung and spoken liturgy, but the technical explanation illustrates the present-day problem of going from a rigid and legalistic pattern of regulations to a greater and greater flexibility."[36]

The document (in article 28) proposes "different degrees of participation" for the sung Mass, much as we have seen earlier in the Instruction of 1958.

This instruction is not only translated and presented to the United States Catholics, but in the months which follow the instruction is "adapted" to the conditions of the Church in America, and the Bishops' Committee on the Liturgy published a document on "The Place of Music in Eucharistic Celebrations."[37]

The instruction of the U.S. Bishops begins:

> While it is possible to make technical distinctions in the forms of Mass—all the way from the Mass in which nothing is sung to the Mass in which everything is sung—such distinctions are of little significance as such, and any combination of sung and recited parts may be chosen. The important decision is whether, in the particular circumstances of the individual celebration, this or that part may or should be sung. The statement attempts to offer criteria: no set or rigid pattern can be proposed.[38]

The Roman instruction retained the distinctions between sacred and profane music. Sacred music is defined as that which "being created for the celebration of divine worship, is endowed with a certain holy sincerity of form."[39] Included in this category are Gregorian chant, sacred polyphony, sacred music, sacred popular music, and religious music. Here again the document preserves the terminology of the instruction of 1958. No particular type of music is excluded, however, in the instruction of 1967, except for article 63 which excludes those musical instruments which are suitable for secular music only.

Commenting on this distinction, McManus writes:

> The fact is that recent writers have made it clear that there is no intrinsic sacredness or holiness in any particular style or piece of music. Often times the norm of holiness means merely to exclude what is incongruous or improper.
>
> Last year two speakers made this point strongly. The chairman of the Music Advisory Board of the Bishops Committee on the Liturgy, Archabbot Rembert Weakland, O.S.B., spoke of the "innate fear of the traditional church musician of anything new and contemporary as being somehow secular and profane. Sacred music must affirm that there is no intrinsic difference in style between sacred and secular in music." Professor Paul Henry Lang of Columbia University explained that the term itself, "sacred music," "makes a false distinction which has done a great deal of artistic harm; . . . No musical composition can be holy by determination."[40]

The statement of the U.S. Bishops approaches the problem from a different aspect. The document first gives a "theology of celebration" and then offers four criteria for music in eucharistic celebrations:

1. The liturgy must be a humanly attractive experience.
2. The amount of singing should be in relation to the degree of solemnity of the celebration.
3. The amount of singing should be in relation to the nature of the congregation.
4. The amount and kind of singing should be in relation to the available resources.

The type of music chosen depends upon a) a musical judgment, b) a liturgical judgment, and c) a pastoral judgment. The statement then adds:

> There is a further problem: it is the problem of faith itself. The liturgy by its nature normally presupposes a minimum of biblical

culture and a fairly solid commitment of living faith. Often enough these conditions are not present. The assembly or many of its members are still in need of evangelization. The liturgy, which is not meant to be a tool of evangelization, is forced into a missionary role. In these conditions the music problem is complex. On the one hand, music can serve as a bridge to faith, and therefore greater liberty in the selection and use of musical materials may be called for. On the other hand, certain songs normally called for in the climate of faith (e.g. psalms and religious songs), lacking such a climate, may create problems rather than solve them.[41]

The statement of the Bishops' Liturgy Committee then applies the principles to the celebration of the Eucharist, making adaptations of the Roman document to the English language. For example, "in the United States it seems that the hearing of God's word is a more meaningful and stirring experience when the lessons are read rather than sung."[42] The statement also mentions that the creed should be spoken rather then sung. (The Roman document listed the creed in the "second degree" of sung participation.)

Speaking of the "Prayer of the Faithful," the statement mentions that "it can be sung in various forms, be spoken by one person, or be *spontaneous*." This is the first time I have found the word "spontaneous" used in the rubrics, Latin or English.[43]

Before leaving the subject of music, we will look quickly at the rubrics concerning music in the Roman Missal of 1969 so that we can see the final stages of this development. The General Instruction (1969 APR 06) no longer makes any distinction between high Mass and low Mass. (What few references are left, for example 242 § 7 which speaks of ". . . the deacon and ministers who exercise their office at a Mass with singing," are changed in the second edition of the missal. For example, the words "with singing" are omitted in the second edition of the above rubric.)

However, the most important change with regard to liturgical law with regard to music in the General Instruction is perhaps the fact that instead of prescribing a particular text or type of music the rubric gives the *purpose* that the rite is to fulfill and leaves the choice of music to fulfill this purpose up to the celebrating community. For example, speaking of the entrance rite, the instruction states: "The purpose of these rites is to make the assembled people a unified community and to prepare them properly to listen to God's word and to celebrate the Eucharist." The following article gives the function of music in this context: "The purpose of the entrance song is to open the celebration, deepen the unity of the people, introduce them to the mystery of the season or feast, and accompany the procession." The following article gives

the different ways in which the entrance song can be sung and
where the text may be found: The Roman Gradual, the Simplified
Gradual, or "another song appropriate for this part of the Mass,
the day, or the season. The text of such a song is to be approved
by the conference of bishops."[44]

In applying this text to the United States, the bishops chose not
to approve specific texts but chose instead to give "criteria" to
be used in selecting such a text:

> The entrance rite should create an atmosphere of celebration. It
> serves the function of putting the assembly in the proper frame
> of mind for listening to the word of God. It helps people to be-
> come conscious of themselves as a worshipping community. The
> choice of texts for the entrance song should not conflict with these
> purposes.
>
> In general, during the most important seasons of the Church year,
> Easter time, Lent, Christmas, and Advent, it is preferable that most
> songs used at the entrance be seasonal in nature.[45]

Thus, with regard to music, the legislation has passed from a
system which indicated a specific text to be sung and gave rules
for the type of music to be used, to a system where the singing
is governed by "criteria" and "function." This new style of legislation will require a corresponding change in the obedience given to
the law.

*1967 MAY 04 A second instruction on the correct implementation
of the Constitution on the Liturgy, Tres abhinc annos.*

The first instruction (1964 SEP 26) invited the bishops to report on the progress of the implementation of the instruction and
many of these replies from the bishops ask that the reform be
extended further. This instruction, issued three years after the
first, continues to apply the general principles of the Constitution
on the Liturgy to those cases where a complete change of liturgical
books is not required. The changes are primarily simplifications:

1-3	More freedom for the choice of Mass texts on week days.
4-6	Simplification of the orations.
7-9	Omission of some genuflections, kisses, signs of the cross.
10	The celebrant may recite the Eucharistic Prayer our loud.
11-16	Simplifications in the Eucharistic Prayer and in Communion and the dismissal.
17-24	Changes in the wedding Mass, the divine office, funerals.
25-27	Simplification of vestments—the maniple need no longer be

worn; for a serious reason the concelebrants need not wear a chasuble.

28 Extension of the use of the vernacular. The Eucharistic Prayer may be said in the vernacular.

Perhaps the most important of the above for our study of obedience to liturgical law is the permission to say the Eucharistic Prayer out loud and in the vernacular. (There was little question of "non-authorized" prayers when they were recited silently in Latin.)

1967 MAY 25 Instruction on Eucharistic Worship.

This instruction, entitled "Eucharisticum Mysterium," follows about a year and a half later the encyclical "Mysterium Fidei." The instruction brings a certain balance to the encyclical. We noted above that the encyclical spoke of the Eucharist in the context of sacrifice and, with reference to *Mediator Dei,* stressed the Eucharist as a public act "in itself." Here the aspect of sacrifice is balanced by "meal"; the act "in itself" is balanced by the act "as sign." In general the perspective is more that of the Council than *Mediator Dei.* Again it is a question of balance and perspective, not a question of contradictions.

Article 3 of the instruction emphasizes that the Mass, the Lord's Supper, is at the same time and inseparably: a sacrifice, a memorial, and a sacred banquet. In the Mass the sacrifice and the sacred meal belong to the same mystery.

Article 4 of the instruction speaks of the "sign value" of the Eucharist and states that the Eucharist, in common with the other sacraments "is the symbol of a sacred reality and the visible form of an invisible grace; consequently, the more intelligible the signs by which it is celebrated and worshipped, the more firmly and effectively it will enter into the minds and lives of the faithful."[46]

The instruction is particularly concerned with the intelligibility of these signs. Because the liturgy is a sign of the unity of the community, care must be taken that two liturgies are not celebrated at the same time in the same church.[47] Article 43 recommends that priests concelebrate rather than communicate like the laity because of the *sign.*

In the celebration of the Eucharist, priests also are deputed to perform a specific function by reason of a special sacrament, namely Holy Orders. For they too "as ministers of the sacred mysteries, especially in the sacrifice of the Mass . . . act in the person of

Christ in a special way." It is therefore fitting that by reason of the sign they participate in the Eucharist by exercising the order proper to them, by celebrating or concelebrating the Mass and not by limiting themselves to communicating like the laity.[48]

In relation to the obedience called for by liturgical laws, article 20 of the instruction is particularly important:

To encourage the active participation of the people and to ensure that the celebrations are carried out as they should be, it is not sufficient for the ministers to content themselves with the exact fulfillment of their role according to the liturgical laws. It is also necessary that they should so celebrate the liturgy that by this very fact they convey an awareness of the meaning of the sacred actions.[49]

Obedience now demands not only attention to the rubrics, but also attention to the *sign value* of the liturgy. The priest must communicate the meaning of the rite so that all can participate in it actively and fruitfully.

1968 MAY 23 The New Eucharistic Prayers and Prefaces

The decree "Preces eucharistica" introducing the three new Eucharistic Prayers and eight new prefaces states that this was done in response to the requests of the bishops and faithful in order to express the Eucharistic Prayer in "richer and more varied forms." We noted above that the "Second Instruction" (Tres abhinc annos) permitted the Eucharistic Prayer to be proclaimed out loud and in the vernacular. At first we experienced the importance of having the central liturgical prayer proclaimed in a way which could be understood by all. But then, as the Bishops' Committee on the Liturgy states: "there was a certain monotony engendered by its constant use, a monotony only partly relieved by the variety of prefaces."[50] (With relation to the context of liturgical law we note here that formerly, when the liturgy was viewed under the aspect of the cult offered to God, there was no question of "monotony." It is only when we consider the "educative and pastoral nature" of the liturgy that the values of "variety" and "change" take on a special importance.)

Another reason for the new Eucharistic Prayers is found in the relation of the liturgy to the Church. The liturgy is to be an expression of the mystery of the Church and consequently no one Eucharistic Prayer can adequately contain or express that mystery. Therefore a variety of texts are necessary. The guidelines introducing the new prayers state:

> A consideration of the variety of anaphoras in the tradition of the universal Church, and of the contents of each, clearly shows that no one anaphora is able to contain all the riches which are desirable from a pastoral, spiritual and theological viewpoint. To complement the naturally inevitable imitations of each one, a plurality of texts is necessary.[51]

A statement such as this is to be understood in the context where the liturgy stands in relation to the Church as taught by the Council. In an earlier context, such as that of *Mediator Dei,* where the sacrifice of the Mass is entrusted to the Church to continue the sacrifice of the cross, it is not as obvious that "a plurality of texts is necessary."

1968 AUG 15 Rite of Ordination of Deacons, Presbyters, and Bishops

The Rite of Ordination is the first of the sacramental rites to by completely revised by the Consilium. The general principle for the revision again refers to the sign value of the rite: that the rite express more clearly the holy things which it signifies (SC 21). The apostolic constitution "Pontificalis Romani recognitio" (1968 JUN 18) promulgating the new rite states that the revision was made so that the Christian people, as far as possible, should be able to understand the rite with ease and to take part in it fully, actively, and as befits a community. The constitution mentions the importance of the "simplicity and clarity of the rites." The values of tradition, organic development, unity, and ecumenism are recognized in the change in the prayer of ordination for a bishop. The constitution states:

> It appeared appropriate to take from ancient sources the consecratory prayer which is found in the document called the "Apostolic Tradition of Hippolytus of Rome," written at the beginning of the third century, and which is still used in large part in the ordination rites of the Coptic and West Syrian liturgies. Thus the very act of ordination may witness to the harmony of the tradition in both East and West concerning the apostolic office of bishops.[52]

In the rite itself, there are several rubrics which are interesting from the point of view of the development of the style of the legislation. Rubric 13 states that after calling those to be ordained deacon, the people give their consent by saying "Thanks be to God," or give their consent according to local custom.[53] As this does not refer to customs already existing, we see that the rubric is a type of *invitation* for such customs to arise and for the bishops to adapt the rite according to local circumstances.

The rubric 14, relative to the homily, states: "Then, everyone is seated, and the bishop speaks to the people and the candidates about the office of deacon: he may use these words:"[54] and then is given a text. Compare this wording of 1968 with the second edition of the rite.

> Then all sit, and the bishop gives the homily. He begins with the text of the readings from Scripture and then speaks to the people and the candidates about the office.

The second edition reflects an increased awareness of the importance of the Scripture readings and the nature of the homily.

Several times during the rite there is the indication "then the following hymn may be sung, or one can sing some other fitting hymn."[55] We see here a change from former legislation of this same type. Formerly when a hymn or psalm was indicated the text was most important and the music secondary. If the hymn could not be sung, the text was recited. Here we see that the rubric is indicating primarily the fact that at this point in the rite singing is called for.

1969 JAN 25 Instruction on the Translation of Liturgical Texts

In January of 1969 the Consilium sent this instruction to the presidents of the Episcopal Conferences to aid them in translating the liturgical texts into the vernacular.[56] To my knowledge this is the first time an instruction has addressed itself to the "communication" aspect of the liturgy. Here the scientific methods of linguistics and oral communication are brought together with the liturgical mystery. The instruction treats the text not only in itself but also as a means of communication.

> The liturgical text, as a ritual document, is a means of oral communication. It is first of all a sensible sign by which praying men communicate among themselves. But for the believer celebrating the liturgy, the word is at the same time "mystery": through the spoken word, Christ himself speaks to his people and they respond to their Lord. The Church speaks to the Lord and expresses itself with the voice of the spirit who gives it life.[57]

When translating a liturgical text, three things must be considered:

1. The content of the text. In translating the text, we must discover the true meaning and sense of the text. For this, the scientific methods of textual and literary criticism must be employed. The type of text and its liturgical function must be considered. Translation of Sacred Scripture requires a different fidelity to the original than an oration. The texts of the sacramental formulas are to be translated "integre et fideliter" (completely and faithfully) without variation, omissions, or insertions. On the other hand, an acclamation is to be translated with care being given to the phonetic and rhythmic nature of the text for the form, the literary genre of acclaiming with the voice, constitutes an essential element of the translation.[58]

2. Those to whom the text is addressed. A translation must also consider the ones who are to hear the text and use it as their prayer.

> The prayer of the Church is always the prayer of a particular group, come together here and now. Therefore it is often not sufficient in the liturgy to translate with a purely verbal and material exactitude texts formulated in another time and culture. The assembled community should be able to take the translated text and make of it its living and actual prayer, in which each member of the assembly can find expression.[59]

3. The literary genre. The instruction notes that there is a difference between a spoken text and a written text. There are also different types of spoken texts. The very way of speaking is an integral part of oral communication. The translator must not have as his final goal the text as it appears on paper, but the text as it is spoken and communicated. There are different kinds of oral communication: it is one thing to proclaim and another to meditate. We do not give thanks in the same tone of voice in which we make a request. "These facts must influence not only the way of speaking, but also the literary form of the translation. "[60]

The instruction on Eucharistic worship (1967 MAY 25, § 20) stated that "it is not sufficient for the ministers to content themselves with the exact fulfillment of their role according to the liturgical laws; it is necessary that they so celebrate the liturgy that they convey an awareness of the meaning of the sacred actions." This would imply an awareness of the principles of oral communication and the different literary genres spoken of in the instruction on translating texts.

The Constitution on the Liturgy spoke of adapting the liturgy to the genius and traditions of peoples (SC 37-40). The instruction states that for this directive to be properly implemented there will be a need for "non-translated" texts, that is texts that are not translations of the Roman documents but original creations growing from the experience of the liturgy as expressed in a particular culture.

> For a completely renewed liturgy, we cannot be content with texts translated from other languages. New creations will be necessary. But translation of texts transmitted through the tradition of the Church is an excellent exercise and the necessary way to learn how to compose new texts so that "the new forms adopted will in some way grow organically from forms already in existence."[61]

1969 MAR 19 Rite of Marriage

The introduction (or *Praenotanda*) to the new rite of marriage begins by treating the "importance and dignity of the sacrament." This type of brief, theological introduction to the sacrament has become characteristic of the new rites and helps to place the legislation in its theological context. The introduction also gives references to the Scriptures, the Council documents, and the instructions which give the spirit of the legislation.

Article 6 of the introduction states that "in the celebration of marriage certain elements should be stressed, especially the liturgy of the word, . . . Also of supreme importance are the consent of the contracting parties, . . . the special nuptial blessing, . . . and finally the reception of Holy Communion. . ."[62] Obviously, we can no longer consider all rubrics to be of equal importance. Furthermore, if those responsible for the celebration are to communicate its meaning, they must be aware of which elements are most important and which are to be stressed. This is part of that "more" spoken of in article 11 of the Constitution: ". . . more is demanded than the mere observance of the laws governing valid and licit celebration."

A further example of the demands of the new liturgical legislation is found in article 9 of the introduction:

> Priests should show special consideration to those who take part in liturgical celebrations or hear the Gospel only on the occasion of a wedding—Catholics or non-Catholics who seldom or never participate in the Eucharist or who seem to have lost their faith. Priests are ministers of Christ's Gospel to everyone.[63]

Looking to the rite itself, the first rubric states that at the appointed time, the priest "greets the bride and bridegroom in a friendly manner, showing that the Church shares their joy." This is, to my knowledge, the first time that a liturgical text has directed the priest to say something and has not prescribed any words. This is another indication of the change in the type of obedience called for by the new legislation.

After the homily we find the rubric: All stand and the priest says, "in these or similar words. . . ." This phrase, "in these or similar words," is found frequently in the new rites and permits the celebrating priest to adapt the text to the occasion. Also, we note that nearly every article of the rite which gives a formula to be used, if it does not say "in these or similar words," gives one or more alternate formulas.

These alternate formulas, options, readings are not given merely to allow variety. The couple to be married, together with the priest or a liturgy team from the parish, when choosing their readings and texts are drawn to reflect on the meaning of the prayers and readings. Thus the liturgy and its preparation become an integral part of the preparation for marriage. As was stated in the "First Instruction" (1964 SEP 26, n. 7-8): "It is necessary that there be a close union between the liturgy and religious formation. . . The bishops and their assistants in the priesthood should relate their entire pastoral ministry ever, more closely to the liturgy." As the understanding of "liturgy" is more closely related to our understanding of the "Church," the liturgy will become more central to the pastoral ministry.

After the publication of the rite, many books and materials were printed to help the couple about to be married plan their liturgy and choose readings and texts. Sometimes these books go beyond the permissions given in the official rite. One such book *Your Wedding: Planning Your Own Ceremony*,[64] contains a section entitled "Writing Your Own Wedding Vows."

> Two different formulas are given in the Catholic rite, but some couples today prefer to choose their own words to state their marriage commitment. Some dioceses require that you use one of the official formulas, but before or after you may add your own words. The Pre-Cana folder from the Archdiocese of Chicago says, "So long as the key elements outlined here are clearly present, the couple may modify the language of the vows or add appropriate elements that have special meaning for them." If you decide to write your own vows, a good place to start is with the traditional formula. Each idea expressed there is important and must be included, in some form, in the vows you compose.[65]

The official text does not invite the couples to compose their own formula for their marriage commitment. If we are to say that the text quoted above goes beyond the permissions given in the official rite, we must note at the same time the context in which this is done. The text proposes a way in which the couple can be led to a deeper reflection on the meaning of the rite as desired by the introduction to the official rite. It directs that the regulations of each local ordinary be observed. It states that the key elements of the formula must be clearly present. It is in harmony with the instruction on translations (1969 JAN 25), which stated that "texts translated from another language are clearly not sufficient for the celebration of a fully renewed liturgy," and Article 23 of the Constitution, "new texts should in some way grow organically from forms already in existence."

1969 MAR 21 General Norms for the Liturgical Year and the Calendar

This legislation was presented in a book of 179 pages; however a note at the beginning states that only the first part of the volume (pages 5-49) is the official document and the second part (pages 53-177) is a non-official commentary given by the Consilium. The Consilium chose to publish not only the liturgical legislation but also the background, history, and theology which motivated the decisions. Again we see an effort made to win a willing obedience to the new legislation by explaining the motivation behind the changes and the spirit of the norms. This documentation provides the materials necessary for using the new calendar intelligently and for making options that are more apt to be pastorally effective. This documentation also provides background material for those who must teach the new rites to others.

The motu proprio approving these norms begins with the key idea: the paschal mystery. "The celebration of the paschal mystery is of the greatest importance to Christian worship." The new calendar has as its principal objective to give proper emphasis to the paschal mystery and its weekly celebration, the Sunday (norms 4 to 7). Secondly, the principle of universality and local adaptation (SC 37-40) calls for the celebration of the universal Church of those saints who have significance for the whole Church, and giving the option to particular Churches, countries, or religious communities to venerate the saints which are of particular importance to them (norms 8 to 15).

The norms speak of 1.) The liturgical day in general; 2.) Sunday; 3.) Solemnities, feasts, and memorials; and 4.) Weekdays. When we compare this division of liturgical days with that of the Code of 1960 which had over a dozen different classifications, we see that the new calendar is greatly simplified. However, if the liturgy is to become in reality the prayer of the whole people of God and not merely an "affair concerning the clerics and professionals" the liturgical law will of necessity direct itself to the entire people of God and the basic laws and norms should be understandable to all. Thus the recognition of the role of the laity in the liturgy will have a corresponding influence on the form and style of the liturgical legislation.

1969 APR 06 General Instruction of the Roman Missal

We have already studied several of the aspects of this General Instruction with regard to concelebration, Communion under both kinds, the homily, and the legislation concerning music in the liturgy. Here we will make only two further comments: the literary genre of this document marks a change in the rubrics of the missal; and second, a word about the interpretation of the document.

A list of rubrics was printed in the front of the missal (according to the use of the Roman Curia) from the time of the reform of the Council of Trent. We have seen an example of this style of rubric in the Code of Pope John (see above 1960 JUL 25) and in the Ordo Missae (1965 JAN 27). The present missal, however, breaks with this usage and is introduced not by an "Ordo Missae" but by a "General Instruction" (Institutio Generalis). Martimort states that this change of vocabulary indicates a radical change in perspective.[66]

Martimort explains that the Latin word "institutio" can mean "general principles" or "method" or "plan of action." However, it can also be used in the sense of an "instruction," that is, instruction in the sense of training and education. This new form of introduction to the missal is designed

> to encourage a new school of thought, a new spirit. It is no longer sufficient today to describe the correct execution of the rites. It is necessary to explain the reason for the rites and to help those who celebrate them to do so intelligently, devoutly, and fruitfully.[67]

Another sign of a "change in perspective" with regard to liturgical law is seen in the way the articles are interpreted. For example, article 11 of the General Instruction reads:

> As president of the congregation, the priest gives instructions and words of introduction and conclusion that are indicated within the rite, proclaims the word of God, and gives the final blessing. He

may also very briefly introduce the Mass of the day (before the
celebration begins), the liturgy of the word (before the readings),
and the Eucharistic Prayer (before the preface); he may make con-
cluding comments before the dismissal.[68]

To interpret this article in the style of the former rubrics we
would note that nowhere does the article mention that the introductions may be made in words other than those indicated
in the missal. To interpret the article in the style of the new
legislation we would note that the role of a president is to actually
"preside." The new legislation requires a respect of literary genre
so that introductions are real introductions and greetings are real
greetings.

However, during the years after the publication of the Instruction
some priests were often occused of being disobedient to the rubrics
when they used a wording for these introductions and admonitions
other than that given in the missal. The Congregation for Divine
Worship, in a circular letter to the presidents of the Episcopal Conferences (April 27, 1973) states that it is the responsibility of the
celebrating priest to consider the possibilities for further accomo-
dation of the texts of the admonitions. The letter states that these
admonitions, such as during the penitential rite, so before the
Lord's Prayer do not require that everyone use the form given
in the missal; they can be adapted to the varying circumstances
of the community.

This interpretation of the article is included in the article itself
in the second edition of the General Instruction which was promulgated March 27, 1975. The second edition of the article reads:

As president of the congregation, the priest gives instructions and
words of introduction and conclusion that are indicated within the
rite. *By their very nature these admonitions do not require that
everyone use them in the form in which they appear in the Missal;
it can be useful, at least in some cases to adapt them in some
measure to the actual conditions of the community. The presiding
priest also* proclaims the word of God, and gives the final blessing.[69]

The words in italics are the words which have been added in
the second edition. (Note: *The Sacramentary* which is the official
text for the United States of America at the present time, was
printed in 1974 and contains the first edition of the Instruction.
The French missal, however, published in one volume in 1974
contains the second edition of the General Instruction. The American Sacramentary, however, does refer to the circular letter of the

Congregation for Divine Worship in an appendix to the General Instruction. This is a further reminder that a correct interpretation of liturgical law at the present time requires that we consider each document in its historical context and in relation to the documents which go before it. A document must be considered in the total context of the post-Conciliar legislation.)

In reference to obedience to liturgical law, the legislation states that the priest is not to change anything on his own authority nor is he to follow his own personal desires. There is danger that the priest "create" a "personal" liturgy. The General Instruction to the Roman Missal makes it clear that the choices and options given are not for the private devotion or decision of the priest. The purpose of allowing the rite to be adapted is so that it may be more pastorally effective:

> 313. The pastoral effectiveness of a celebration depends in great measure on choosing readings, prayers, and songs which correspond to the needs, spiritual preparation, and attitude of the participants. This will be achieved by an intelligent use of the options described below.
>
> In planning the celebration, the priest should consider the spiritual good of the assembly rather than his own desires. The choice of texts is to be made in consultation with the ministers and others who have a function in the celebration, including the faithful, for the parts which belong to them.
>
> Since a variety of options is provided, it is necessary for the deacon, readers, cantors, commentator, and choir to know beforehand the texts for which they are responsible, so that nothing shall mar the celebration. Careful planning and execution will help dispose the people to take their part in the Eucharist.[70]

The publication of the apostolic constitution and the General Instruction of the Roman Missal caused a very vociferous reaction from the traditionalists, and Pope Paul wrote a motu proprio answering their objections and stressing the fact that the new missal is a witness to an unbroken tradition. However, it is hardly good form for a pope to apologize for an apostolic constitution in a motu proprio and consequently the motu proprio was incorporated into the General Instruction. This accounts for the difference in tone and content of the first 15 paragraphs of the instruction, and also explains why the paragraph numbering starts over after 15: it seemed more practical to retain the original numbering of the articles in the instruction.

1969 MAY 15 Rite of Baptism for Children

The sacrament of baptism was revised in two stages: a rite for children and a rite for adults. This first rite contains an introduction to Christian Initiation in General, (baptism, confirmation, Eucharist), and then (articles 3 and following) an introduction to baptism in general. This is complemented by the introduction to the baptism of children and the introduction to the "Rite of Christian Initiation of Adults" (1972 JAN 06).

The introductions to these rites contain many examples of the theological context spoken of in Chapter III of this study treating of the Vatican Council. The rite of baptism is seen in relation to the Church; the Church is formed by the sacraments of initiation. When speaking of the "offices and ministries of baptism," mention is first made of the role of the "Church." "Christian instruction and the preparation for baptism are a vital concern of God's people, the Church, which hands on and nourishes the faith it has received from the Apostles."[71] The document then speaks of the importance of catechists and those who help prepare the candidate for baptism.

Another example of this new theological context is seen in the fact that the bishop is listed in first place among the ordinary ministers of the sacrament. The bishop is no longer spoken of as the one who must watch that priests observe the liturgical laws, but the bishop himself is viewed as "the principal dispenser of the mysteries of God and leaders of the entire liturgical life of the Church committed to them."[72]

The introduction also treats of those adaptations which can be made by the Conferences of Bishops, the local Ordinary, and the minister of baptism. The Constitution on the Liturgy spoke of "adaptation within the limits of the typical editions" (SC 39) and places where "more radical adaptations" are required (SC 40). The distinction has disappeared in the legislation, and the introductions to the rites of baptism join these two paragraphs of the Constitution and the "typical editions" themselves make provision for "more radical adaptations."

The notes to the introduction to baptism in general and the baptism of children do not contain any reference to the canons of the Code concerning baptism.

An example of change in the style of the legislation can be seen in number 7 of the introduction to the rite for children. We noted above that the former legislation was primarily directed to specific actions and prayers—"The celebrant, vested as indicated above, takes the chalice in his left hand, carries it at the height of his chest, and places his right hand on the burse covering the chalice; he makes the proper reverence to the crucifix in the sacristy and goes to the altar. . ." The new legislation looks more to the pastoral effectiveness of the rite and addresses the rite as a whole and the purpose of the rite:

> It is also the duty of the priest to arrange that baptism is always celebrated with proper dignity and, as far as possible, adapted to the circumstances and wishes of the families concerned. Everyone who performs the rite of baptism should do so with care and devotion; he must also try to be understanding and friendly to all.[73]

1969 MAY 15 Instruction on Masses for Special Gatherings

This instruction was prepared in order to respond to a felt pastoral need. After the Council, as the Eucharist became more central in the spiritual life of the Christian people, the priests found that they were called upon to celebrate the Eucharist with the faithful in many more diversified circumstances than formerly. These Eucharistic celebrations, frequently held in homes, seemed to call for a certain adaptation of the liturgical legislation. The instruction addresses this need.

The instruction states that the Mass can be the crowning point of certain reunions within the parish and experience has shown the importance of pastoral activity in these gatherings. The participation of the faithful is to be encouraged in the fullest way possible (6a). Readings adapted to the particular celebration can be chosen from an approved lectionary (6e) and the readings before the Gospel should be read by one of the participants (man or woman) (6f). In the prayer of the faithful "a particular intention, properly prepared, can be proposed by the participants" (6h).

However, this is about the limit of the adaptation allowed in the document. The instruction repeats the options given to the priest to make an initial admonition and to introduce the liturgy of the word and to say something before the preface, and to intervene again before the dismissal. And then adds: "He should abstain from this (admonitions and introductions) during the Eucharistic Prayer." (Ab hoc tamen abstineat durante Prece Eucharistica. 6c) The English text distributed by the American Bishops translates this as: "Any other interruption is excluded during the Eucharistic liturgy."[74] In translating the term "Prece Eucharistica" as "during the Eucharistic liturgy," the English text can seem more restrictive than the Latin.

Article 7 of the instruction states that Communion under both species is excluded when Mass is celebrated in houses. The English text adds another phrase which is not in the Latin text (and there is no indication that this is an American addition): "Giving communion to oneself and receiving it in the hand are likewise excluded."[75]

Article 6d states that (with the exception of readers, commentator, and one who gives a petition prepared in advance during the prayer of the faithful) the faithful will refrain from any interventions in the way of reflections, exhortations and the like.[76]

Article 11 states that all other rules given in the missal are to be observed with regard to Mass texts, furnishings and vestments, gestures and ceremonies. "Every change is arbitrary and therefore rejected."[77]

The instruction closes by stating that:

In our day and age there are those who think they are up-to-date only when they can show off novelty, often bizarre, or devise arbitrary forms of liturgical celebrations. Priests, religious and diocesan, considerate of the true welfare of the faithful, realize that only in a generous and unyielding fidelity to the will of the Church, expressed in its directives, norms and structures, lies the secret of a lasting and sanctifying pastoral success.

Those who wander from this line, even if it is alluring, finish in creating bewilderment in the faithful. At the same time they are killing and rendering sterile their sacerdotal ministry.

This instruction, prepared at the request of higher authority by the Sacred Congregation for Divine Worship, will regulate every type of Mass celebrated in special gatherings until the Apostolic See disposes otherwise.[78]

Before going to the next document of our study, it is perhaps useful to our study of obedience to liturgical law to see the way in which the instruction on Masses for special gatherings was presented in France. The instruction was translated and printed in *La Documentation Catholique,* number 1558, (mars 1970); in the following issue, number 1559 (15 mars 1970), the Episcopal Commission for the Liturgy published a "note" on the celebration of Mass in small groups.[79]

The bishops refer to the Instruction on Masses for Special Gatherings, and state that they have been attentive to this problem for several years; they have studied it during their assembly at Lourdes in 1968 and since January 1969 "principles of pastoral judgment and action" were proposed. The bishops now represent the following norms:

There are different kinds of "special groups" which celebrate the Eucharist: Masses for large gatherings, Masses of pilgrimae, Masses for children, for the handicapped, etc. The present document is addressed to "small groups" and this designates, not so much the number, but "a certain type of relation between the participants" in which each participant sees the others as individuals, not as a group or crowd.[80]

The French document notes the importance of these "small groups" and states that prayer of this type can greatly aid the participants to deepen their faith and to integrate their lives with the Church and their apostolic activity. The document first gives the general orientation of such celebrations and then turns to "practical directives."

The Eucharist may be celebrated in any fitting place; the directives are not of a juridical nature but rather directed toward allowing the celebration to be a truly human and spiritual experience. The document speaks of a place where a prayerful atmosphere can be experienced. The place must be festive and aid the participants to pray. Similar directives are given for the altar; rather than speak of the legal requirements, the document speaks of the *functional* requirements: the beauty of the altar cloth, the role of flowers, the importance of simplicity and beauty.

The priest and the role of the priest are to be clearly able to be seen; however, the document states that this is accomplished not only by vestment but by the general attitude of the priest. The document allows a simplification of the vestments.

The Latin document stated that the Eucharist can never be preceded by a meal or an agape. If an agape or meal follows it should not be at the same table where the Eucharist was celebrated (10c). The French document states that "if there is a meal or an agape, care must be taken that there is no confusion between a friendly meal or a meal of brotherhood and the celebration of the Eucharist."[81]

The French text makes reference to the instruction on liturgical translations (1969 JAN 25) and states that the priest can, for example, adapt the idea of the oration found in the missal, and give it a form and wording which communicate the content of the prayer to those participating.[82] The text also states that during the homily, the priest can invite those participating to express their ideas also, for this often leads to a better assimilation of the word of the Scriptures.[83] The document also indicates that Mass in small groups is a good occasion for receiving Communion under both bread and wine for it allows a proper catechesis to be given and also the sign of the Eucharist as a sacred banquet is more clearly expressed.[84]

1969 MAY 25 Lectionary for Mass

From the introduction to the Lectionary for Mass it is clear that the principle behind this new lectionary is the desire to bring the people of God into closer contact with the Scriptures. The Council directed that the treasures of the Bible should be opened up more lavishly so that richer fare might be provided for the faithful at the table of God's word (SC 35, 51).

The more important texts were placed on Sundays, and other readings which to some degree complement these texts are assigned to the weekdays. The introduction to the lectionary explains the principles which directed the choices of texts and then gives "guidelines" for those times when options are to be made. The introduction also contains a "discription of the order of the readings" which is intended to "help clarify the structure of the entire lectionary and its relationship to the liturgical year." This section of the introduction gives ample material not only for understanding the arrangement of the lectionary but much material that is most helpful in giving homilies and teaching the use of Scripture in the liturgy. The introduction states:

> The purpose of this lectionary is primarily a pastoral one, in the spirit of the Second Vatican Council. The general principles governing it and the wealth of texts within it are all pastorally oriented.[85]

This "pastoral orientation" calls for an obedience which is also pastorally orientated. A mere observance of the given order of texts is not the intention of the lawgiver. The law itself makes this clear, as for example, in the case of the weekday lectionary:

> When the weekday lectionary is used, it is important to determine in advance whether any feasts will occur in a given week to interrupt the course of the weekday readings. Then the priest, considering the entire week's readings may omit less important selections from the weekday lectionary or combine them with other readings when this will give a unified presentation of a specific theme.[86]

1969 MAY 29 Instruction on the Manner of Administering Communion

This instruction is occasioned by "the desire expressed in some places to return to the practice by which the Eucharistic bread is placed in the hand of the faithful who communicates himself by putting it in his mouth."[87]   The reasons for this practice are that it is a better sign of the Eucharist as a meal and it is a sign which is more in keeping with the dignity of the laity and their role in the liturgy as taught by the Council. (Note again that the question is a question of "sign value" and not principally a doctrinal question.)

The instruction argues for the traditional way of receiving Communion (that is, the bread placed on the tongue of the communicant) and states:

> In view of the state of the Church as a whole today, this manner of distributing Holy Communion must be observed, not only because it rests upon a tradition of many centuries but especially because it is a sign of the reverence of the faithful toward the Eucharist. The practice in no way detracts from the personal dignity of those who approach this great sacrament, and it is a part of the preparation needed for the most fruitful reception of the Lord's body.[88]

The instruction then states that in spite of these reasons of continuing the traditional practice, certain Episcopal Conferences have asked that the usage of placing the consecrated bread in the hand of the faithful be admitted in their territories.

In view of these requests, and in view of such an important matter resting on a very ancient and venerable tradition, and in view of the dangers involved in this new practice (a lessening of reverence toward the noble sacrament, its profanation, or the adulteration of correct doctrine), the Supreme Pontiff decreed that each bishop of the entire Latin Church should be asked his opinion concerning the appropriateness of introducing a change.

The instruction then publishes the results of this correspondence. This is the first time I have found such a "questionnaire" incorporated into an instruction of the Holy See. It reads as follows:

1. Does it seem that the proposal should be accepted by which, besides the traditional mode, the rite of receiving Holy Communion in the hand would be permitted?
   Yes: 567; No: 1,233. Yes, with reservations: 315; Invalid votes: 20.

2. Should experiments with this new rite first take place in small communities, with the assent of the local Ordinary?
   Yes: 571; No: 1,215; Invalid votes: 70.

3. Do you think that the faithful, after a well planned catechetical preparation, would accept this new rite willingly?

Yes: 835; No: 1,185; Invalid votes 128.

From the responses received it is thus clear that by far the greater number of bishops feel that the present discipline should not be changed at all; indeed that if it were changed this would be offensive to the sensibilities and spiritual appreciation of these bishops and most of the faithful.[89]

However, this is not the end of the matter. The instruction then states that if the bishops still want to have permission to change the practice, the Holy See will weigh the individual cases with care, remembering the bonds which exist between the several local Churches among themselves and with the entire Church, in order to promote the common good and edification and the increase of faith and piety which flow from mutual good example.

The instruction states that the bishops should study the question carefully and make their decision by two-thirds majority by secret ballot. The instruction is given with a special mandate of Pope Paul VI and signed by Cardinal Gut, prefect of the Congregation for Divine Worship. There then follows a second part of the instruction (sent to those bishops' conferences which had asked for Communion in the hand, and consequently not published in the English edition of the text provided by the USCC) which gives the practical norms for introducing the new practice. The letter, also signed by Cardinal Gut, states that the new practice is not to exclude the old, but the proper religious sensibilities of each communicant are to be respected. The new practice is to be introduced gradually, starting with those groups which are best prepared. The placing of Communion in the hand is not to lessen respect for the sacrament but to increase the respect for the dignity of each member of the Mystical Body of Christ—the dignity given by baptism to those into whose hands the sacrament is placed. The letter also states that the bread can be placed in the hand of the communicant or, simpler, the communicant may take the bread from the sacred vessel.[90]

The instruction was issued May 29, 1969. Permission was given for Communion in the hand to the Episcopal Conference of Belgium two days later, May 31, 1969. Permission was given for France and Germany on June 6, one week after the instruction was published. Many other permissions follow: Holland, September 18; Chad, September 18; South Africa, February 3, 1970; Canada, February 3; etc.[91] The first part of the instruction must not be read without the final paragraphs, and we must consider the way in which the document was implemented.

We note also, that the fact that this change allowed each communicant to have the option to receive in the way he or she preferred, enabled the change to take place easily and without much opposition in those countries where the permission was granted. The method which the faithful preferred and the method which proved more pastorally effective gradually became the accepted practice while not forcing others to accept this practice. Thus many questions of authority and obedience were avoided.

1969 AUG 15 The Rite of Funerals

In the rite of funerals we find again many of the themes we have already treated. The rite begins with the key theological element: the paschal mystery. The rite is the concern of the whole Christian community, not just the priest.

> In funeral celebrations all who belong to the people of God should keep in mind their office and ministry: the parents or relatives, those who take care of funerals, the Christian community as a whole, and finally the priest. As teacher of the faith and minister of consolation, the priest presides over the liturgical service and celebrates the Eucharist.[92]

The rite gives the Bishops' Conferences extensive powers to adapt the rite to local conditions, admitting elements and traditions of the cultures of the individual countries in the rite. The text speaks of adding texts and adding other formulas—evidently the intention of the law is not that the bishops restrict the options given, but enlarge them.

We noted in the discussion of the theological context of the Council that the priest is to be in close contact with those to whom he ministers, he is to deal with others as with his brothers and sisters, he cannot be of service to them if he is a stranger to their life and conditions. This relation of priest and people is necessary for the proper implementation of the new rites. For example, the rite of funerals states:

> In preparing and arranging funeral celebrations priests should consider the deceased and the circumstances of his life and death and be concerned also for the sorrow of the relatives and their Christian needs.[93]

Another article states that the priest should consider the particular circumstances of each funeral and in particular the wishes of the family and the community.[94] The options of the new rites are not to be exercised in isolation from the community for the liturgy is the prayer of the entire community.

What type of obedience is called for by this rite? The introduction states that the priest is to make free use of the choices afforded in the rite.[95] The following article gives remarkable liberty in this regard:

> In general, all the texts are interchangeable and may be chosen, with the help of the community or family, to reflect the individual situation.[96]

This is the first time that I have found the rubrics to give such freedom to the celebrants.

In the English text for the United States, a paragraph is added to this text which reads:

> If an individual prayer or other text is clearly not appropriate to the circumstances of the deceased person, it is the responsibility of the priest to make the necessary adaptation.[97]

When the liturgical law is stated in this way, it is difficult for a priest who sincerely tries to adapt the rite in view of its pastoral effectiveness to be guilty of "disobedience" to the new rite of funerals.

1970 FEB 02 Rite of Religious Profession

The Second Vatican Council called for the revision of the rite of consecration to a life of virginity and the creation of a rite of religious profession that would have a greater unity, sobriety, and dignity (SC 80). In the course of history, the rites for profession in the various religious orders and congregations had developed in many different ways. The intention of the new rite of religious profession is not to achieve a strict uniformity in the rites but to give them a structure so that they will conform with the general principles and the theological context of the liturgical reform of the Council.

The text given in the new rite is more a "model" than a text to be translated and used as in the typical edition. The introduction states that

> Religious families should adapt the rite so that it more clearly reflects and manifests the character and spirit of each institute. For this purpose the faculty of adapting the rite is given to each institute, the adaptation to be submitted to the Apostolic See.[98]

Even the formula for profession not only *may* be adapted but *should* be changed and adapted. This is true for many other formulas also:

> As stated in the appropriate places, many formulas in the rite of profession may be changed, and in fact should be, to reflect more clearly the character and spirit of each institute.[99]

Article 12 of the introduction states that the norms given here are not obligatory, unless they are stated to be obligatory, or unless they are demanded by the very nature of the liturgy.

We noted above that the Council teaches a very close relationship exists between "Church" and "liturgy." The rites must express this relationship; for example, with regard to the rite of religious profession, the act of entering a novitiate does not involve the Church in the same way as a perpetual profession. Consequently, the rite for entering a novitiate indicates that this is to be done simply, in the presence of the religious community. Perpetual profession, however, which is a sign of the unbreakable union between Christ and his bride the Church, concerns the whole Church in a different way than entrance into a novitiate. Consequently, the rite of Perpetual Profession takes place during a Eucharistic celebration and it is fitting that it take place on a Sunday or a solemnity of the Lord, the Blessed Virgin Mary, or a saint distinguished in the living of the religious life. The faithful should be invited to come "in great numbers" for this is an act which signifies an aspect of the Church and "speaks" of the nature of the Church. In this respect, the act is more "liturgical" than the act of entry into novitiate; and the liturgical legislation reflects this fact in that the rite of perpetual profession is more structured by the Church than is the rite of entry into novitiate.

The rite as presented in the typical edition speaks of preserving the "arrangement of the parts of the rite."[100] The text does not speak of the "structure" of the rite but we will see this word enter the vocabulary of liturgical law later is our study. However, we can already see a progression from legislation which will be concerned with the invidual parts of the rite, to a legislation which will be concerned with the "arrangement" of the parts while leaving many of the individual parts optional.

The rite also states several general liturgical principles: The practice of performing publicly during Mass what belongs to private devotion is not to be commended; and, the celebration of several rites in the same liturgical action is to be avoided completely.

The introduction to the ICEL translation of the rite states that "it is anticipated that many communities will wish to use these translations as interim texts and as a basis for making their own adaptations in these rites." Thus, starting with the typical edition, each institute can develop a rite which, in the words of the Council, "grows organically from already existing forms" (SC 23). We will speak more about "interim" texts and "transitional forms of the rites" below, when speaking of confirmation.

1970 SEP 05 The Third Instruction (Liturgicae Instaurationes) on the correct implementation of the Constitution on the Liturgy

This "third" instruction is somewhat different in tone than the first instruction (1964 SEP 26) and the second (1967 MAY 04); the first two instructions were concerned with the gradual introduction of modifications into the rites to bring them into harmony with the principles of the Council. The purpose of the Third Instruction is to exercise a "breaking action" to slow down those who want to make too many changes too fast.

The document is not against flexibility and adaptation; however, these qualities are to be exercised within the limits given in the official texts.

> The wide choice of texts and the flexibility of the rubrics make it possible to adapt the celebration to the circumstances, the mentality and the preparation of the assembly. Thus there is no need to resort to arbitrary adaptations, which would only weaken the impact of the liturgy.[101]

In the introduction to this instruction we find a statement which is most important to the understanding of obedience to liturgical law. The document first speaks of the bishop and states that he is not only to watch that his priests observe the laws of the Church concerning the liturgy, but he himself is to be a "shining example in carrying out the genuine renewal of the liturgy."

> With the help of their liturgical commissions, the bishops should be accurately informed about the religious and social condition of the faithful which they serve; in order to meet their spiritual needs in the best way possible, they should learn to make full use of the means offered by the rites. By thus evaluating the situation in their diocese, they will be able to note what helps and hinders true renewal and engage a wise and prudent work of persuasion and guidance, a work which both recognizes the real needs of the faithful and follows the guidelines laid down in the new liturgical laws.

A well-informed bishop will be a great help to the priests who must exercise their ministry in hierarchical fellowship with him; his knowledge will make it easier for them to work together with him in obedience for the more perfect expression of divine worship and for the sanctification of souls.[102]

One of the "crises" of obedience with regard to liturgical law at the present time is the conflict which can arise between the priest who is exercising a leadership role in the liturgical celebrations and the bishop. The more their pastoral experiences are harmonized, the more they are motivated by the same liturgical spirit, the more easily they will be able to cooperate in their common mission.

The third instruction then turns to some of the specific problems that had come to the attention of the Congregation. The list gives an indication of the areas where "priests were going too far" according to the instruction; for example, no non-Scriptural readings may ever be used; the faithful should not add comments to the homily; no one may make changes, substitutions, additions in the official texts. This legislation, or rather, this reminder of the legislation already existing, is to be read in the total context of the legislation and the documents giving the spirit of the legislation. As the Church is a living and dynamic reality, there will always be need for encouraging those who are timid and for restraining the over-zealous.

1971 FEB 02 The Liturgy of the Hours

The *General Instruction on the Liturgy of the Hours* was published under the date of February 2, 1971 and the actual text followed later because of the time required to print and distribute the four volumes. As was said above with regard to the "General Instruction on the Roman Missal," this type of presentation is a change from previous editions of the Hours. The breviary of Pius V was introduced by a set of "general rubrics" to be followed in the recitation of the Hours and this style of presentation continued in the Roman usage to the present time. We saw that the Code of 1960, while changing many of the individual rubrics, retained the same style of legislation. The present text, however, is introduced by an "Institutio generalis" and "this change in vocabulary," Martimort says,[103] "reveals a profound change of perspective."

Official approval was given to the Hours in the Apostolic Constitution "Laudis Canticum" November 1, 1970. The statement is made in this form, an apostolic constitution and not merely a *motu proprio,* because of the importance of the Hours in the life of the Church.

About two years before this constitution, the Consilium sent to each of the bishops a short description of the new Hours (January 1969); among the principles listed in this letter are the following:

> The new Roman breviary will be composed in such a way so that it will:
>
> a) open the riches of this prayer to the faithful in general, and not reserve them only for priests and religious.
>
> e) provide for a certain flexibility in many different ways, keeping the essentials of the structure of the office and the liturgical year.
>
> f) lessen the strictly juridical or legal obligation of saying the office in order that the heart might be better taken up with praying.[104]

When studying the theological context of the liturgical legislation in the teachings and documents of the Council, we noted the relation between the liturgy and the Church. The liturgy forms and structures the Church; the Church reveals its true nature most clearly when it prays. It is in this context that the Hours, as "liturgical" prayer, must be the prayer of the "Church." This is perhaps the most important change in the liturgy of the Hours— the fact that they are no longer viewed as the prayer of the whole Church, for in the perspective of the Council, all liturgy belongs to the whole Church. The fact that a prayer engages the whole Church and makes the Church visible to the world has entered into our understanding of the nature of liturgical prayer. In the first article of the apostolic constitution *Laudis Canticum,* Pope Paul states that the Hours are the prayer of the entire people of God:

> The office has been drawn up and arranged in such a way that not only clergy but also religious and indeed laity may participate in it, since it is the prayer of the whole people of God. People of different callings and circumstances, with their individual needs, were kept in mind, and a variety of ways of celebrating the office has been provided, by means of which the prayer can be adapted to suit the way of life and vocation of different groups using the liturgy of the Hours.[105]

The General Instruction states that "the Church's praise is not to be considered the exclusive possession of clerics and monks either in its origin or by its nature, but belongs to the whole Christian community."[106]

This change in perspective is reflected in the change in the vocabulary used in speaking about the prayer. The code of 1960 spoke of "breviary" in the title, but the text of the code usually used the term "divine office." However, as we noted above when treating the code of 1960, the rubrics which treated of the time for saying the canonical Hours stressed the importance of saying the Hours at their proper times:

> By their very makeup the canonical Hours of the divine office are ordained to the sanctification of the various hours of the natural day. Hence it it best, both for the real sanctification of the day and for the spiritually fruitful recitation of the Hours themselves, that each canonical Hour be recited at the time which most nearly approaches its own true time.[107]

Msgr. Jounel, in an article in *Notitiae,* outlines the evolution in the terminology. The word "breviary" looks mainly to the book itself; the term divine office has the double advantage that it indicates the dignity of the prayer and that it indicates the action itself, not just the book.[108] However the term divine office does not express the specific nature of this prayer: the sanctification the hours of the day and night.

Mgr. Jounel states it was only when the first volume of the Hours was going to press, in the fall of 1970, that the editors decided to introduce the word "Hours" into the title. "Liturgy of the Hours" was preferred to "Prayer of the Hours" because the word "liturgy" better emphasizes the ecclesial nature of the prayer. However, as the Council had legislated for the "divine office" this term was kept in the subtitle: "The divine office revised by decree of the Second Vatican Ecumenical Council and published by authority of Pope Paul VI."

The realization of the relation of the Hours and the praying Church developed, in large part, after the Council. This is another example where the implications of the change of the theological perspective brought about by the Council are only gradually realized and implemented. In the schema of the Constitution of January 1962, there is no reference to the Hours as the prayer of the whole people of God. Jounel writes:

> At that time, such an understanding of the office would seem (outside of certain circles) to be but an archaic vision of the prayer of the Church taken from the *Pilgrimage of Etheria.* Nearly all of the future Fathers of the Council saw the breviary as the book of the priest, the guarantee of his fidelity to prayer, and the guardian of his chastity.[109]

The change of perspective which causes the Hours to be viewed as the prayer of the whole Church involves, at the same time, a change in the structure of the prayer. As the new rites allow the laity to take their proper liturgical role, we find that they must be flexible enough to adapt to the various needs of the laity, and simple and clear in their structure so that everyone, and not just the "professionals," can understand and profit from them.

The General Instruction lists many options possible in the Hours.[110] There are also the options which result from the new calendar and the number of days on which an optional memorial may be celebrated (GI 244). There is the possibility of a votive office which corresponds to a need or certain occasion (GI 245). Articles 246-252 allow a certain flexibility to the choice of psalms, the Scripture readings, and the use of an optional lectionary.

Furthermore, if the Hours are to become the prayer of the people of God in fact and not just in theory, it is necessary that certain adaptations be made according to the capacities and understanding of the group praying the Hours. The Instruction states that "in the case of an office celebrated with the people, other psalms especially chosen to lead them step by step to an understanding of the psalms" may be substituted for those given in the text (GI 247).

The recognition that the prayer is the prayer of the Church leads us to emphasize the specific characteristics of this liturgy: namely, the sanctification of the hours. The instruction repeats the directive of article 94 of the Constitution on the Liturgy: That the day may be truly sanctified and the Hours themselves recited with spiritual profit, it is preferable that they should be recited at the hour nearest to the one indicated by each canonical Hour (SC 94, GI 11). This regulation concerning the time for reciting the Hours also states the end to be achieved: that the day may be truly sanctified and the Hours themselves recited with spiritual profit. The Hours are to be a source of devotion, "a means of gaining God's manifold grace, a deepening of personal prayer, and an incentive to the work of the apostolate" (GI 19). It is in this context that the obligation of the Hours is treated.

The Instruction first speaks of the importance of the liturgy of the Hours in the life of the Church (Chapter 1). This chapter speaks of the relation between *Church* and *prayer*. It speaks of the prayer of Christ, and the Church continuing the prayer of Christ. The references to the Scriptures given in the footnotes to this section of the instruction would give anyone who takes the time to study them thoroughly a rich understanding of the place of prayer in a biblical spirituality. To take these articles seriously, and not merely as a pious introduction, is to realize that the primary obligation lies in the fact that "Jesus has commanded us to do as he did. On many occasions he said: Pray, ask, seek in my name" (GI 5).

The Instruction then speaks of "those who celebrate the Hours" and first mention is made of the fact that the Hours pertain to the whole body of the Church; it manifests the Church and has an effect upon it. Its ecclesial celebration is best seen and especially recommended when it is performed with the bishop surrounded by his priests and ministers, that is, by the local Church (GI 20).

Next the instruction speaks of those who have a special mandate to celebrate the liturgy of the Hours. First among these the instruction mentions the bishop.

> The bishop represents the person of Christ in an eminent and visible way and is the high priest of his flock. In a certain sense it is from him that the faithful who are under his care derive and maintain their life in Christ. Therefore the bishop should be the first in prayer among the members of his Church. When he recites the liturgy of the Hours he always does so in the name of and on behalf of the Church committed to him.[111]

The mandate of priests to celebrate the Hours is placed in this same context:

> Priests, united to the bishop and the whole presbytcrium, also represent the person of Christ the priest in a special way. They share the same duty of praying to God on behalf of all the people entrusted to them and indeed for the whole world.[112]

However, this duty cannot be divorced from the task to lead the community in prayer:

> The task of those who are in sacred orders or who have a special canonical mission is to direct and preside over the prayer of the community; they should devote their labour to this end, that all those committed to their care may be of one mind in prayer. Pastors of souls should see to it that the faithful are invited and helped by requisite instruction to celebrate the chief Hours in common, especially on Sundays and feasts. They should teach them to draw sincere prayer from their participation and so help them to understand the psalms in a Christian way that they may gradually come to use and appreciate the prayer of the Church more fully.[113]

The obedience called for by liturgical law in regard to the celebration of the Hours has changed in the following ways: The
Hours are seen in relation to the prayer of the whole Church
and the relation of the clergy to people of God; the Hours are
seen as the prayer of the Church sanctifying the day and night
and consequently the obligation of the Hours is more closely
related to the specific times when the Hours are intended to be
celebrated. The General Instruction on the liturgy of the Hours
intends to "lessen the strictly juridical or legal obligation of saying
the office in order that the heart might be better taken up with
praying."[114]

Another aspect, however, of this style of legislation is that
presenting the "reasons" for the law can weaken the law. The
reasons behind the legislation, the function of the legislation, and
the end the laws are to achieve are often incorporated in the
new legislation in order to call forth a more willing and intelligent
obedience—and thus strengthen the law. However, this style of
legislation can weaken the law in that the law is sometimes set
aside by those who find that the reasons for the law are not
present, or that observing the law does not achieve the end stated
in the law.

*1971 JUN 14 Note on the date when the new missal and Hours
may be used*

Due to the difficulties of translating and publishing the new
missal and liturgy of the Hours, several Episcopal Conferences
asked for more time to implement these new rites. Cardinal Tabera
issued a "notification" concerning this matter and also mentioned
certain interpretations of the calendar for 1972 and 1973: The
solemnity of St. Joseph, and the date for celebrating the solemnity
of St. John the Baptist, for example. This "notification" would
not be of sufficient importance to single out for our attention
at this point were it not for the fact that it also mentions that the
entire Mass and Hours, with the people or without, can be celebrated in the vernacular language.

The permission to celebrate the liturgy in the vernacular was
given gradually during the years following the Constitution. However, this permission is presented in a simple "notification." Once
again we have occasion to note that the liturgical reform was implemented without always giving proper consideration to canonical
form. The rites we have studied thus far have often modified
the Code of Canon Law, but have seldom made reference to
this fact. In this present instance, we recall that the use of the

vernacular in the liturgy was one of the most discussed questions at the Council. During the voting on the Constitution we find the following:

> That the vernacular language at Mass be only "permitted" and not "advised." In favor, 2215 bishops out of 2275.

> That the vernacular languages be limited to "those parts which concern the people" (sic). In favor, 2212 bishops.

> That the people retain some contact with the Latin. In favor, 2193 bishops.[115]

The point we are making is not that the notification of June 14, 1971 contradicts the wishes of the bishops eight years earlier— rather it shows something of how their thinking evolved. The point here is that a matter of such importance should not be decided in a document which has the form of a simple "notification."

1971 AUG 22 Rite of Confirmation

The rite of confirmation continues along the lines of development we have noted above concerning the other rites reformed by the Council. However, in the introduction to the rite we read:

> In view of contemporary pastoral circumstances, it is desirable that the godparent at baptism, if present, also be the sponsor at confirmation; canon 796 § 1 is abrogated.[116]

We wish to draw attention to the fact that explicit mention is made that the Code of Canon Law is here being modified. Such explicit references to the Code are rare in the new rites. The liturgical legislation has on many occasions altered the Code, but reference to this fact and explicit mention of the canons in question is seldom made.

The Rite of Christian Initiation of Adults (1972 JAN 06) mentions canon 790 and canon 1153 in the footnotes, and the Rite of Anointing and Pastoral Care of the Sick (1972 DEC 07) mentions explicity canons 938, 941, 943, 822 § 4, and 468 § 1. Perhaps we can see here a growing concern for coordination between the liturgy and canon law. Earlier rites, however, do not often mention this relation. The Rite of Baptism for Children (1969 MAY 15) has no footnotes referring to the Code. The Rite of Confirmation, although it mentions explicitly that canon 796 § 1 (sponsors) is abrogated, makes no mention that canons 782 (minister) and 788 (age) are also changed. The rite adopts the terminology of the Constitution on the Church and speaks of the bishop as the "original minister" of confirmation (LG 26); the rite also mentions others who have the faculty to confirm "by law." Article 8 of the introduction speaks of cases where the minister of confirmation can associate other priests with himself in the administration of the sacrament. Clearly, this legislation changes canon 782 even though no mention is made of this fact.

One other point might be made in reference to the ICEL text presented for use in the United States. In the "Foreword" we read:

> The present text is the English translation approved for provisional use. It is provisional in another sense, namely, that no regional or national adaptations (SC 37-40) have been introduced at this time. Instead, it is hoped by the Bishops' Committee on the Liturgy that a period of several years' use will help to discern and develop such adaptations.[117]

Although this is the first time I have found an explicit statement that the rites are to serve as "provisional" rites to allow the development of rites which are more adapted to the United States, a comparison of the ICEL translations and the Latin texts show that the ICEL text is a translation and not an adaptation. A comparison of the English translations of the new rites and their French or German equivalents shows that the French and German texts have a much larger proportion of adaptations and additions.

Perhaps this fact reflects a change in the way ICEL sees its role. In the presentation of the International Committee on English in the Liturgy, printed in *Notitiae* 1965, we read that the hierarchies of the member countries give the International Advisory Committee on English in the Liturgy the following mandate:

> To work out a plan for the translation of liturgical texts and the provision of original texts where required. . .[118]

However, at a preliminary meeting of part of the International Committee held in London, in January of 1965, general norms were reached which included:

> 1. The task of the Advisory Committee and of its associates is limited to the provision of acceptable English translations from the Liturgical books of the Latin rite. It does not extend to the composition of new (and in places possibly better) texts.[119]

At the end of the first year's work, Archbishop Gray, President of ICEL, gave a report in which he stated:

> A major problem of English translations of Latin liturgical texts, which of course is not solved, is the extent of adaptation demanded by contemporary pastoral considerations and the literary character of the English language. While remaining within the limits of faithful translation, such adaptation is necessary for the project, but it is distinct from the creation of new liturgical texts and rites, which is outside the province of the International Committee on English in the Liturgy.[120]

In the fall of 1975, the constitution of ICEL was published in *Notitiae.* It is stated there that the ICEL has received the mandate of the bishops to "work out a plan for the translation of liturgical texts and the provision of original texts."[121] "The advisory committee is entrusted with the following mandate: to implement the English translation of liturgical texts and to provide original texts where required. . ."[122] There is no mention in the document of the fact that "the creation of new liturgical texts and rites is outside the province of the committee;" rather, it seems that the Constitution indicates that this creation is an important part of the work.

If the present texts are to serve as the basis for future adaptations to regional and national conditions, a certain flexibility is necessary if they are to fulfill this role. New creations will not be able to grow organically from the existing forms if the existing forms do not permit such a development, often coming from the grass-roots, to take place orderly yet freely.

1972 JAN 06 *Rite of Christian Initiation of Adults*

The Constitution on the Liturgy listed among the norms for the revision of the rites "norms following from the catechetical and pastoral nature of the liturgy." The present rite is based on an analysis of how one ordinarily comes to the faith and the way in which faith grows and matures. The rite presupposes a certain catechetical analysis and expresses a relation to the different states of the "spiritual journey" of the one to be baptized.

> The rite of initiation is suited to the spiritual journey of adults, which varies according to the many forms of God's grace, the free cooperation of the individuals, the action of the Church, and the circumstances of time and place.[123]

An analysis of the prayers and texts of the rite shows that they too reflect this progressive nature of conversion. In the rite of becoming a catechumen, for example, the prayers are not yet explicitly trinitarian. The rite does not start with a "complete" theology, but allows the theological expression of the faith to progress and deepen within the rite itself. The former rite looks more to the accomplished fact of conversion; the present rite looks more to the spiritual progress of the candidate.

Clearly, a rite which intends to respect the "many forms of God's grace" will demand a special pastoral concern and adaptation on the part of the celebrants:

> It is for the celebrant to use fully and intelligently the freedom which is given to him either in the General Introduction (no. 34) or in the rubrics of the rite. In many places the manner of acting or praying is intentionally left undetermined or two possibilities are offered, so that the celebrant may accommodate the rite, according to his prudent pastoral judgment, to the circumstances of the candidates and others who are present. The greatest freedom is left in the introductions and intercessions, which may always be shortened, changed, or even increased with new intentions in order to correspond with the circumstances or special situation of the candidates (for example, a sad or joyful event occurring in a family) or of the others present (for example, a joy or sorrow common to the parish or town).[124]

1972 DEC 07 Rite of Anointing and Pastoral Care of the Sick

One of the more important principles of liturgical obedience which we have traced through this study is the fact that it is not sufficient for the ministers to content themselves with the exact fulfillment of their role according to the liturgical laws. The Rite of Anointing and Pastoral Care of the Sick exemplifies this principle. The very title of the rite places the sacrament in a larger pastoral context. The introduction begins with a section on "Human Sickness and Its Meaning in the Mystery of Salvation." The celebration of the sacraments of the sick is seen in the context of the continuation and prolongation of the concern which Christ himself showed for the bodily and spiritual welfare of the sick (Number 5). When speaking of the "offices and ministries for the sick," the rite places this ministry in its larger liturgical and ecclesiastical context:

> If one member suffers in the body of Christ, which is the Church, all the members suffer with him (I Cor 12:26). For this reason, kindness shown toward the sick and works of charity and mutual help for the relief of every kind of human want should be held in

special honor. Every scientific effort to prolong life and every act of heartfelt love for the sick may be considered a preparation for the gospel and a participation in Christ's healing ministry.

It is thus fitting that all baptized Christians share in this ministry of mutual charity within the body of Christ: by fighting against disease, by love shown to the sick, and by celebrating the sacraments of the sick. Like the other sacraments, these too have a communal aspect, which should be brought out as much as possible when they are celebrated.[125]

This perspective requires that the priest not only adapt the rite but that he see the rite as part of his concern for the sick. He must visit the sick and help them by acts of charity in whatever way he can (Number 35). In adapting the rite he should be aware that the sick tire easily—if the rite is going on too long he is to shorten it. He is to be aware of others who may be present, for example, in a hospital.

When the priest prepares for the celebration of the sacraments, he should ask about the condition of the sick person. He should take this information into account when he arranges the rite, in choosing readings and prayers, in deciding whether he will celebrate Mass for viaticum, and the like. As far as possible he should plan all this with the sick person or his family beforehand, while he explains the meaning of the sacraments.[126]

The final paragraph of the introduction is especially important for our study of liturgical law:

The priest should follow the structure of the rite in the celebration, while accommodating it to the place and the people involved. . .[127]

Formerly the rubrics did not speak of the "structure" of the rite. The practice of allowing so many variations in a rite brings with it the recognition that the rite is not merely a chain of unrelated prayers but that it is a structured whole. The new rites often allow variable parts within the structure of the rite. To adapt a rite in this way is not the same as what was often forbidden in the rubrics, the creation of a new rite.

For example, the rite for the visitation and communion of the sick first gives an introduction explaining this ministry and then presents the rite. The rite is composed of a greeting, a penitential rite, a reading and homily, prayer, communion, silence, prayer, and a final blessing. The rite mentions that several of these elements are optional and gives alternate texts for the various parts. The ritual, then, presents a basic structure into which the priest is to place approved prayers and other elements in order to "create" a rite that is pastorally adapted to the individual circumstances.

1973 JAN 29 Instruction facilitating Sacramental Communion

This instruction intends to preserve the respect for the Eucharist and at the same time modify some of the signs accompanying this reverence. However, in practice, the change in the theological context of the Eucharist brought about by the Council had already changed certain attitudes in this matter. The instruction treats four areas of pastoral concern.

1. The distribution of Communion by the laity. Reverence for the eucharist traditionally limited the distribution of Communion to deacons and priests. Canon law (C. 1306) forbids the laity to touch the host or chalice—even an empty chalice. However the emphasis on the Eucharist as a meal and the practice of Communion in the hand caused a change in the way reverence to the Eucharist was viewed. The instruction wishes to "facilitate" the reception of Communion. Often the lack of priests or the size of many parishes and the increased number of communicants have either made the reception of Communion difficult, or caused the Communion of the Eucharistic celebration to be out of proportion with the length of the total celebration. For these reasons "it has seemed appropriate to the Holy Father to establish extraordinary ministers, who may give Holy Communion to themselves and to other faithful under the following conditions. . ."[128] The conditions which follow serve to safeguard the reverence due to the Eucharist; however, it is not the sole purpose of the instruction to safe-guard the Eucharist. The instruction is directed to facilitate the reception of Communion. It is in this light which we must inter-pret the conditions. An interpretation which would negate the very purpose of the document cannot be considered consistent with the obedience called for by the instruction.

2. Receiving Communion more than once a day. We have seen above that this legislation has changed frequently. The instruction states that beyond the circumstances which have been mentioned already, there are similar occasions which suggest that Communion might fittingly be received twice on the same day. The instruction states that the tradition remains intact and is not to be set aside merely to repeat the reception of the Eucharist. However, when it is not a case of a mere "repetition" of Communion the case is different. The instruction then extends the list of times when

this is permitted. There is no indication that the list is taxative or restrictive. The fact that the ordinary can grant permission in other particular circumstances is an indication of this. It is doubtful that the ordinary is to be consulted in each case which is not literally included in the list but which seems to fit the general principles. The new legislation requires that a certain responsibility for interpreting the legislation be assumed by each of the people of God.

3. The Eucharistic fast for the sick and aged. Again the purpose of the document is to free the reception of Communion from unnecessary restrictions, that is, from restrictions which are not made necessary by the reverence due to the sacrament. The fact that the fast is reduced to "approximately 15 minutes" is an indication that the document does not intend a strict interpretation of this law. The concern is to be directed toward the worthy reception of the Communion and not be distracted by clock-watching. Even in the pre-Conciliar moral texts, the authors would not consider 15 minutes "serious matter" in itself.

4. The reception of Communion in the hand. This final section of the instruction treats of the "piety and reverence" towards the Eucharist when it is placed in the hands of the faithful. No new legislation is given here; however, the fact that the matter is treated in the instruction indicates the number of Bishops' Conferences who have asked for permission to use this rite and also the growing preference among the faithful for this manner of receiving Communion.

1973 APR 27 Letter concerning the Eucharistic Prayers

This letter to the presidents of the national Conferences of Bishops is the response to a very important pastoral and liturgical question: is the flexibility and possibility to adapt the rite to the needs of the faithful sufficient in the new missal, or should it be extended? Should new Eucharistic Prayers be allowed? There is a need to establish a balance between variety and unity. "The celebration of the Eucharist is, in itself, a profession of faith whereby the entire Church recognizes and expresses its nature. Nowhere is this more apparent than in the Eucharistic Prayer."[129]

The question is larger than the question of allowing other Eucharistic Prayers. The real question is what makes a Eucharistic Prayer Catholic? The Church is constituted by the union of all the baptized; the Church is made visible as the people of God celebrate the Eucharist with their apostolic ministers. How much variety can be tolerated in the prayer which is central to the

manifestation of the one Church? "By using the various texts
contained in the Roman missal, various Christian communities,
as they gather to celebrate the Eucharist, are able to sense that
they themselves form the one Church praying with the same faith,
using the same prayer."[130]

The unity of the Church does not depend on the fact that there
be only one Eucharistic Prayer; the existence of many different
Eucharistic Prayers in the Church demonstrates this fact. Furthermore, the Council states that this very diversity of liturgical usage
has come about by divine Providence and is a sign of the catholicity of the Church (LG 23). "This variety of local churches with
one common aspiration is particularly splendid evidence of the catholicity of the undivided Church."[131]

The letter then states that "upon mature consideration of the
entire matter, it does not seem advisable at this time to grant
Episcopal Conferences the general faculty of either composing or
approving new Eucharistic Prayers."[132]

However, the letter does not stop here, but mentions the importance of variety in the liturgy. Furthermore, the letter speaks
of variety not only in relation to the text but also speaks of variety
in its psychological and catechetical dimensions:

> Tradition makes proper provision for the immutability of the text
> as a whole, while not excluding any appropriate variations. Thus
> the people can more readily associate themselves with the presiding
> priest with the frequent proclamation of the same texts. At the same
> time, the variations within the text, however few in number, are not
> only useful but welcome, for they foster devotion and attentiveness,
> and embellish the prayer in a unique way.[133]

This letter also speaks of the "different forms of oral communication." The incorporation of this type of vocabulary into
the liturgical laws gives yet another dimension to the problem of
the obedience demanded by liturgical law:

> In addition to the selection of appropriate texts, a truly living and
> communal celebration requires the president and all other ministers
> to carefully examine different forms of verbal communication with
> the congregation; this refers to the readings, homily, admonitions,
> introductions, and similar parts.[134]

It is also in this letter that we find the explicit mention of the
fact that the introductions and invitations given in the new Roman
missal do not have to be used word for word: "By their very
nature these brief admonitions do not require that everyone use

them in the form in which they appear in the missal."[135] If communities celebrating the Eucharist took full advantage of the possibilities given in the new rites to adapt them to their needs, there would be less "need" to change the Eucharistic Prayer.

1973 NOV 01 Directory for Masses with Children

The letter to the presidents of the national Conferences of Bishops concerning the *Directory for Masses with Children* is interesting to our study of liturgical law not only from the point of view of the rubrics but also because of the vocabulary it employs. The document speaks of the "pedagogical force" of the liturgy and speaks of the results of "recent psychological study." We see again the growing importance of the liturgy in its catechetical and communication dimensions. The directory also speaks of the human values that are found in the liturgy: the exchange of greetings, capacity to listen and to seek and grant pardon, expression of gratitude, the experience of symbolic actions, a meal of friendship, and festive celebration. In this context, liturgical law makes demands on the priest and all those responsible for the celebration, demands beyond the former system of rubrics; for example:

> It is the responsibility of the priest who celebrates with children to make the celebration festive, fraternal, meditative.[136]

> It will help in reaching the hearts of the children if the priest sometimes uses his own words when he gives invitations, for example, at the penitential rite, the prayer over the gifts, the Lord's Prayer, the sign of peace, and Communion.[137]

The directory states that the text of the presidential prayers may be chosen at will from the prayers of the missal and may even be adapted to the needs of the children. The directory states that the priest must "avoid anything foreign to the literary genre of a presidential prayer."[138] The mention of the "literary genre" of the prayers is the natural complement to the "structure" of the rite. This type of rubric implies that the president of the assembly be aware of the "literary genre" of the different parts of the liturgy, the "style" of an oration, the vocabulary, the structure. The former rubrics did not make this type of demand upon the celebrating priest, and formerly liturgy courses did not always give this type of training.

1973 DEC 02 Rite of Penance

Many aspects of the new rite of penance could be examined

in this study relating to the theological context of liturgical law: the new rite shows the hierarchical and communal nature of the liturgy, the sacrament is placed in an ecclesial context, the importance of Scripture, the emphasis on reconciliation. However, we will note only one aspect of the rite: the different degrees or levels of obligation to follow the rite as presented in the rite itself. Formerly nearly all parts of a rite or celebration were considered equally important; the present rite demonstrates how this has changed.

The appendix to the rite gives sample penitential services which are not proposed to be translated literally but are given as *models* to be used by liturgical commissions and individual Christian communities in preparing celebrations suited to their proper circumstances.

In the first chapter of the rite, we note that certain elements are "optional" (ad libitum); for example, number 43 mentions that a reading from the Scriptures at this point is "optional." We also find rubrics which state a possibility: The priest *may* do . . . (pro opportunitate). Furthermore, we find rubrics which indicate that a prayer may be said "in these or similar words" (his vel similibus verbis).

While certain parts of the rite are optional others are not. For example, in the introduction we read that the priest may adapt the rite but he must not change the *essential structure* of the rite, nor the "entire form of absolution."

It is for priests in reconciling individuals or the community, to adapt the rite to the concrete circumstances of the penitents. The essential structure and the entire form of absolution must be kept, but if necessary they may omit some parts for pastoral reasons or enlarge upon them, they may select the texts of readings or prayers, and they may choose a place more suitable for the celebration according to the regulations of the Episcopal Conference, so that the entire celebration may be rich and fruitful.[139]

Article 27 of the introduction states that in adapting the rite, the Lord's Prayer "is never omitted." This indicates that this prayer has a special importance in the rite.

There are indications of which parts of the rite pertain to the "essential structure," for example: "When pastoral needs dictate, the priest may omit or shorten some parts of the rite but must always retain in their entirety the confession of sins and the acceptance of the act of penance, the invitation to contrition and the form of absolution and the dismissal."[140]

The form of absolution has been enriched in the new rite and it is to be "retained in its entirety" even when the rite is shortened.

> The form of absolution indicates that the reconciliation of the penitent comes from the mercy of the Father; it shows the connection between the reconciliation of the sinner and the paschal mystery of Christ; it stresses the role of the Holy Spirit in the forgiveness of sins; finally, it underlines the ecclesial aspect of the sacrament because reconciliation with God is asked for and given through the ministry of the Church.[141]

These elements of the sacrament are of such an importance that the rubric which allows omitting or shortening the rite requires that this prayer be kept intact.

However, the same article speaks of the "essential words" of the formula: ". . . the priest extends his hands . . . and pronounces the formula of absolution, in which the essential words are. . ." We see reference to the "essential words" also in number 21 of the introduction which states that "in imminent danger of death, it is sufficient for the priest to say the essential words of the form of absolution, namely, "I absolve you from your sins in the name of the Father, and of the Son, and of the Holy Spirit."[142]

Consequently, not everything in the new rite is of equal importance. At the same time, the rite does not attempt to give an organized hierarchy of which parts are more important than others. When we list the facts mentioned above, we find:

1. The rite gives "models" for composing other similar services.
2. The rite gives optional elements and elements which may or may not be used.
3. The rite gives prayers that may be said "in these or similar words."
4. The rite indicates some prayers which are "never omitted."
5. The rite indicates that the essential structure and entire form of absolution are to be always kept intact.
6. The essential formula suffices in imminent danger of death.

Obedience or disobedience to this type of legislation must be seen in a different perspective than in the context of the pre-Conciliar legislation. The rite of penance requires both an understanding of the rite, its structure, and its function, and an understanding and concern for the pastoral situation and condition of the penitent. Obedience to this legislation requires knowledge of the rubrics, their spirit, and their theological context.

1974 NOV 01 Eucharistic Prayers for Masses with Children and for Masses of Reconciliation.

The Eucharistic Prayers for Masses of reconciliation are the first examples of Eucharistic Prayers in the Roman liturgy composed around a special "theme." However, when we speak of "literary genre" and "structure" of a rite, it is necessary to consider the question of "theme" also. If there is a basic structure and we are going to choose elements to fill the structure, there must be some guiding principle for this choice. Not all aspects of the Paschal Mystery can be presented at the same time for our celebration and thanksgiving; a theme is one way of selecting among the different aspects of the mystery. Consequently the question is not whether or not a liturgy is unified by a theme; rather, the question deals with the use of the theme and which themes are suitable for liturgical celebration.

In the introduction to the Eucharistic Prayers, we read that "the translation of these texts may be made with a measure of freedom so that it corresponds fully to the requirements and nature of the respective language. . . . The structure of the Eucharistic Prayer and the meaning of the text are to be maintained, however, and the formulas of consecration, which must be the same in all Eucharistic Prayers, are to be translated faithfully and literally."[143]

There is a hierarchy of values presented:

1. The consecration formula is to be translated "faithfully and literally."
2. The structure and meaning of the text are to be maintained.
3. The translation of the text is to be made with a measure of freedom.

The introduction to the Eucharistic Prayers for Masses with children states that the Latin text is not intended for liturgical use. Latin never developed a special style for speaking with children, and the translators are to keep in mind that the text is not "simply to be translated." The texts presented are to be used as models upon which the Episcopal Conferences should base their Eucharistic Prayers for children which are "adapted to the spirit of the respective language as well as to the manner in which one speaks with children concerning matters of great importance."[144]

Conclusion

In this chapter of our study we have examined some of the

legislation concerning the liturgy which has appeared since the Council. In each case we have pointed out one of the other aspects of the rite or document which related to our theme. In the next and final chapter of this study we will attempt a synthesis of the facts which we have examined in this and the previous chapters.

NOTES

1964 JAN 25 The motu proprio "Sacram Liturgiam"

[1] AAS 56 (1964) 140-141. NCWC 38-39. (Note: the complete references for each of the documents in this section are listed in the Bibliography. For the official documents, see the date corresponding to the date given in the title.)

[2] AAS 140.

[3] SC 14.
Sed quia, ut hoc evenire possit, nulla spes effulget nisi prius ipsi animarum pastores spiritu et virtute Liturgiae penitus imbuantur in eaque efficiantur magistri, ideo pernecesse est ut institutioni liturgicae cleri apprime consulatur.

[4] AAS 144.
. . . atque idcirco nemini omnino alii, ne sacerdoti quidem, licere quidquam in re liturgica vel addere, vel demere, vel mutare.

1964 SEP 26 The First Instruction (Inter Oecumenici)

[5] SEP 14, 1964 Pope Paul VI. Opening address to the Third Session, NCWC p. 10.

[6] "Spirit of the liturgy"—See SC 14. 17. 29. 37. 116. 121. 127.

[7] Art. 1.
. . . eaque tanto abundantiores fructus feret quanto altius animarum pastores atque christifideles genuinum eiusdem spiritum perspexerit et volenti animo in usum deduxerint.

[8] Art. 5.
Attamen, in primis necesse est ut omnes sibi persuasum habeant Constitutionem Concilii Vaticani II de sacra Liturgia non sibi proponere tantum formas et textus liturgicos mutare, sed potius illam fidelium institutionem illamque actionem pastoralem excitare, quae sacram Liturgiam veluti culmen in fontem habeat. Mutationes enim in sacram Liturgiam usque adhuc inductae atque in posterum inducendae ad hunc finem ordinantur.

⁹ Article 7.
Praesertim autem necesse est ut intima unio vigeat liturgiam inter et catechesim religiosam institutionem atque praedicationem.

¹⁰ Article 20.
Sacrae Liturgiae moderatio ad Ecclesiae auctoritatem pertinet; nemo proinde alius in hac re suo marte procedat, cum detrimento, saepius, ipsius Liturgiae eiusque instaurationis a competenti auctoritate peragendae.

¹¹ Notitiae 1 (1965) 137.
Breviter: cum unum celebratur Officium, etsi iteratum, unica conceditur accessio ad sacram mensam; cum duplex celebratur Officium, duplex conceditur Communio.

¹² See the alphabetical list following the list of official documents, under the heading COMMUNION MORE THAN ONCE A DAY.

¹³ Notitiae I (1965) 109-135; 167-184.

¹⁴ Ibid. 113.
Magis quam nova forma celebrationis, vera initiatio sensui instaurationis desideratur; et sacerdotes hanc exspectant. Multi receperunt formationem quoad rubricas, pauci quoad mysterium contentum et actum in liturgia. Dialogus cum laicis, in hac re, est elementaris, etsi revera incepit. Diversitas munerum in actione liturgica non ab omnibus intelligitur: sacerdos usque nunc omnia faciebat.

1965 JAN 27 The Order of Mass.

¹⁵ See "Alphabetical List" under the heading HOMILY.

¹⁶ Post Evangelium, celebrans, ad sedem aut ad altare, vel in ambone aut ad cancellos, homiliam, si facienda est, habet.

¹⁷ Jounel, LMD 80 (1964) 46.

1965 MAR 07 Rite for Concelebration

¹⁸ Article 11.
Curent animarum pastores ut fideles qui concelebrationi intersunt, per aptam catechesim, de ipso ritu eiusque significatione opportune edoceantur.

¹⁹ Decree "Ecclesiae semper," beginning:
Ecclesiae semper curae fuit, in sacrorum mysteriorum celebrationibus ordinandis et instaurandis, ut ipsi ritus inexhaustas divitias Christi, quas continent et bene dispositis communicant, etiam optimo quo fieri potest modo, manifestent, atque ita facilius animos et vitam fidelium imbuant, qui eos participant.

²⁰ His itqaue rationibus, multo magis quam aliis ordinis mere practici, . . .

1965 MAR 07 Communion under both kinds

²¹ SC 55 (second paragraph)
Communio sub utraque specie, firmis principiis dogmaticis a Concilio Tridentino statutis, in casibus ab Apostolica Sede definiendis, tum clericis et

religiosis, tum laicis concedi potest, de iudicio Episcoporum, veluti ordinatis in Missa sacrae suae ordinationis, professis in Missa religiosa suae professionis, neophytis in Missa quae Baptismum subsequitur.

[22] Praenotanda, number 2.
Simul tamen fideles hortentur ut sacrum ritum, quo signum eucharistici convivii plenius elucet, impensius participare satagant.

[23] Institutio Generalis Missalis Romani.
240. Formam ratione signi pleniorem habet sacra Communio cum fit sub utraque specie. In ea enim forma signum eucharistici convivii perfectius elucet, et clarius exprimitur voluntas qua novum et aeternum testamentum in Sanguine Domini ratum habetur, eschatologicum in regno Patris.

1965 JUN 30 Letter of Cardinal Lercaro

[24] Notitiae 9-10 (1965) 257-258.

[25] Ibid. 258.

[26] Ibid. 259.

[27] Karl Rahner, S.J. *Strukturwandel der Kirche als Aufgabe und Chance* (Freiburg-im-Breisgau: Herder, 1972), translated by Edward Quinn, *The Shape of the Church to Come* (London: SPCK, 1974), pp. 59-60.

[28] Notitiae 9-10 (1965) 260.

[29] Rev. Gommar A. Depauw publicly launched the movement on March 15, 1965. The history and activities of the movement can be found in their publications issued from Suite 303 east, Pan Am Building, 200 Park Avenue, NY 10017. The quotation here is taken from "The New Mass, WARNING!" page 8.

The theological arguments against the "new" Mass have been systematically answered by Dom Guy Oury, *La Messe de S. Pie V à Paul VI* (Solesmes, 1975), 127 pp.

[30] Notitiae 9-10 (1965) 260.

1965 SEP 03 Encyclical Letter on the Holy Eucharist

[31] AAS 57 (1965) 755. English: NCWC 10.
10. Compertum namque habemus inter eos, qui de hoc Sacrosancto Mysterio loquendo scribendoque disserunt, esse nonnullos qui circa Missas quae privatim celebrentur, circa dogma transsubstantiationis et cultum Eucharisticum tales vulgent opiniones, quae fidelium animos perturbent. . .

[32] AAS 755. NCWC 11.
11. Non enim fas est, . . . Missam quam "communitariam" dicunt, ita extollere, ut Missis quae privatim celebrentur derogetur.

[33] AAS 761-762.
(The theological controversy has been treated in other books, for example see: *Die vielen Messen und das eine Opfer*, by Karl Rahner, volume 31 of the Quaestiones Disputatae.)

[34] See Bibliography 1963 NOV 18, Modi, Caput I, nn 16-31, page 21. Articles 26 to 32 remain unchanged except for the following addition to article 27: "Quod valet praesertim pro Missae celebratione, salva semper natura publica et sociali cuiusvis Missae, et pro Sacramentorum administratione." The reference given for this addition is to Pius XII, Mediator Dei, AAS 39 (1947) 557, where Pius XII states that each time the Sacrifice is offered it is a public and social act because the Sacrifice of the Cross was a public and social act.

1966 APR 17 The Prayer of the Faithful

[35] Page 5.
Praesens libellus . . . intendit hos textus explanare seu illustrare, ita ut competenti Auctoritati territoriali suppeditentur rationes ad recte, pro sua dicione, formulas parandas, vel criteria ad eas approbandas. Schemata proinde quae exhibentur non sunt *obligatorie* accipienda.

1967 MAR 05 Instruction on Music

[36] USCC 27.

[37] Bishops' Committee on the Liturgy, "The Place of Music in Eucharistic Celebrations," USCC, November 12, 1967.

[38] Ibid. 1.

[39] Instruction, article 4.
. . . ad cultum divinum celebrandum creata, sanctitate et bonitate formarum praedita est.

[40] McManus, commentary, USCC 31-32.

[41] Bishops' Committee: "The Place of Music. . ." page 3.

[42] Ibid. 4.

[43] Ibid.

[44] 1969 APR 06 General Instruction on the Roman Missal.
24. . . . Finis horum rituum est, ut fideles in unum convenientes communionem constituant et recte ad verbum Dei audiendum digneque Eucharistiam celebrandam sese disponant.

25. . . . Finis huius cantus est celebrationem aperire, unionem congregatorum fovere, eorumque mentem in mysterium temporis liturgici vel festivitatis introducere atque processionem sacerdotis ministrorumque comitari.

Note: similar rubrics are given for the chant between the readings 36-39; the offertory song, 50; and the communion hymn 56. Article 39 states that "the alleluia or the verse before the Gospel may be omitted if not sung; article 50 states that if the antiphon for the offertory is not sung, it is omitted.

26. . . . Adhiberi potest sive antiphona cum suo psalmo in Graduali Romano vel in Graduali simplici exstans, sive alius cantus, actioni sacrae, diei vel temporis indoli congruus, cuius textus a Conferentia Episcopali sit approbatus.

45 Appendix to the General Instruction for the Dioceses of the United States of America. Approved November 1969. Article 26.

1967 MAY 25 Instruction on Eucharistic Worship

46 Article 4. Latin page 10, English page 5.
. . . symbolum esse rei sacrae et invisibilis gratiae formam visibilem. Unde eo securuis et efficacius in mentem et vitam fidelium penetrabit quo aptiora et clariora erunt signa quibus celebratur et colitur.

47 Article 17.

48 Article 43.
In celebratione Eucharistiae etiam presbyteri ob speciale sacramentum, scilicet Ordinem, delegantur ad munus sibi proprium. Nam et ipsi "ut sacrorum ministri, praesertim in sacrificio Missae . . . personam specialiter gerunt Christi." Unde consentaneum est, ratione signi, ut, munere suo secundum proprium ordinem fungentes, id est Missam celebrantes aut concelebrantes nec tantum laicorum more communicantes, Eucharistiam participent.

49 Article 20.
Ad fovendam rectam ordinationem sacrae celebrationis atque actuosam fidelium participationem, ministri non tantum munus suum recte expleant, ad normam legum liturgicarum, sed ita se gerant ut eo ipso sensum rerum sacrarum insinuent.

1968 MAY 23 The New Eucharistic Prayers and Prefaces

50 Bishops' Committee on the Liturgy, "Introduction: The New Eucharistic Prayers," Washington, November 7, 1968, page 5.

51 Guidelines for the Episcopal Conferences For a Catechesis of the Faithful Concerning the Anaphoras of the Mass, Prepared by the Consilium for the Implementation of the Constitution on the Sacred Liturgy, June 14, 1968, page 6 of English text.

1968 AUG 15 Rite of Ordination

52 Latin, page 8 of the Rite. English, ICEL.

53 Number 13 for ordination of deacons. Similar references can be found in the ordination of priests and bishops.

Omnes dicunt: "Deo gratias," vel alio modo, iuxta morem regionis, electioni assentiunt.

54 Number 14.
Deinde, omnibus sedentibus, Episcopus alloquitur populum et Electos de munere Diaconi: quod facere potest his verbis:

55 For example, number 26.
Interim cani potest: . . . (psalm 145 is listed) . . . Cani potest etiam alius cantus aptus.

1969 JAN 25 Instruction on Translation

[56] This instruction does not contain in the text any mention of papal approval. Furthermore, it is issued only by the Consilium and not by the Congregation of Rites. This fact would seem to indicate that it does not have the same canonical force as an instruction issued by a Congregation. However, during this period we notice a certain "flexibility" in the forms of the official documents. Strictly speaking the statements of the Congregations issued as a "decree" and ratified by the pope have the binding force of law. Instructions have a directive force and must be observed but do not constitute the law of the Church. Declarations are interpretations of laws or answers to disputes.

This instruction on translation of liturgical texts, as stated above, does not contain any special mention of papal approval: however it is quoted in number 12 of the introduction for the "Eucharistic Prayers for Masses with Children" which states that the translation of these texts is to be made in accordance with the principles which were expressed in the instruction of January 25, 1969. The Eucharistic Prayers were in turn made public law, together with their introductions November 1, 1974 (Notitiae 101 page 4: . . . die 1 novembris 1974 impresso, publici iuris facimus Normas a Summo Pontifice statutas, necnon Praenotanda.) Thus the instruction on translation has received a kind of approval by implication or use.

[57] Article 5.

[58] Articles 9, 33, and 35.

[59] Article 20.

[60] Article 26.
Ces données influent non seulement sur la manière de parler, mais aussi sur la redaction littéraire.

[61] Article 43, quoting SC 23.

1969 MAR 19 Rite of Marriage

[62] Article 6.
. . . Celebrationis Matrimonii . . . praecipua elementa eluceant, nempe. . .

[63] Article 9. English, author's translation.
Specialem insuper rationem habeant pastores de iis qui occasione Matrimonii liturgicis celebrationibus assistunt vel Evangelium audiunt, sive sunt acatholici sive catholici qui Eucharistiam numquam vel vix umquam participant, vel fidem amississe videntur: sunt enim sacerdotes ministri Evangelii Christi pro omnibus.

Note: this same rubric is repeated in the "Rite of Funerals" number 18, and in the General Instruction on the Roman Missal, number 341.

[64] Jeremy Harrington, *Your Wedding: Planning Your Own Ceremony* (St. Anthony Messenger Press, Cincinnati, 1974) 122 pp. Imprimatur: Joseph L. Bernardin, Archbishop of Cincinnati.

[65] Ibid. p. 35.

1969 APR 06 General Instruction of the Roman Missal

[66] Martimort, Notitiae 64 (1971) 220.

[67] Ibid. 221.

[68] Article 11, first edition. Latin text as below, with the omission of the words in italics.

[69] Article 11, second edition.
Item ad sacerdotem, munere prasidis coetus congregati fungentem, spectat proferre quasdam monitiones atque formulas introductionis et conclusions in ipso ritu praevisas. *Natura sua hae monitiones non exigunt ut omnino ad verbum proferantur forma qua in Missali exhibentur; unde expedire poterit, saltem in aliquibus casibus, veris communitatis condicionibus aliquatenus eas aptare.* Sacerdoti praesidi etiam spectat verbum Dei nuntiare, necnon benedictionem finalem ipertire. . .

[70] Article 313.

1969 MAY 15 Rite of Baptism for Children

[71] General Introduction, article 7.
Ad populum Dei, hoc est Ecclesiam, quae fidem ab Apostolis acceptam tradit et nutrit, praeparatio Baptismi et christiana institutio summopere pertinet.

[72] Ibid. article 12.
Episcopi, quippe qui praecipui dispensatores mysteriorum Dei, sicut et totius vitae liturgicae in Ecclesia sibi commissa moderatores.

[73] Rite for Children, Introduction, 7 n. 2.

1969 MAY 15 Instruction on Masses for Special Gatherings

[74] USCC 6c.

[75] USCC 7.

[76] Article 6d.
Firmo praescripto litteris f et h, quae sequuntur, notato et his exceptis quae ab aliquo "commentatore" aguntur, fideles sese abstineant considerationibus, adhortationibus hisque rebus similibus in ipsa celebratione.

[77] Article 11.
. . . Reprobatur, ut arbitraria, quaevis commutatio, salvo praescripto sub n. 6, e). (Note: 6e refers to the possibility of choosing other readings for the liturgy of the word.)

[78] Final paragraphs (not numbered in Latin text, AAS page 811).
Quamvis his diebus nonnulli sint qui ex rebus novis quandoque insanis, quas ostendunt, vel ex liturgicarum celebrationum arbitrariis formis, quas excogitant, sese existimant esse renovatos, tamen sacerdotes, saeculares et regulares, vere de fidelium bono solliciti, compertum habeant actionis pastoralis mansurae et sanctificantis viam in constanti et magnanima fidelitate erga Ecclesiae voluntatem inveniri, quae eius praceptis, normis et structuris exprimitur.

Quod autem ab huiusmodi ratione abducit, quamvis specie alliciat, fidelium mentes perturbat atque sacerdotale ministerium languidum infructuosumque reddit.

Haec Instructio, quam de mandato Summi Pontificis, Sacra Congregatio pro Cultu Divino confecit, et ipse Summus Pontifex approbavit, omnes Ss. Missarum celebrationes pro coetibus particularibus posthac ordinabit.

[79] See Bibliography 1969 MAY 15B.

[80] DC 1559, p. 279.

[81] Ibid. 280.

[82] Ibid. 282.

[83] Ibid.

[84] Ibid. 283.

1969 MAY 25 Lectionary for Mass

[85] Article 10.

[86] Article 8d.

1969 MAY 29 Instruction on the Manner of Administering Communion

[87] AAS 61 (1969) 541. English, page 8.

[88] AAS 542. USCC 9.

[89] AAS 543-544. USCC 10.
1. Videturne exaudiendum votum, ut praeter modum traditum, etiam ritus recipiendi sacram Communionem in manu permittatur?
    Placet: 567
    Non placet: 1.233
    Pl. iuxta modum: 315
    Suffragia invalida: 20

2. Placetne ut experimenta huius novi ritus in parvis communitatibus prius fiant, assentiente Ordinario loci?
    Placet: 751
    Non placet: 1.215
    Suffragia invalida: 70

3. Putasne fideles, post praeparationem catecheticam bene ordinatam, hunc novum rituum libenter esse accepturos?
    Placet: 835
    Non placet: 1.185
    Suffragia invalida: 128

Ex redditis igitur responsis patet Episcopos longe plurimos censere hidiernam disciplinam haudquaquam esse immutandam; quae immo si immutetur, id tum sensui tum spirituali cultui eorundem Episcoporum plurimorumque fidelium offensioni fore.

(Note: The high percentage of invalid votes needs an explanation.)

[90] Notitiae 48 (1969) 353.

[91] See Notitiae Vol 5 (1969) p. 361. Vol 6 (1970) p. 62, 239, 332. Vol 7 (1971) 121, 260. Vol 8 (1972) p. 8, 113, 210. Vol 9 (1973) p. 124, 258. Vol 10 (1974) 116, 324. Vol 11 (1975) p. 40, 237.

1969 AUG 15 The Rite of Funerals

[92] Article 16.

[93] Article 18.

[94] Article 23.

[95] Ibid.

[96] Article 24 1.

[97] USCC page 10.

1970 FEB 02 Rite of Religious Profession

[98] Article 14.

[99] Article 14d.

[100] Article 14b. The text does not speak of "structure." Partium distributio minime perturbetur.

1970 SEP 05 The Third Instruction

[101] AAS 62 (1970) 693. USCC 2.
Etenim facultas aliquos textus eligendi et flexibiles rubricae sane celebrationi actuosae, acceptae ac spiritualiter salutari favent, cum eam ad locorum condiciones fideliumque ingenium et cultum accommodent, ideoque nihil erit opus inventis et arbitriis propriis uti, quibus celebratio ipsa extenuatur.

[102] AAS 694. USCC 3.
Hi igitur, liturgicis Commissionibus auxiliantibus, diligenter edoceantur de religiosa et sociali condicione fidelium, suis curis .creditorum, de spiritualibus eorum necessitatibus, deque aptiore via illos adiuvandi, omnibusque utantur facultatibus quas novi dant ritus. Hac ratione expendere valent ea quae verae renovationi conveniunt vel adversantur, et ita caute ac sapienter agenda proponere et moderari, ut iustis agnitis necessitatibus, integrum tamen opus secundum normas, novis legibus liturgicis editas, fiat.

Congrua enim rerum cognitio, quam Episcopi habent, non parvo auxilio est sacerdotibus in ministerio, quod sane in communione hierarchica est exsequendum, eaque debitam reddit oboedientiam faciliorem, quae ad perfectiorem cultus significationem atque ad animarum sanctificationem postulatur.

1971 FEB 02 The Liturgy of the Hours

[103] Martimort, Notitiae 64 (1971) 221.

[104] Notitiae 45 (1969) 75.

Novum Romanum ea ratione compositum est ut:
a) thesaurus eius non solis prebyteris regularibusque reservaretur, sed fidelibus etiam pateret. . .
e) multis modis praevideretur quaedam flexibilitas, servata tamen essentiali structura Officii et anni liturgici;
f) mitigaretur obligatio stricte iuridica vel legalis ut meliore libertate cor in orando dilataretur.

[105] Laudis Canticum, number 1.
Ita autem Officium est concinnatum et instructum, ut idem, cum sit oratio totius populi Dei, participare possint non solum clerici, sed etiam religiosi, quin etiam laici. Diversi ordinis et gradus hominibus ac peculiaribus eorum postulatis eo consultum est, quod variae formae celebrationis sunt inductae, quibus oratio accommodari potest variis coetibus ad Horarum Liturgiam incumbentibus, secundum eorum condicionem atque vocationem.

[106] General Instruction, number 270.
. . . et ceterum laus Ecclesiae neque ex sua origine neque ex sua natura censenda est propria clericorum vel monachorum, sed ad totam communitatem christianam pertinet.

[107] See above, Chapter II, note 94.

[108] Jounel, Notitiae 97 (1974) 312.

[109] Ibid. 313.

[110] See also: Martimort, "Souplesse et flexibilité. . ." Not 64 (1971) 237-238. And: E.J. Lengeling, "Les options générales de la nouvelle liturgie des heurs," LMD 105 (1971) 7-34.

[111] General Instruction, number 28.
Episcopus, utpote qui eminenti et aspectabili modo Christi personam gerat et sui gregis sacerdos magnus sit, a quo vita suorum fidelium in Christo quodammodo derivatur et pendet, primus in oratione inter Ecclesiae suae membra esse debet, eiusque oratio in Liturgiae Horarum recitatione semper Ecclesiae nomine ac pro Ecclesia sibi commissa peragitur.

[112] Ibid.
Presbyteri, cum episcopo cunctoque presbyterio coniuncti, et ipsi personam specialiter gerentes Christi sacerdotis, idem munus participant, Deum deprecantes pro toto populo sibi commisso, immo pro universo mundo.

[113] Number 23.
Munus autem eorum, qui sacro ordine insigniti vel peculiari missione canonica praediti sunt, est indicere et dirigere orationem communitatis: "laborem impendant ut omnes quorum cura sibi est commissa, unanimes sint in oratione." Curent ergo ut fideles invitentur et debita catechesi formentur ad celebrandas in communi, diebus praesertim dominicis et festis, potiores Liturgiae Horarum partes. Eos edoceant sinceram orationem ex eius participatione haurire, ideoque per aptam institutionem illos dirigant ad psalmos sensu christiano intellegendos, ita ut gradatim ad ampliorem gustum et usum orationis Ecclesiae manuducantur.

[114] See above, note 104.

1971 JUN 14 Note on the date for new Missal and Hours

[115] See Bibliography, 1962 OCT 22 Emendationes.

1971 AUG 22 Rite of Confirmation

[116] Article 5.
Attentis hodiernis pastoralibus adiunctis, expedit partrinum Baptismi, si adsit, esse etiam patrinum Confirmationis, abrogato can. 796, 1.

[117] NCCB 1.

[118] Notitiae 11 (1965) 341.

[119] Ibid. page 343.

[120] Notitiae 25 (1967) 17.

[121] Notitiae 108-109 (1975) 245.

[122] Ibid. page 246.

1972 JAN 06 Rite of Christian Initiation of Adults

[123] Article 5.
Ordo initiationis aptatur spirituali adultorum itineri, quod varium est secundum Dei gratiam multiformem, liberam ipsorum cooperationem, actionem Ecclesiae et adiuncta temporis et loci.

[124] Article 67.

1972 DEC 07 Rite of Anointing and Pastoral Care of the Sick

[125] Articles 32-33.

[126] Article 37.

[127] Article 41.
In celebratione proinde structuram ritus servet, accommodatam tamen adiunctis loci et personarum.

1973 JAN 29 Instruction facilitating Sacramental Communion

[128] Notitiae 83 (1973) 158. USCC. 2.
. . . Summo Pontifici opportunum visum est extraordinarios constituere ministros, qui sibi aliisque fidelibus s. Communionem praebere valeant, certis his definitisque condicionibus: . . .

1973 APR 27 Letter concerning the Eucharistic Prayers

[129] Number 11, quoting the Instruction "In quibus rerum circumstantiis," June 1, 1972, N. 2b. AAS 64 (1972) 520.

Missae celebratio in se ipsa est iam professio fidei in qua Ecclesia tota se ipsam agnoscit et exprimit. Quae omnia agregie apparent in ipsa Prece eucharistica.

[130] Number 2.

[131] LG 23.
Quae Ecclesiarum localium in unum conspirans varietas indivisae Ecclesiae catholicitatem luculentius demonstrat.

[132] Number 5.
Omnibus denique mature perpensis, visum est hoc tempore non convenire ut Conferentiis Episcopalibus facultas generalis concedatur exarandi aut approbandi novas Preces eucharisticas.

[133] Number 10.
Ex his patefit proprium esse eiusdem traditionis et immutabilitatem textus magni facere et opportunas variationes non excludere. Si enim fideles eundem textum pluries percipiendo facilius quodammodo cum sacerdote celebrante in oratione socientur, illius textus aliquae, sed numero paucae, variationes gratae et utiles evadunt, eoquod attentionem excitant, peitatem movent et orationem peculiari quodam colore ornant.

[134] Number 17.
Sane celebratio, ut sit communitaria et viva, praeter selectionem partium, requirit ut praeses aliique munus peculiare implentes diligenter perpendant diversa genera communicandi per verba cum ipsa congregatione, ex quibus sunt lectio, homilia, monitio, introductio et his similia.

[135] Number 14. See above, note 69.

1973 NOV 01 Directory for Masses with Children

[136] Number 23.
Sacerdoti Missam cum pueris celebranti cordi sit reddere celebrationem festivam, fraternam, meditativam.

[137] Number 23, continued.
Ad corda purerorum movenda iuvabit, si eos sacerdos quandocumque propriis verbis invitaverit, v.gr. ad actum paenitentialem, ad orationem super oblata, ad orationem dominicam, ad pacem dandam, ad Communionem.

[138] Number 51.
Interdum principium selectionis non sufficiet, ut pueri orationes considerare possint tamquam expressionem vitae propriae et suae experientiae religiosae, cum orationes compositae sint pro fidelibus adultis. In hoc casu nil impedit, quin textus orationum Missalis Romani necessitatibus puerorum aptentur, ita tamen, ut, fine et quodammodo etiam substantia servatis, omnia vitentur, quae a genere litterario orationis praesidentialis aliena sunt, uti adhortationes de moribus et modus loquendi nimis puerilis.

1973 DEC 02 Rite of Penance

[139] Article 40.

[140] Article 21.

Quando necessitas pastoralis id suadet, sacerdos potest quasdam partes ritus omittere aut breviare, attamen semper integre servanda sunt: confessio peccatorum et acceptatio satisfactionis, invitatio ad contritionem (n 44), formula obsolutionis et formula dimissionis.

[141] Article 19.

[142] Article 21.

Si vero mortis periculum imminet, sufficit ut sacerdos dicat verba essentialia formulae absolutionis, scilicet: Ego te absolvo a peccatis tuis, in nomine Patris, et Filii et Spiritus Sancti.

1974 NOV 01 Eucharistic Prayers for Masses with Children and for Masses of Reconciliation

[143] Article 3.

Interpretatio popularis textus selecti cum quadam libertate fieri potest ut exigentiis et indoli cuiusque linguae plene respondeat et a textu latino aliquantulum differre potest, iuxta eaque in Praenotandis pro Missis cum pueris, nn. 9-11, dicuntur. *Structura* tamen Precis eucharisticae et significatio formulae consecrationis, quae eaedem esse debent in omnibus Precibus eucharisticis.

[144] Article 11.

Talis coetus semper prae oculis textum latinum hac vice destinatum non esse ad usum liturgicum; exinde eum non simpliciter vertendum esse . . . . Quorum loquela sit in omnibus adaptata genio diversarum linguarum simul et modo quo in diversis linguis cum pueris sermo fit, quando agitur de rebus magni momenti.

V.

Synthesis Of The Change In Liturgical Laws And Their Context: Conclusions. Projections For The Future

---

In the preceding chapters of this study we have seen an evolution in the style and vocabulary used in issuing liturgical laws. We have also seen a change in the understanding of the nature of the liturgy and its relation to the Church. These changes have caused the legislation to have a new *spirit* and to call for a new *style* of obedience.

The Change in the Style of the Liturgical Legislation

The liturgical legislation has undergone several changes: first, a change from a legislation which governed each detail of the liturgy and gave little possibility for the minister or the community to change the rite, to a legislation which indicates certain "limits" within which there is a measure of freedom and flexibility. Second, we have seen a change from legislation which was directed to the external elements of the rite to a legislation which looks to the celebration of the rite as a whole and to its effects. The new legislation places the details in their pastoral context and gives indications as to the end or purpose which the rite is to achieve.

With regard to the first of these changes, the change from "rigid" to "flexible" rubrics, we have seen that *Mediator Dei* and the documents issued before the Council left little room for choice or adaptation on the part of the minister. There were few rubrics which were facultative or optional. For example, the rubrics permitted a choice in the hymns to be sung during the procession on Palm Sunday; but such rubrics were the exception, not the rule.

The rubrics were generally considered to be binding with the same degree of moral obligation. Of course, rubrics which concerned matters of less importance did not bind under pain of mortal sin. Yet, because of the sacred nature of the liturgy, very few rubrics were considered "less important." In general, nearly all matters concerning the rubrics were seen to be serious because of their relation to the sacred mystery: for example, the number of candles, the use of a missal, the vestments, etc.

The moral books taught that not all rubrics were equally binding, but these distinctions were hard to apply in actual practice. Prümer said that the distinction between prescriptive rubrics which bind under pain of sin and directive rubrics which appeal to a filial spirit of obedience and a sense of good order was "very difficult, if not impossible" to apply.[1] McManus was quoted above as saying that "it must be insisted that it is almost impossible to find rubrics in the liturgical books which are merely directive, that is, which give a direction or command while leaving complete liberty of action."[2]

We have seen an evolution in this legislation during the period following the Second Vatican Council. However, even before the Council we found that the simplification of the rubrics in 1955 allowed a certain freedom in the choice of the office during Lent. The rubrics of 1960 allowed bishops of mission countries to adapt the liturgical colors to local cultures. But the possibility for local adaptations is infrequent in the pre-Conciliar liturgy.

The "fixed" or "rigid" nature of the rubrics during this period is related to the fixed nature of the liturgy. The Code of Canon Law and the Instruction of 1958 both state that it is this "fixed" and legislated character of the prayer that identifies it as liturgical. The liturgical and official prayer of the Church is that which is determined in the liturgical books and regulated by the Church.

Elements of the liturgy which are unable to be determined in this juridical sense are accepted into the definition of liturgy only with certain reservations. The homily appears in the missal in 1955, in the rite for Holy Thursday, and is mentioned in the Code of 1960. However, it is only with the Council that the homily can be seen as an integral part of the liturgical action.

With the Council, the liturgy is seen not only in its juridical and legal aspects but also in its mystical and symbolic dimensions. Consequently the rubrics lose their rigidity. We find the appearance of the rubric ". . . in these or similar words." Beginning with the rite of marriage, we find rubrics where the minister is directed to say something but no words are given; for example: ". . . the priest greets the bride and bridegroom in a friendly manner, showing that the Church shares their joy." The rites begin to give "alternative" formulas for introductions and admonitions and for the prayers of the rites. Finally, in 1973, we read that introductions and admonitions "by their very nature" do not require the verbatim use of the text given in the liturgical book.[3]

Along with these options in the rites, we have seen that the rubrics begin to speak of "structure," "literary genre," and "themes." Sometimes the priest celebrating is permitted to change the prayers but keep the structure of the rite, or to adapt the prayer preserving its literary genre. The new rites list those adaptations which are to be made by the Episcopal Conferences, the local ordinary, and the minister. In the introduction to the Eucharistic Prayers for Masses with children, we read that these Latin texts are not to be translated but are to serve as models according to which the Episcopal Conferences are to create prayers adapted to the children of their countries.

This new style of legislation implies a new *type* of obedience. The options in the new rites are no longer merely, or even principally, given for the devotion of the minister. The adaptations are to be made in view of the pastoral effectiveness of the rite. The new legislation often not only gives the possibility of choice but demands that choices be made. The possibility of choice involves a higher level of principles upon which a choice can be responsibly based.

The former legislation was directed to the individual elements of the rite. Often these elements were regulated very precisely: the tone of voice, the position of the hands, etc. The understanding was that if these rubrics were properly carried out, the effectiveness of the rite would be achieved. The minister had the responsibility to follow the rubrics precisely, and in so doing he was assured that the rite would be posited in such a way that there would be no doubt as to the validity of the sacrament and its intrinsic (*ex opere operato*) effectiveness.

Already in 1955 we find that *more* is demanded than the mere literal observance of the rubrics. We saw that with the restoration of Holy Week, the bishop is directed to see to it that the priests "understand the meaning of the rites." The instruction of 1958 states that the priest is to pray in a voice so that "he can be heard and understood." He is not only to sing, but to sing well. He is to be able to explain the meaning of the rites, the degrees of festivity, and the meaning of the sacred silence. This type of directive becomes much more frequent and demanding in the rites published after the Council.

The rubrics for the rite of marriage direct the priest to "first of all strengthen and nourish the faith of those about to be married."[4] This statement is an example of the demands of the new obedience. The minister and the celebrating community are responsible not only for the exact fulfillment of the individual rubrics, but also they are responsible that the celebration is a "manifestation, by signs perceptible to the sense, of the sanctification of man" (SC 7). They are responsible for making possible the special liturgical presence of Christ in his Church, so that He may be experienced praising God and making men holy. The new legislation looks not only to the rite itself, but to the purpose of the rite: the mystical experience of the passion, resurrection and glorious ascension of Jesus Christ, in the way proper to each liturgical celebration.

The minister is responsible for celebrating the rite in such a way that its purpose can be fulfilled. The rite for baptism states that the minister is to take into account "existing circumstances and needs, as well as the wishes of the faithful." The rite for the anointing and pastoral ministry of the sick states that the ministers are to care for the sick, visit them, help them by works of charity; the sacrament is more apt to achieve its fullest expression when it is placed in the total context of ministry to the sick. The sacrament is to "stir up the hope of those present and strengthen their faith." Ministers are instructed in the marriage rite and the funeral rite to be aware not only of the faithful who are present, but also to "be especially aware of their responsibility to those present, whether Catholic or non-Catholic, who never or almost never take part in the Eucharist or who seem to have lost their faith."[5]   Priests are to be ministers of the Gospel to all.

We see that the rubrics are not only different in their style and vocabulary than they were at the time of *Mediator Dei,* but we also see that the rubrics are now directed to a different function. They do not merely legislate the external details and words of the rites and prayers. They look to the totality of the rite and its communicative and symbolic function and to the ability of the rite to produce a spiritual effect in those celebrating it. This requires not only obedience to the new rubrics but an obedience to the spirit of the new legislation: thus, a new obedience.

This new obedience can cause problems which did not exist formerly. A priest may feel that in a particular circumstance he has to go beyond the limits of the adaptation permitted by a rite in order to achieve the purpose of the rite and fulfill the spirit of the legislation. This can be difficult and an emotional decision. It is especially difficult because many priests were not trained to make this type of decision. It can be emotional because we formerly associated any variation of the rubrics with an act of disobedience—a disobedience that was usually caused by carelessness or ignorance. Rubrics were disobeyed by those who "didn't care" about the liturgy and its laws. Now, however, a priest may feel that he must be "disobedient" to a specific directive in order to achieve the spirit of the directive. For those who are unaware of the added dimensions of the post-Conciliar liturgical legislation, such a priest trying to be obedient to this dimension of the law is seen as "doing whatever he wants" and changing the rites according to whim on his own authority.

The Change in the Theological Context of the Legislation

The flexibility and spirit of the new legislation is made possible and caused by the change in the theological context in which the new legislation has been formulated. Before the Council liturgical law was seen to be those laws which governed the official public prayer of the Church. The Church as an institution has the right and duty to regulate its various activities—especially the most important of its activities, the public worship offered to God.

This remains true after the Council. However, we now see the Church not only as a society or an institution founded by Christ but also as the mysterious union with her founder. "By her relationship with Christ, the Church is a kind of sacrament or sign of intimate union with God and of the unity of all mankind; she is also an instrument for achieving such unity" (LG 1). This sacrament or sign is most visible when the Church prays. The holy people of God, gathered around the altar, led by the apostolic minister, giving thanks and breaking bread is the pre-eminent sign of the mystery that is the Church (SC 41).

In this context, the liturgy is not only something which the Church *does;* the liturgy is the sign and revelation of what the Church *is.* The Church makes laws which regulate the liturgy; but the liturgy also "makes laws" for the Church in the sense that the Church is constituted and structured by the liturgy.

The former legislation considered the sacraments primarily as symbolic *things* and stressed the importance of the matter and form which constituted the essence of the sacrament. The law insisted on the observance of the rubrics by the priest both because of the importance placed on the material aspects of the sacrament and because of the corresponding lack of importance placed on the role of the priest as an active liturgical agent.

This theological context changes with the Council. The liturgy is associated not only with *things* (matter, form, prayers, gestures) but with symbolic *actions* and with the agent of the action. The liturgy becomes more closely associated with *persons:* the minister, the faithful, and with Christ himself.

The word "liturgical" is applied not only in relation to specific rites and prayers, but in relation to a specific sign: the sacramental union of God and his people. Actions are liturgical to the degree that they call into being and manifest the praying Church. Liturgy is a public prayer, not merely because it is so defined juridically, but it is experienced as publicly placing the sign of the mystery of the Church.

The minister is not only "delegated to perform the rite" but is seen in his active role as the leader of the prayer of the people of God. The bishop is not only "one who must guard that the precepts of the sacred canons regarding divine worship are faithfully observed" (canon 1261); the bishop is the symbol and sacrament of Christ present in the Church and the symbol of the liturgical personification of the people of God worshipping the Father.

The Change in the Spirit of the Liturgical Legislation

The new style of the liturgical legislation together with the theological changes in the context of the laws give the present legislation a new *spirit* which was not a property of the former law. Formerly, a pastoral approach to the sacraments called for a faithful observance of the rubrics. Now, pastors must not only fulfill the letter of the law but also its spirit.

The options and adaptations demanded by the new legislation imply that there exists "higher principles" which allow these choices to be made reasonably. The *Memoria* spoke of "principi fondamentali." Pope John, introducing the Code of 1960, spoke of "altiora principia." The first chapter of the Constitution on the liturgy speaks of "General Principles."

What are these general principles? They are not so much "legislated" as "discovered." They are not extrinsic laws but intrinsic principles—implications flowing from the nature of the Church, the nature of the liturgy, and the relation between the Church and the liturgy.

They are not the type of principle which allows an exact listing. We can only give indications of the type of principle involved and list here the principles which have become evident in this study.

Principles based on the Church as Mystery

1. There is a need for continual development. Pope Paul stated at the beginning of the second session of the Council that "the Church is a mystery; she is a reality imbued with the divine presence and, for that reason, she is ever susceptible of new and deeper investigation." If the Church is susceptible to continual

investigation, the liturgical manifestation of this Mystery will also need continual re-examination.

The liturgy manifests the mystery of the Church. "The liturgy is the outstanding means by which the faithful can express in their lives, and manifest to others, the mystery of Christ and the real nature of the true Church" (SC 2). Consequently, as the mystery of the Church is ever open to new understanding, the liturgy is continually open to the changes necessary to reflect this Mystery.

The Council called for a liturgy which would be an authentic sign—"the texts and rites should be drawn up so that they express more clearly the holy things which they signify" (SC 21). The relation liturgy-mystery, if it is to be authentic, implies that the liturgy cannot be completely fixed, rigid, and defined. We can never say: "Now that the liturgical reform has been completed. . . ."

2. The new liturgical forms must develop organically from existing forms. The progressive understanding of the Church develops organically from our tradition. Our understanding of the Church must always be in close contact with its origins. Liturgy also must develop organically (SC 23). The Scriptures will be of paramount importance to the celebration of the liturgy and also in the organic development of new liturgical forms. The liturgy must be in contact with its history; its development will require experts in the sources and history of liturgical prayer.

In this context a word might be said about the rate of liturgical change. We saw in the introduction to this study that after the Council of Trent, when the liturgical form became too rigid and fixed, the liturgy became divorced from the expression of the devotion of the faithful. Life moved on; the liturgy did not keep pace.

In *Mediator Dei* we saw that in a context where the liturgy is stable and unchanging, there was a need to point out that change was possible: "the human components admit of various modifications as the needs of the age, circumstances, and the good of souls may require." This situation has changed so radically in the ten years after the Council that it is now important psychologically to give expression to the need for continuity, stability, and tradition.

Perhaps much of the problem of those who express an extreme liturgical conservatism could have been avoided if the changes had come more slowly. Perhaps the changes could have come more slowly if they were not so urgent—due to the long period of too little change. In the future we must watch that the liturgy continues to change in pace with our understanding of the mystery of the Church and in pace with the needs of the people of God. For the present, we must balance the experience of nearly "total change" with an experience of continuity and stability.

3. The liturgy and the Church have the same concerns. The liturgy as a manifestation of the Church implies that the liturgy will have the same ends and goals. The liturgy is primarily directed toward the worship of God (SC 33); however, it must often serve other ends: it must also be missionary, catechetical, ecumenical. The liturgy is not primarily missionary; but in circumstances where the liturgy is the only contact that some people have with the Church, the liturgy is called upon to serve this role also. The liturgy is not primarily an instrument to further unity between the churches and ecclesial communities; but at a time when these values are so urgent, individual rubrics must be interpreted in the light of these needs.

4. If the liturgy is to manifest the true nature of the Church, it will need to be catholic and universal. No one prayer, no one rite can express the Mystery of the Church adequately. The need for different rites and expressions of liturgical prayer is called for by the very nature of the liturgy. Variety and adaptation to different cultures is not only permitted or tolerated but demanded by the catholicity of the Church.

The experience of the new Roman liturgy translated into the vernacular and celebrated in different countries and cultures leads us to project that this adaptation of the years immediately following the Council is only the first step of the liturgical reform. The rites currently in use in the United States are basically the translations of the Roman texts. As we read in the forward to the rite of confirmation, the present text is provisional in that no regional or national adaptations have been introduced at this time; it is hoped that a period of several years' use of the rite will help to discern and develop such adaptations.

If these adaptations are to be allowed to grow organically from the tradition of the Church and from the experience of the local communities, the next period in the evolution of the liturgy will need to allow a flexibility in the interpretation of the legislation in order to permit this type of adaptation to take place.

The implications of the spirit of the Council and the experience of the effectiveness and fruitfulness of the liturgy when it is properly celebrated can only lead us to project what might be the beauty and experience of a liturgy which is even more closely adapted to the genius of the various local churches. There is the possibility, if this next stage of the reform is successful, of a liturgy containing a richness of expression which will not only increase our appreciation of the liturgy but give us a fuller insight into the mystery and catholicity of the Church.

5. The liturgy will continue to be legislated by the central authority of the Church; however, this power may be exercised in a different manner. The renewed relation between liturgy and the mystery of the Church does not mean the end of the liturgical law.

The "unchanging" can be mistakenly identified with the "sacred," The former liturgical law, by the very fact that it was very "unchanging" was considered "sacred" in a sense that was not historically justified. The very fact that the legislation has changed can have the positive value of giving a clearer picture of the function of liturgical law and can allow us to apply the ordinary principles of interpreting law to liturgical law also (for example, epikia, custom, dispensation, cessation of law, etc).[7]

On the other hand, the fact that the laws have changed so drastically in the past ten years has led some not only to desacralize the laws but to begin to ignore liturgical legislation altogether and to consider it a relic from an age that is now past.

Liturgical law still demands an obedience, but a different obedience than formerly. Formerly the legislation was often concerned with the externals of the rites and ceremonies. The Church was concerned with the rites because they must be properly performed to fulfill their purpose. The Church had to safeguard the validity of the sacraments. The Church regulated the liturgy because of the close relation between the liturgy and faith and morals. The liturgy must be the expression of correct doctrine. Pius XII stated in *Mediator Dei* that the rule of faith is the rule of prayer (Lex credendi legem orandi constituit).

The theological context of liturgical law taught by the Council places this maxim back into its original order. The Church as mystery, the Church as the assembly of the baptized discovers her identity in praying. The sacraments give structure to the people of God and order the community. The Church regulates the liturgy not only because of an extrinsic relation to "faith and morals" but because the liturgy must be a faithful manifestation and reflection of the way the Church views herself. The liturgy is a theological source (*locus theologicus*); it is in the liturgical experience of the paschal mystery that we find one of the principal sources of the faith. The maxim "The rule of prayer is the rule of faith" (Lex orandi legem credendi constituit) takes again its proper theological importance.

And when the liturgy is seen as a source of theology, liturgical law also takes on a particular importance. Liturgical law is necessary not only because it governs an *activity* of the Church; liturgical law is necessary to preserve the authenticity of the self-expression of the *essence* of the Church.

Principles Based on the Hierarchic and Communal Nature of the Liturgy

1. The liturgical assembly should reflect the nature of the Church. The Church is not made up of only the hierarchy, nor is the liturgy the affair of the clergy alone. The Church is the people of God and the liturgy is their prayer. It concerns individual members in different ways, however, according to the diversity of holy orders, functions, and degrees of participation (SC 26). In many of the documents issued before the Council we saw a stress placed on the "active participation of the laity." The perspective has changed. This active participation is no longer seen as the participation of the laity in an act which is essentially the affair of the clergy for they alone were delegated for it. The Council described the Church as the whole people of God, including the laity. The liturgy is the prayer of the Church and consequently the prayer of the whole people of God. No special delegation is needed. Christian initiation makes one apt to participate in liturgical prayer—each member of the Church performing his own role.

This is more than a change of vocabulary. It will require a new outlook and a new perspective in liturgical education. "Community" must become more than a word; it must be an experience integral to the liturgy as an experience of our corporate salvation. The priest must no longer appropriate the liturgy to himself as though he alone celebrated the liturgy; he must see his priestly role in relation to the total community's responsibility for the liturgy.

2. The liturgy is the public prayer of the Church not only because it is publicly and officially regulated by the Church, but because it is a sign. It makes visible the Mystery. This principle must play a role in determining the appropriateness of certain liturgical celebrations. Even though every Eucharistic celebration "has of itself a public and social nature" (SC 27) because of its relation to the sacrifice of Christ, even when celebrated entirely alone, the appropriateness of the sign value of each celebration must be considered.

3. The liturgy must be celebrated in such a way that it can express and nourish the devotional life of the people of God. We have witnessed the liturgy move to a more central position in the Christian life. Along with this change we have seen a lessening of the previously over emphasized distinction between the external rites and internal devotion, and between liturgical prayer and devotional

exercises. The juridical distinction between liturgical prayer and non-liturgical prayer is modified by the new relation between the liturgy and the Church. Obviously, not all prayer engages the Church in the same way. The celebration of the Eucharist and the other sacraments expresses the nature of the Church in a way in which other prayers cannot; however all prayer and devotion should be animated by the liturgical spirit, and consequently, by the general liturgical principles in so far as they are applicable.

The liturgy will need to respect the individual differences of the people of God. We noted above that the vocabulary used in the rite of Christian Initiation for Adults speaks of "the spiritual journey" of the individuals and the "many forms of God's grace." The liturgy must respect the indivudal within the communal structure. And as the liturgy becomes more central to the spiritual life, it will have to possess the flexibility to be truly expressive of the devotion of the faithful. The liturgy can only be legislated in every detail when it is removed from the devotional life of the Church. When this happens, the void is filled with non-liturgical devotions. We have seen that *Mediator Dei* and the other pre-Conciliar documents left a large measure of freedom in the area of devotions and pious exercises. The liturgy will need to incorporate some of the flexibility. Is one of the reasons why many Catholics are turning to charismatic prayer to be found in the fact that the liturgy is still not sufficiently adapted to the expression of the devotional lives of individual Catholics?

The new rubrics give the largest measure of flexibility in those cases where the rite must be adapted to the needs of the people. The Hours, for example, permit much flexibility to allow and invite the laity to pray the Hours. The communal celebration of the liturgy always demands a certain "simplicity" of form; the rubrics for the Breviary of 1960 would be found difficult by many Christians. However, this "simplicity" is not to be viewed as a sign of the "poverty" of the liturgy and the cause for regretting the loss of many beautiful antiphons and responses. When the liturgy is celebrated with full awareness of its communal nature, there is much less danger of the rubrics becoming a complicated system of laws reserved only for clerical experts—a system of details which is inconsistent with the spirit of freedom given us in the New Testament.

4. The liturgical celebration must reflect the hierarchic nature of the Church by giving proper value to the role of the bishop. Formerly we often considered that the role of the bishop was to assure that the liturgical laws were properly observed. As the Church-as-institution is balanced by the Church-as-mystery, the

role of the bishop as guardian of the liturgy is balanced by the role of the bishop as the principal liturgist of the local Church. He is not only to see to it that the laws are observed; he himself is to be the model and example of liturgical leadership. The ecclesiology of Vatican II and its liturgical implications reunite in one person the liturgical authority and the liturgical leadership.

In areas where the organizational structure of the Church is so important that the balance with the image of the Church as mystery and sacrament of our union with God is not sufficiently realized, it is difficult to see the bishop in his true liturgical role. Dioceses with large school systems and many charitable and social organizations and serious financial commitments to providing services demand much time and much administrative skill on the part of the bishop. This fact in itself, however, does not exclude the possibility of the bishop fulfilling his liturgical role. It will demand much delegation of responsibility and authority according to the principles of subsidiarity and the utilization of the different ministries and charisms of the local Church. Efforts to realize this situation where the bishop can be the leader of prayer for his diocese are crucial to the problem of obedience to liturgical law. The image of the bishop as the liturgical leader reunites in a much closer way the one celebrating the rites and the one having authority over the celebration. This is a return to the situation in the early Church. We no longer have a division between the one who must observe the laws and the one who is responsible for the faith of the Church.

The hierarchical nature of the liturgy also gives new importance to the local Church. This can be advantageous in those dioceses where the liturgical function of the bishop is a fruitful and effective reality. However, we might ask to what extent the reforms of the Second Vatican Council would have been implemented if the decisions were left to each individual bishop. A corrective for this danger is found in the theology and practice of the collegiality of the bishops.

However, if the Episcopal Conferences are to be given more and more responsibility for liturgical decisions and adaptations, they must have something of the nature of a decision making body. They must meet in regular legislative sessions. Is a meeting once a year sufficient for this task? The increased responsibility given to territorial bodies for liturgical decisions seems to imply that they should be structured in such a way as to be able to fulfill such a responsibility.

5. The communal and hierarchic nature of the liturgy implies that the priest is to be placed in a new relationship with both

the bishop and the laity.

The theology of the bishop as the principal liturgist of the local Church implies that the liturgical role of the priest must be seen as somehow related to that of the bishop. The Council documents speak of the priest as acting for the bishop when he is not present. The Constitution on the Liturgy states that the pastor "takes the place of the bishop" (SC 42).

Here again, the conditions of the Church in the United States make it difficult to have a liturgy which reflects this theology. For most Catholics the priest is the only liturgical leader they see. Often the sacramental meaning of confirmation is lost in the fact that it is the only time the parish sees the bishop. The large proportion of parishes that are staffed by religious order priests in the United States also makes this problem visible. How many religious order priests look upon their liturgical ministry as directly related to the task of the bishop?

The priest must not only "often" but "usually" lead the liturgical assembly and the real presence of the bishop is the exceptional instance. And although the Council documents say that the priest must act "in place of the bishop" the priest does not always have the liturgical authority of the bishop. Here again we have a division between the one who acts with the liturgical authority and the one who has the responsibility to lead the celebration and be responsible for its pastoral effectiveness.

In order for this relation of bishop-priest to function pastorally, we must put into practice not only the theological relationship called for by the Constitution on the Liturgy, but also the relation of friendship and mutual trust and understanding called for by the Decree on the Bishops' Pastoral Office, and the Decree on the Ministry and Life of Priests.

We have seen above that one of the strengths of the theological context of the liturgy as found in the Council documents is the fact that the bishop is the liturgical minister and a minister possessing liturgical authority. One of the causes of the problems with regard to obedience to liturgical law is found in the fact that the priest must often exercise the ministerial role—but without the corresponding authority. Furthermore, it may happen that the pastoral perspective of the priest and the bishop are not the same. The bishop may be less aware of the needs of the local community; the priest may be less aware of the needs of the total diocese and the whole Church.

A large step is taken toward resolving this problem when the bishop is in contact with the pastoral experience of his priests. The Third Instruction was quoted as saying:

With the help of their liturgical commissions, the bishops should be accurately informed about the religious and social conditions of the faithful which they serve; in order to meet their spiritual needs in the best way possible, they should learn to make full use of the means offered by the rites.

. . . A well-informed bishop will be a great help to the priests who must exercise their ministry in the hierarchical fellowship with him; his knowledge will make it easier for them to work together with him in obedience for the more perfect expression of divine worship and for the sanctification of souls.

In the context of the relation between the bishop and the priest, we might note that it is not a proper reflection of the ecclesiology of Vatican II to have the rite for baptism and marriage and the care of the sick in a book "exclusively" for the use of priests; and to have the rite of confirmation and the conferral of ministries in a book reserved for the bishop. The forthcoming "second typical editions" of the sacramental rites will no doubt reflect the relation of the bishop and priest in the way in which these rites are published.

The priest also sees his relation to the laity in a new perspective. The priest is no longer the one "officially delegated" to perform a clerical action in which the people are invited to participate. For example, the second edition of the General Instruction on the Roman Missal systematically refuses to speak of the priest as "the celebrant" as though the priest alone celebrates. It is the community who celebrates the liturgy. The priest celebrating has different responsibilities than the laity, but it is not the priest alone who celebrates. The priest sees his role more as a leadership role within an action which belongs to the community. This understanding demands a much closer relation between priests and people; and this need is felt at the very time when the number of priests in relation to the number of laity makes this relationship even more difficult.

We have seen that the new rites require the priest to be aware of the circumstances in which the rite is to be celebrated. He is to help the community plan the rite. The options and the alternative prayers are to be chosen for their pastoral effectiveness. The rite, and the theological understanding of the priesthood, have moved the priest into closer contact with the people. The liturgy has become much more central in the pastoral activity of the priests.

However, it is often this very contact with the people demanded by the rite which causes the priest and people to modify the rite beyond what is allowed in the liturgical legislation. Here we have another paradox of the new obedience. It is often in trying to be obedient to the new rites and to plan a celebration with the laity which will be pastorally effective that they are led to go beyond what is permitted in the rubrics.

Principles based on the Pastoral and Instructive Nature of the Liturgy

1. When we speak of the instructive nature of the liturgy, it is with the realization that the liturgy always has a twofold regard: to God and to the community. From 1951 (in the restoration of the Easter Vigil) the rubrics have taken note of the fact that there are people present. The Council stated that the worship of the divine majesty contains abundant instruction for the faithful (SC 33). The Constitution lists "norms based on the educative and pastoral nature of the liturgy" (SC 33-36). The fact that the liturgy is directed not only to God but also to man has become more and more important.

As in any change of this nature, the present concern must be one of preserving the proper balance between these two elements. This liturgy must always have this double orientation; although different elements may be orientated more toward God or more toward man, they are never so orientated exclusive of the other dimension. For example, prayers are addressed to God and are for his praise (not his instruction). The prayers are not addressed to the people (as though they were really "sermons" in the form of prayers); yet at the same time they are not directed exclusively towards God for they are spoken in the name of the congregation and must help them to willingly give their "amen." On the other hand, a homily is addressed to the people, not to God. Yet here too there is a dimension of worship and participation in the liturgical mystery which makes a homily different from an instruction that might be presented in a school context.

The problem of balance between the cultic and instructive ends of the liturgy is related to the tension between the worship of a God who is transcendent and the worship of a God who is immanent. The God of the Scriptures reveals himself as both transcendent and immanent and our liturgy must reflect this tension. In a liturgy which placed high values on mystery, the sacred, distance in cult, we saw value given to those elements reflecting the transcendence of God. These values must not be lost as the liturgy tries to bring into balance the relation between transcendence and immanence.

2. The liturgy must be an authentic human experience. The

Bishops' Committee on the Liturgy stated that

> the primary goal of all celebration is to make a humanly attractive
> experience. The signs of sacramental celebration are vehicles of
> communication and instruments of faith. They must be good signs,
> simple and comprehensible; they must be humanly attractive.[8]

The directory for Masses with children also spoke of human values
found in the Eucharistic celebration: the activity of the community,
exchange of greetings, capacity to listen and to seek and grant
pardon, the expression of gratitude, the experience of symbolic
actions, a meal of friendship, and festive celebration.

We have seen other references in the legislation to this type of
value. The priest is sometimes directed to greet the people or to
invite them to pray. Obviously these invitations and greetings are
to real, human acts. The people are to be actually greeted or invited.

A human experience demands a certain variety; the liturgy
must never bore people. A human experience requires beauty;
vestments must not only fulfill the rubrics but must be clean and
fit properly. A human experience must take account of the sen-
sitivities of those present: the role of gestures, touch, repetition
vary from culture to culture. A human experience demands an
awareness of the dynamic between the people participating; the
relation existing between those present in a parish Mass on Sunday is different from the dynamic of a home Mass.

It is impossible to expect the rubrics to give us a list of what
is required to make a human experience. They cannot legislate
"common sense." However, they presume that the celebrating community take these principles into account when interpreting and
applying the rubrics.

The pastoral and instructive nature of the liturgy implies that the
liturgical celebrations take into account the principles which govern
the communication arts. A prayer of thanksgiving must be spoken
differently than a prayer of supplication. The written text of the
liturgical book must become the living word communicating life
to the people.

The liturgical communication, as it is essentially symbolic, must
be aware of the importance of beauty, art, and music. The cultural
treasures preserved by the Roman liturgy must not be sacrificed
merely in the name of simplicity. Only when they are no longer
capable of expressing the essential nature of the liturgy can these
elements be replaced by forms which in themselves may be less
artistic.[9] The new texts and rites must not only be simple and

understandable; they cannot fulfill their function without the dimension of the beautiful and the artistic.

The Contemporary Problem of Obedience to Liturgical Law.

Unless we are aware of both the rubrics and the general principles (such as those listed above) we lack the necessary norms for judging the obedience or disobedience of a particular act. No one, not even a priest, may change, add, or omit anything in the liturgical rite on his own authority (SC 22 § 3). However, it is one thing to change the order of psalms at Tuesday morning prayer and to change the Eucharistic Prayer. It is one thing to use a Eucharistic Prayer for children when there are only adults present, and quite another thing to use a Eucharistic Prayer which makes no reference to the Last Supper. However the difference between these situations and the seriousness of the reasons which may justify disobedience to the rubrics in one case and not another cannot always be found in the rubrics themselves; the general principles and the spirit of the legislation play an important role in these decisions. For priests who are unaware of this dimension of the legislation, every act of disobedience to the rubrics can appear to be wrong and consequently sinful.

At the time when this study is being written, the Code of Canon Law is being revised. The canons which treat of the liturgy will need to be sufficiently different in style from the Code of 1917 to be able to embody the general liturgical principles and to reflect the spirit of the Council. Such a work must involve the careful and close collaboration of legal and liturgical experts. (We have noted above that the liturgical renewal did not always acknowledge changes in the Code nor observe strictly the rules for changing the canons.) A Code which is formed in the spirit of the Council would have a positive role to play in safeguarding the proper interpretation of the general principles so that they can be translated into pastorally effective action.

Today, the priest often finds himself in conflict between his responsibility to the rubrics, the principles, the bishop, the people. . . . Are there ways to solve these problems? Does the degree of responsibility on the part of the priest required by the new legislation place unreasonable demands on him? Can each pastor be a poet, public relations director, administrator, musician, public speaker, theologian, and mystagogue?

Indications of a solution

1. Education. The new liturgy and the new liturgical legislation

call for a different type of liturgical education and training in seminaries. The Constitution[10] and the motu proprio which promulgated the first of its reforms[11] insist on the importance of liturgical formation if the new legislation is to be understood. This change is already taking place. Liturgy is no longer presented only in its rubrical aspects but is being integrated into its theological and historical context; liturgy is taking its place as a source of theology.

Part of the present crisis of liturgical law is due to the fact that many priests are now called upon to give one type of obedience, but they were trained and prepared to give another style of obedience. Hopefully, this problem will be temporary.

Furthermore, the candidates must become real leaders of prayer. Attention must be given to the development of communication arts, catechetics, pedagogy, group dynamics, music, and aesthetics. It is not necessary or possible that every priest be a poet and a musician. However, there is much room for training in this regard; there are many ways in which this help can be given to become better qualified in these areas. However, this will require a different approach to the teaching of liturgy.

2. A closer relation with the bishop. If the relationship between priest and bishop as described by the Council is taken seriously, another problem area will be diminished. As bishops become more aware of their own liturgical role, as they devote more time and importance to presiding at the liturgy; and as they become more closely involved in the formation of those who will aid them in their liturgical ministry, it is probable that the pastoral viewpoints of the "chief pastor" and "those who assist" him will grow closer together. The sharing of authority and the dialogue we are experiencing in priests' senates and lay councils all give promise of a movement in this direction.

3. The role of liturgical commissions and committees. Because of the many practical decisions which have to be made by the celebrating community, it is more important than ever that they receive help in understanding and planning the rites. In the United States the effort at the national level has thus far been primarily directed toward translating and distributing the Roman documents in English. Now there is need (and action is being taken in this direction) of providing materials to explain the rites, of providing helps to introduce the rites in parishes, and of providing programs of education for clergy and laity. In the future the committees at the various levels (Roman, national, local) will have to be concerned not merely with listing what is permitted and what is forbidden; they will need to guide the ongoing work of local adapta-

tion. They will be called upon to help in the preparation of economic and pastorally adapted editions of the liturgical books. They will have to encourage and publicize the best of the prayers and rites which are created at the local level. This direction and assistance will be crucial if the next phase of the liturgical reform is to be successful.

4. A new respect for the liturgical books. Once the initial period of transition is passed and once the newness of being able to create prayers and exercise spontaneity and flexibility in the rites has worn off, the beauty and the effectiveness of the new rites celebrated in the spirit of the new legislation will become more apparent. Constant creation on the part of each celebrating community is neither necessary or possible. We have the liturgical books restored in the light of our liturgical tradition and contemporary needs. They are not a substitute for a certain necessary local adaptation, but if the restoration of the liturgical books has been successful, the rites themselves will inspire a new trust and confidence in the liturgical books and their legislation.

5. A proper expectation of the liturgy. On the tenth anniversary of his election, Pope Paul VI, speaking to the college of cardinals, said that although the liturgical reform has been introduced and the liturgical books published, "all this is only a beginning. Our aim and purpose as pastors of the Church is to try—without ever being satisfied with the result—to celebrate the liturgy in such a way that it leads contemporary man to come into personal contact with the Father."[12]

The liturgy is the summit toward which the activity of the Church is directed (SC 10), but at the same time we must not expect too much of the rite itself or place too much hope in the liturgical renewal. In our study of liturgical law and in the celebration of the rites we must not lose sight of the fact that the liturgical action is directed toward "leading contemporary man to contact with the Father." The liturgy goes not exhaust the entire activity of the Church (SC 9).

The importance of the liturgical legislation is related to the importance of the liturgy. An understanding of the obedience called for by the new legislation and by faith in the Church is necessary if the liturgy is to become in fact "the outstanding means by which the faithful can express in their lives and manifest to others the mystery of Christ and the real nature of the true Church" (SC 2). It is the hope of the author of this study that this end may be served by clarifying the fidelity that is called for by the present liturgical legislation and the freedom that is ours in the Spirit.

NOTES

1 Prumẹr, Manuale Theologiae Moralis, p. 58.

2 McManus, The Congregation of Rites, p. 136.

3 See 1973 APR 17 Letter concerning the Eucharistic Prayers.

4 Ordo Celebrandi Matrimonium, praenotanda, article 7.

Imprimis pastores foveant nutriantque fidem nupturientium: Sacramentum enim Matrimonii fidem supponit atque expostulat.

5 See also General Instruction of the Roman Missal, 341.

6 1949 DEC 30, p. 14.

7 McManus, "Liturgical Law and Difficult Cases," Worship 48 (1974) 347-366.

8 1967 NOV 12.

9 Gy, "Situation historique de la Constitution," La Liturgie apres Vatican II. Paris: Cerf, 1967, p. 124.

10 See SC 14-19.

11 1964 JAN 25.

12 Address to the College of Cardinals, June 22, 1973. AAS 65 (1973) 382 (Italian text). French translation: DC, July 15, 1973, p. 651.

A SELECT BIBLIOGRAPHY

The principle sources for this study have been the liturgical documents published by the Holy See. In this bibliography, these documents have been listed chronologically together with some of the events which help to put the documents in their historical context.

It is understood that the dates of the documents are, in a sense, fictitious. The documents are often given a date which relates to the liturgical year rather than a "secular" date. The English translation is listed under the date of the Latin text.

In spite of these inconsistencies, this method of listing the documents has proved more helpful to the readers of this study than several other systems which were tried. At the end of the chronological list is an alphabetical summary by subject: baptism, Eucharist, Hours, etc. The dates which are in italics indicate documents which were treated more at length in this study.

The second part of this bibliography gives an alphabetical listing of secondary sources, divided into books and articles. Because the official sources occupy such a prominent place in this study, the list of secondary sources is short. It contains primarily those books and articles which are related directly to the topic of obedience to liturgical law. It also contains those books and articles which the author has used for the background of this study.

A Select Bibliography, Part One: Documents
1. Chronological List of Documents and Events Related to this Study

1946 MAY 10 Pope Pius XII asks the Prefect of the CSR (Cardinal Salotti) to begin forming a project for a general reform of the liturgy.

1946 JUL 27 A special commission is established for the study of the general liturgical reform; however two years pass before the work is begun (See 1948 MAY 28).

1947 OCT 24   Cardinal Salotti dies. He is later succeeded by Cardinal Micara.

1947 NOV 20   Pius XII. Encyclical letter *Mediator Dei.* AAS 39 (1947) 521-600.

The references to this encyclical (abbreviated MD) are to page number as the AAS does not number the paragraphs. The English translation quoted in this study is the Vatican Library Translation published by the National Catholic Welfare Conference (NCWC), Washington. "Mediator Dei: Encyclical Letter of Pope Pius XII on the Sacred Liturgy." References are to page number.

1948 MAY 28   The members for the commission to form a project for a general liturgical reform are appointed. Rev. Ferdinando Antonelli, O.F.M., is the general director (Relatore Generale), and Rev. Joseph Löw, C. Ss. R., is his assistant. Rev. A. Bugnini, C.M. is appointed secretary. The commission holds its constitutive meeting on June 22.

1948 DEC 30   CSR. Sectio Historica. *Memoria sulla Riforma Liturgica.* S. Hist, N. 71. Tip. Pol. Vat. 1948. Notes on the Liturgical Reform.

I have been able to study this document and numbers 75, 76, 79, 90, and 97 of the Historical Section of the CSR through the courtesy of Msgr. Pierre Jounel.

1949 JUN 25   The *Memoria* is printed and given to the members of the commission.

1949 JUL 22   The *Memoria* is presented to Pope Pius XII.

1949 NOV 03   The *Memoria* is given to three experts for their comments (Dom Capelle, Rev. Jungmann, and Msgr. Righetti).

1950 MAR 25   CSR. Historical section. *Memoria sulla riforma liturgica.* Supplemento I: Intorno alla graduazione liturgica. Tip. Pol. Vat. 1950. CSR Sec. His. 75.

1950 APR 21   CSR. Historical section. *Memoria sulla riforma liturgica.* Supplemento II: Annotazioni alla "Memoria" presentate, su richiesta, dai Rev. mi Dom Capelle O.S.B., P. Jungmann S.J., Mons. Righetti.

Tip. Pol. Vat. 1950. CSR S. Hist. n. 76.

1950 NOV 22 Cardinal Lienart, president of the Cardinals and Archbishops of France, petitions the Holy See to permit the celebration of the Easter Vigil in the evening or at night. The German bishops also petition the Holy See.

1951 FEB 09 CSR. Decree. "De Solemni Vigilia Pashchali Instauranda." (The restoration of the Solemn Paschal Vigil.) AAS 43 (1951) 128-137.
These rites were approved experimentally for one year.

1951 JUN 19 CSR. Historical section. *Memoria sulla riforma liturgica.* Supplemento III: Materiale storico, agiografio, liturgico per la riforma del calendario. Typ. Pol. Vat. 1951. S. Hist. n. 79.

1952 JAN 11 The "Ordo Sabbati Sancti" is approved for three more years. AAS 44 (1952) 48-63.

1953 JAN 06 Pius XII. Apostolic constitution "Christus Dominus."
Promulgation of the new discipline for the Eucharistic fast. AAS 45 (1953) 15-24.

1953 SEP 14 to 18 The liturgical congress meeting in Lugano, Switzerland takes as its theme: The reform of Holy Week and Pastoral Liturgy.

1953 DEC 07 Cardinal Cicognani becomes Prefect of the CSR.

1954 NOV 02 Pius XII, in an allocution (AAS 45, 1954, page 670) warns priests not to change anything in the liturgy on their own authority. Together with MD page 538, this reference is given as the note to SC 22 § 3.

1955 MAR 23 CSR. Decree, "De rubricis ad simpliciorem formam redigendis." (On the simplification of the rubrics.) AAS 47 (1955) 218-224.

1955 MAY 25 CSR. Historical Section. *De Instauratione liturgica Maioris Hebdomade: Positio.* Typ. Pol. Vat. 1955. S. Hist. n. 90.

1955 NOV 16 CSR. Decree, "Liturgicus Hebdomadae Sanctae Ordo instauratur." (The restoration of the liturgy of Holy Week). AAS 47 (1955) 838-847.

1955 DEC 25   Pius XII. Encyclical letter, "Musicae sacrae disciplina." AAS 48 (1956) 5-25.

1956 MAY 17   Letter from the Congregation of Rites to the Episcopate asking for their advice concerning a reform of the Breviary.

1956 SEP 18   to 22 The International Congress of Pastoral Liturgy meets in Assisi with the theme: The renewal of the liturgy during the pontificate of Pius XII.

1957 JUL 29   SCR. Historical Section. *Memoria sulla Riforma Liturgica.* Supplemento IV. Consultazione dell' Episcopato intorno alla riforma del Breviario Romano (1956-1957). Risultati e Deduzioni. (Consultation of the Episcopate concerning a reform of the Roman Breviary: Results and Conclusions). Typ. Pol. Vat. 1957. S. Hist. N.97.

1958 FEB 11   to JUL 16 The one hundredth anniversary of the apparitions at Lourdes. The question of the possibility of concelebration for this jubilee arises.

1958 SEP 03   CSR. Instruction, "De musica sacra et sacra liturgia ad memtem litterarum encyclicarum Pii Papae XII 'Musicae sacrae disciplina' et 'Mediator Dei.' " AAS 50 (1958) 630-663.
   The Sacred Music and the Sacred Liturgy according to the norms of the encyclical letters of Pope Pius XII 'The Art of Sacred Music' and 'The Mediator between God and man.'

1958 OCT 09   Death of Pope Pius XII.

1958 OCT 28   Election of Pope John XXIII. AAS 50 (1958) 837.

1959 JAN 25   Pope John, at St Paul's Outside the Walls, first announces his intention to call a council.

1959 MAY 17   Pope John names the General Preparatory Commission and asks them to consult the bishops of world to determine what topics should be discussed at the coming council. Cardinal Tardini is named president. Archbishop Felici, secretary.

1959 JUN 18   Cardinal Tardini sends a circular letter to the

Cardinals, Bishops, and heads of religious orders and certain other communities to ask for their suggestions for the Council.

These suggestions of the bishops, together with the letters of Pope John XXIII, the suggestions of the Sacred Congregations, and the rectors of the catholic universitites, are printed in:

Acta et Documenta Concilio Oecumenico Vaticano II Apparando. Series I (Antepraeparatoria). Typ. Pol. Vat. 19. I have consulted these documents at the Bibliothèque du Saulchoir. 267-B-121.

Beginning of the ante-preparatory phase of the Council.

1960 JUN 05 Pope John. Motu proprio, "Superno Dei nutu." Establishes the preparatory commissions and secretariats for the Council. One of these preparatory commissions is for the liturgy.

The acts and documents of these commissions are published in:

Acta et Documenta Concilio Oecumenico Vaticano II Apparando. Series II (Praeparatoria). Typ. Pol. Vat. 19.

Beginning of the preparatory phase of the Council.

1960 JUN 06 Cardinal Gaetano Cicognani, Prefect of the Congregation of Rites, is named president (relator) of the preparatory liturgical commission.

The prefects of the various congregations of the Curia were named presidents of the corresponding preparatory commissions. However, no other members of the Sacred Congregations were to be members of the preparatory commissions in order that the commissions could work freely in the preparation of the Council.

1960 JUL 09 Cardinal Tardini gives Cardinal Cicognani, president of the preparatory liturgical commission, the report listing the themes to be treated by the Council concerning the liturgy as suggested by the letters from the world's bishops. (See 1959 MAY 17).

The topics listed:
1. De calendario recognoscendo: Apta criteria hac de re proponantur.
2. De missa: Rationes edantur de textibus et rubricis recognoscendis.
3. De sacris ritibus: De reducendis ad simpliciorem formam Missa pontificali, ecclesiae consecratione, campanarum benedictione, etc.
4. De sacramentis: Batismi, confirmationis, extremae unctionis, matrimonii ritus ita recognoscentur, ut magis significent ea quae efficiunt.
5. De Breviario: Aptetur Breviarium sacri ministerii necnon spiritualibus cleri necessitatibus.
6. De lingua liturgica: Diligenter perpendatur an expediat linguam vulgarem in quibusdam missae et sacramentorum administrationis partibus permittere.
7. De vestibus liturgicis ad simpliciorem formam reducendis.

1960 JUL 11   Rev. A. Bugnini, C.M., is appointed secretary of the preparatory liturgical commission.

1960 JUL 25   John XXIII. Motu proprio, "Rubricarum instructum." AAS 52 (1960) 593-595.

CSR. "Decretum Generale quo novus rubricarum Breviarii ac Missalis Romani Codex promulgatur." AAS 52 (1960) 596.

Rubricae Breviarii et Missalis Romani. Ibid. 597-705.

Variationes in Breviario et Missali Romano, etc. Ibid. 706-740.

The English translation of the motu proprio and of the *Rubrics of the Roman Breviary and Missal* is that of the NCWC (translated by Leonard J. Doyle).

1960 AUG 22   The members for the preparatory liturgical commission are announced. Originally there were 18 members and 29 consultants (periti); others are added until final membership is achieved September 2, 1961: 26 members and 37 consultants.

1961 JAN 01   The Code of rubrics of 1960 JUL 25 goes into effect.

1961 FEB 14 CSR. Instruction "De calendariis particularibus et Officiorum ac Missarum Propriis ad normam et mentem CSR revisendis." AAS 56 (1961) 160-180.

1961 APR 05 The CSR publishes a new typical edition (that is, a model edition from which all other editions must be taken and to which they must conform) of the *Roman Breviary.*

1961 APR 13 CSR publishes a partial revision of the *Pontifical* giving a new rite for the consecration of altars and the consecration of churches. AAS 54 (1962) 52.

1961 APR 12 TO 22 The second general meeting of the preparatory liturgical commission. During this meeting a first schema for the liturgy is prepared from the recommendations of the bishops (see 1959 MAY 17 and 1960 JULY 9).

I have not examined this text. I know of it only from the references made to it in the schema of 1961 AUG 10. There, for example, on page III, mention is made of the text approved in the plenary session of the commission during April (". . . textum in sessione plenaria Commissione, mense aprili, aprobatum.") At the beginning of each chapter of the second schema, there is a comparison of the items as found in the schema of April. Apparently, this first text did not have an introductory theological chapter, but consisted of the specific suggestions of the bishops.

1961 APR 16 CSR publishes a new, modified rite for the baptism of adults. AAS 54 (1962) 310-315.

1961 MAY 15 Historical section. *Memoria sulla riforma liturgica.* Supplemento IV: Consultazione Dell'Episcopato intorno alla riforma del Breviario Romano (1956-1957). Risultati e Deduzioni. Typ. Pol. Vat. 1957. S. Hist. N. 97.

1961 JUN 23 CSR publishes a new typical edition of the *Roman Missal.*

1961 AUG 10 The secretariat for the preparatory liturgical commission (Rev. A. Bugnini, secretary) publishes a revised schema for the liturgy.

Pontificia Commissio de Sacra Liturgia Praeparatoria Concilii Vaticani II. *Constitutio de Sacra Liturgia Fovenda atque Instauranda.* Schema transmissum Sodalibus Commissionis die 10 augusti 1961.

The text is mimeographed; 23 x 31 cm. XIV + 252 pages. The text consists of 121 articles divided into eight chapters. There is an introduction by Bugnini which gives the norms for changing the text of 1961 APR 12 to the present text.

I have been able to study this document and the schemata of 1961 NOV 15, and 1962 JAN 11 through the courtesy of Rev. Pierre-Marie Gy, O.P.

1961 NOV 15   The secretariat for the preparatory liturgical commission publishes a third schema for the liturgy.

Pontificia Commissio de Sacra Liturgia Praeparatoria Concilii Vaticani II. *Constitutio De Sacra Liturgia.* Schema transmissum Sodalibus Commissionis die 15 novembris 1961. Romae. 1961.

The text is mimeographed. 23 x 31 cm. XII + 96 pages. The introduction states that during the meeting of October 11 to 13, the subcommission for the first chapter changed much of this theological introduction.

The first chapter, when comparing the text with the previous text, is rearranged. There appears mention of radio and TV liturgies and mention of a commission for art and music. There is also an article on a central Roman office for pastoral liturgical action but this suggestion disappears in the next schema and does not reappear. However, in general, all of the articles which appear in this schema appear in the final text approved 1963 DEC 04. (This fact certainly bears witness to the insight of Rev. Bugnini in guiding the document through the different schemata.) There is added the mention of the homily in the chapter on the Mass. The former text had no mention of the sacrament of penance in the chapter on the sacraments; this text mentions penance in N. 59.

The principal difference between this text and the previous one is that this text is much shorter (96 pages as compared with 252 pages) due to the omission of much of the explanatory material (declaratio voti).

1961 NOV 26 Cardinal Cicognani, president of the Commission for the liturgy and prefect of the CSR celebrates his 80th birthday.

1961 DEC 15 John XXIII. Apostolic constitution, "Humanae Salutis." Convokes the twenty-first ecumenical council.

1962 JAN 11 to 13 The preparatory liturgical commission holds its third plenary session and revises the schema for the liturgy.

Pontificia Commissio de Sacra Liturgia Praeparatoria Concilii Vaticani II. *Constitutio de Sacra Liturgia.* Textus approbatus in Sessione plenaria diebus 11-13 ianuarii 1962. Romae. 1962.

The text is mimeographed; 23 x 31 cm. IX + 79 pages. This is the fourth schema of the document listed in this bibliography. This schema was unanimously approved and given to the president of the commission, Cardinal Cicognani.

1962 FEB 01 Cardinal Cicognani signs the schema of January 11 and sends it to the Secretary General. It is printed under the title: "Quaestiones de Sacra Liturgia. Schema Constitutionis de Sacra Liturgia a Commissione Liturgica propositum Em.mo ac Rev.mo Domino Cardinali Commissionis Praeside Relatore."

The text contains the following Chapters:
1. De principibus generalibus ad S. Liturgiam instaurandam atque fovendam.
2. De Sacrosancto Eucharistiae Mysterio
3. De sacramentis et sacramentalibus
4. De Officio Divino
5. De anno Liturgico
6. De sacra supellectile
7. De musica sacra
8. De arte sacra

1962 FEB 02 John XXIII. Motu proprio, "Concilium." Convokes

for Council for October 11, 1962, in St. Peter's Basilica.

1962 FEB 05   Cardinal Cicognani dies.

1962 FEB 22   John XXIII. Apostolic Constitution, "Veterum Sapientia." On Latin as the Official Language of the Church. English translation: NCWC.

The constitution has two parts:
1. The Excellence and Merits of the Latin Language.
2. Provisions for the Rebirth of the Study and Use of Latin.
Bishops and religious superiors are to see to it that no one writes against the use of Latin in the sacred rites of the liturgy. NCWC p. 7.

1962 FEB   Rev. A. Bugnini, secretary of the preparatory liturgical commission and its acting head after the death of Cardinal Cicognani, is removed from office. The schema for the liturgy, prepared under the direction of Fr. Bugnini, advocated a limited use of the vernacular in the liturgy.

1962 FEB 22   Cardinal Larraona succeeds Cardinal Cicognani as prefect of the CSR and president of the preparatory commission for the liturgy.

1962 MAR 23   to APR 03   The fifth General Session of the Central preparatory commission. The schema for the liturgy (1962 JAN 11, 1962 FEB 01) is studied. It is given to a subcommission to be prepared for distribution to the future Fathers of the Council.

1962 JUL 13   Sacrosanctum Oecumenicum Concilium Vaticanum Secundum. *Schemata Constitutionum et Decretorum de quibus disceptabitur in Concilii sessionibus. Series Prima.* (sub secreto) Typ. Pol. Vat. 1962.

This document contains six schemata, the fifth of which (pages 157-204) is the "Schema Constitutionis de Sacra Liturgia."

I have consulted these documents at the Bibliothèque du Saulchoir. 267-B-123.

1962 OCT 06   John XXIII. Motu proprio, "Appropinquante Concilio." Promulgates the rules governing the procedure for the Council.

1962 OCT 11 The solemn opening of the Second Vatican Council.

The interventions and discussions of the Council are published in:

Acta Synodalia Sacrosancti Concilii Oecumenici Vaticani II. 15 Vol. Typ. Pol. Vat. 1970.

1962 OCT 12 The Council adjourns at its first meeting to prepare to elect ·its own commissions rather than those members suggested on the prepared list.

1962 OCT 13, 16, and 20. The first three general sessions of the Council are devoted to the election of the Conciliar Commissions.

Six of the bishops elected to the Conciliar Commission for the liturgy had served on the preparatory commission. Rev. Antonelli, who had served as director of the commission for liturgical reform under Pius XII (see 1948 MAY 28 above) is appointed secretary.

1962 OCT 20 The Council issues "A message to humanity."

1962 OCT 22 The Council begins the discussion on the schema on the liturgy. It is presented to the Council Fathers by Fr. Antonelli. He gives the principles which have guided the commission in writing the schema (AS Vat II, Vol. I, Pars I, pages 307-308).

The text is discussed in the next 15 sessions, October 22 to November 13. These discussions are taken by the Commission for the Liturgy and incorporated into a new schema:

Sacrosanctum Oecumenicum Concilium Vaticanum Secundum. *Schema Constitutionis de Sacra Liturgia. Emendationes a Patribus Conciliaribus postulate a Commissione Conciliari de Sacra Liturgia examinatae et propositae.* Typ. Pol. Vat. 1962.

This series of booklets gives in two columns the schema of 1962 JULY 13 and the schema emended. The minor changes and the stylistic changes are printed in italics in the second text. The more important changes are printed in capital letters and are proposed to the Fathers for a vote.

The *Emendationes* also give some of the explanations (declarations) for the articles which were
given in the first schemata but which were omitted
from the text of 1962 JUL 13 which was given
to the Council Fathers. This new text also gives a
complete list of references and footnotes. This is
the last such listing for the final text gives references only to Scripture, the Fathers, and the Councils.

I examined this document in the Bibliothèque du
Saulchoir: Collection of R.P. Camelot. 267-B-123,
Vol. II.

1962 NOV 10   Sacrosanctum Oecumenicum Concilium Vaticanum
Secundum. *Schemata Constitutionum et Decretorum
de quibus disceptabitur in Concilii sessionibus. Series
Secunda. De Ecclesia et De B. Maria Virgine.*
(Sub secreto). Rome. Typ. Pol. Vat. 1962.

I examined this document at the Bibliothèque du
Saulchoir: Collection of R.P. Camelot.

1962 DEC 08   Solemn closing of the first session of the Council.

1963 JAN 06   John XXIII. Letter, "Mirabilis ille," addressed to
each of the Council Fathers indicating the direction
to be taken in the future work of the Council.

1963 JUN 03   Death of Pope John XXIII. In virtue of Article
33 of the Constitution "Vacantis Apostolicae Sedis,"
the Council is suspended.

1963 JUN 21   Cardinal Montini is elected Pope Paul VI.

1963 JUN 22   Paul VI gives his first public address during which
he says that "the pre-eminent part of Our pontificate will be the continuation of the Second Vatican
Ecumenical Council."

1963 JUN 27   Rescript, "Ex audientia." Fixes the date for the
reopening of the Council: September 29, 1963.

1963 JUL 01   Paul VI. Coronation address.

1963 SEP 12   Paul VI. Letter to Cardinal Tisserant, stating the
ends which the Council should achieve.

1963 SEP 14   Paul VI. The letter "Horum temporum" is sent
to the Council Fathers convoking them to the

second session.

1963 SEP 21 Paul VI. Address on the Roman Curia.

1963 SEP 29 Solemn opening of the second session of the Council.

1963 NOV 18 to 22 The final votes on the schema on the liturgy according to the changes printed in the *Emendations* (see above 1962 OCT 22).

Certain explanations why some changes were not made are contained in:

Sacrosanctum Oecumenicum Concilium Vaticanum Secundum. *MODI a patribus Conciliaribus Propositi a commissione Conciliari de Sacra Liturgia examenati.* Rome. Typ. Pol. Vat. 1963.

1963 NOV 22 Approval, in principle, of the schema on the Liturgy. Of 2178 votes: 2158 for; 19 against; 1 null.

1963 DEC 04A Final vote on the Constitution on the Sacred Liturgy. Of 2151 votes: 2147 for; 4 against.

1963 DEC 04B Promulgation of two Council documents:

(1) *Constitutio de Sacra Liturgia.* (Sacrosanctum Concilium.) Constitution on the Sacred Liturgy. AAS 56 (1964) 97-138.

(2) *Decretum de Instrumentis Communicationis Socialis.* (Inter Mirifica.) Decree on the Instruments of Social Communication. AAS 56 (1964) 145-157.

Solemn closing of the second session of the Council.

1964 JAN 04 to 06. Pope Paul VI makes an ecumenical journey to the Holy Land and meets with Patriarch Athenagoras.

1964 JAN 10 Holy Office. Decree, "In Apostolica constitutione," reducing the Communion fast for priests celebrating Mass. AAS 56 (1964) 212.

1964 JAN 25 Paul VI. Motu proprio, "Sacram Liturgiam." On the implementation of the Constitution on the Liturgy. Original text: OR January 29, 1964. Emended text: AAS 56 (1964) 139-144. English translation: NCWC.

1964 FEB 16   First Sunday of Lent. Sacram Liturgiam (Jan 25) goes into effect.

1964 FEB 29   Cardinal Secretary of State. Letters to Cardinal Lercaro indicating the specific competence of the Consilium. OR Jan 31, Mar 5, and June 24. List of members: EL 79 (1965) 160-162.

1964 APR 25   CSR. Decree, "Quo actuosius." Changes the formula for Holy Communion to "Corpus Christi. Amen." AAS 56 (1964) 337-338.

1964 MAY 17   The "Secretariat for Non-Christian Religions" is established.

1964 SEP 14   The solemn opening of the third session of the Council.

1964 SEP 26   CSR and Consilium. Instruction, "Inter Oecumenici." The first instruction on the proper implementation of the Constitution on the Liturgy. AAS 56 (1964) 877-900. English: NCWC.

1964 OCT 16   Cardinal G. Lercaro. Letter to the president of the Episcopal Conferences, "De unica interpretatione liturgica populari in linguis pluribus in locis usitatis." States that each vernacular language is to have a unique liturgical translation. Not 5 (1965) 194-196.

1964 OCT 29   Paul VI. Allocution to the members of the Consilium. AAS 56 (1964) 993-996.

1964 NOV 21A Paul VI reduces the time of the Communion fast to one hour before receiving Holy Communion. AAS 57 (1965) 186.

1964 NOV 21B Promulgation of three Council documents:

> (3) *Constitutio Dogmatica de Ecclesia.* (*Lumen Gentium.*) Dogmatic Constitution on the Church. AAS 57 (1965) 5-71.

> (4) *Decretum de Ecclesiis Orientalibus Catholicis.* (*Orientalium Ecclesiarum*). Decree on the Eastern Catholic Churches. AAS 57 (1965) 76-89.

> (5) *Decretum de Oecumenismo.* (*Unitatis Redintegratio*). Decree on Ecumenism. AAS 57 (1965) 90-112.

Paul VI, in his closing address, proclaims Mary "Mother of the Church."

Solemn closing of the third session of the Council.

1964 DEC 14A CSR and Consilium. *Cantus qui in Missali Romano desiderantur iuxta Instructionem ad exsecutionem Constitutionis de sacra Liturgia recte ordinandum et iuxta Ritum concelebrationis.* Typ. Pol. Vat.

1964 DEC 14B CSR and Consilium. *Kyriale simplex.* Editio typica. Typ. Pol. Vat. 1965.

1965 JAN 15 The first issue of *Notitiae*: the communication of the Consilium ad exsequendam Constitutionem de Sacra Liturgia. The first issue was not actually printed until April but the issues are numbered beginning with January.

1965 JAN 27 CSR and Consilium. *Ordo Missae. Ritus servandus in celebratione Missae et De defectibus in celebratione Missae occurrentibus.* Editio typica. Typ. Pol. Vat. 1965. pp. 69.

1965 MAR 04 CSR. Decree, "Pientissima Mater Ecclesia." Ordinaries can permit priests to carry the Oil of the Sick when on a journey. AAS 57 (1965) 409.

1965 MAR 07A CSR and Concilium. *Ritus servandus in concelebratione Massae et Ritus Communionis sub utraque specie.* Editio typica. Typ. Pol. Vat. 1965. pp. 104.

Rite to be observed in the Concelebration of Mass and the Rite for Communion under both kinds with the Text of the Canon of the Mass and Chants for Concelebration. trans: Frank Rodimer. New York: Joseph F. Wagner, 1965. pp. 71.

1965 MAR 07B CSR and Consilium. *Variationes in Ordinem Hebdomadae Sanctae inducendae.* Editio typica. Typ. Pol. Vat. 1965. pp. 23.

The document treats 1. de Missa Chrismatis feriae V; 2. de simplificatione ritus consecrationis Oleorum. 3. de quibusdam orationibus sollemnibus feriae VI (for example, for the Jews).

1965 MAR 07C The instruction "Inter Oecumenici" of 1964 SEP 26 goes into effect.

1965 MAR 25   CSR. Decree "Plures locorum Ordinarii." The Passion may be read by a non-deacon. AAS 57 (1965) 413-414.

1965 JUN 15   Consilium. Declaration, "Passim quandoque." On the permission necessary for liturgical experimentation. Not 6 (1965) 145.

1965 JUN 30   Lercaro, Cardinal G., president of Consilium. Letter to the presidents of the Episcopal Conferences, "Le renouveau liturgique."
    The official text was given in the five principal languages. The text used here is that printed in Not 9-10 (1965) 257-264 in French.

1965 JUL 17   CSR. "Partes quae in collatione Ordinum lingua vernacula dici possunt." Not 9-10 (1965) 277-279. A list of those parts of the Rite of Ordination which may be said in the vernacular.

1965 SEP 03   Paul VI. Encyclical Letter, "Mysterium fidei." AAS 57 (1965) 753-774.
    English translation: "On the Holy Eucharist." NCWC.

1965 SEP 14   Opening of the fourth and final session of the Council.

1965 SEP 14   *Missae in quarta periodo Concilii Oecumenici Vaticani II celebrandae.* Typ. Pol. Vat. 1965. pp. 120.

1965 OCT 04   and 05. Pope Paul goes to New York to address the United Nations General Assembly.

1965 OCT 28   Promulgation of the following Council documents:

    (6) *Decretum de Pastorali Episcoporum Munere in Ecclesia. (Christus Dominus).* Decree on the Bishops' Pastoral Office in the Church. AAS 58 (1966) 673-701.

    (7) *Decretum de Accommodata Renovatione Vitae Religiosae. (Perfectae Caritatis).* Decree on the Appropriate Renewal of the Religious Life. AAS 58 (1966) 702-712.

    (8) *Decretum de Institutione Sacerdotali. (Optatam Totius.)* Decree on Priestly Formation. AAS 58 (1966) 713-727.

(9) *Declaratio de Educatione Christiana.* (*Gravissimum Educationis*). Declaration on Christian Education. AAS 58 (1966) 728-739.

(10) *Declaratio de Ecclesiae Habitudine ad Religiones non-Christianas.* (*Nostrae Aetate.*) Declaration on the Relationship of the Church to Non-Christian Religions. AAS 58 (1966) 740-744.

1965 NOV 18   The promulgation of two Council documents. Pope Paul also announces the beginning of the reform of the Roman Curia, the introduction of the process for the beatification of Pope Pius XII and Pope John XXIII, a Jubilee period, and the convocation of the Episcopal Synod not later than 1967.

(11) *Constitutio Dogmatica de Divina Revelatione.* (*Del Verbum.*) Dogmatic Constitution on Divine Revelation. AAS 58 (1966) 817-835.

(12) *Decretum de Apostolatu Laicorum.* (*Apostolicam actuositatem.*) Decree on the Apostolate of the Laity. AAS 58 (1966) 837-864.

1965 NOV 23   CSR and Consilium. Instruction, "De lingua in celebrandis Officio Divino et Missa 'conventuali' aut 'communitatis' apud religiosos adhibenda." AAS 57 (1965) 1010-1013.
"Instruction on the language to be used in the recitation of the Divine Office and the celebration of the 'Conventual' or 'Community' Mass among Religious."

1965 DEC 07   The promulgation of the following Council documents:

(13) *Declaratio de Libertate Religiosa.* (*Dignitatis Humanae.*) Declaration on Religious Freedom. AAS 58 (1966) 929-946.

(14) *Decretum de Activitate Missionali Ecclesiae.* (*Ad Gentes divinitus*) Decree on the Church's Missionary Activity. AAS 58 (1966) 947-990.

(15) *Decretum de Presbyterorum Ministerio et Vita.* (*Presbyterorum Ordinis.*) Decree on the Ministry and Life of Priests. AAS 58 (1966) 947-1024.

(16) *Constitutio Pastoralis de Ecclesia in Mundo Huius Temporis.* (*Gaudium et Spes.*) Pastoral Constitution on the Church in the Modern World. AAS 58 (1966) 1025-1120.

1965 DEC 08 Solemn closing of the Second Vatican Council.

1966 JAN 25 Lercaro, Cardinal G., president of Consilium. Letter to the presidents of the Episcopal Conferences, "L'héureux développement de la reforme liturgique." Not 18 (1966) 157-161.

1966 JAN 27 CSR and Consilium. Decree, "Cum nostra aetate." On the printing of liturgical books. AAS 58 (1966) 169-171.

1966 FEB 17 Paul VI. Apostolic constitution, "Paenitemini." On penance. AAS 58 (1966) 177-198.

1966 APR 17 Consilium. *De Oratione Communi seu Fidelium: Natura, momentum ac structura. Criteria atque specimina Coetibus territorialibus Episcoporum proposita.* Libreria Editrice Vaticana, 1966. Latin and French. 182 pp.

The Common Prayer, or Prayer of the Faithful: Its nature, importance and structure. Criteria and examples offered to the National Bishops' Conferences.

1966 AUG 05 Paul VI. Apostolic letter, "Ecclesiae sanctae." Statutes for Episcopal Conferences, AAS 58 (1966) 757-787.

1966 DEC 15 Consilium (unsigned article in Notitiae.) " 'Experiences' liturgiques." Not 24 (1966) 345-346.

1966 DEC 29 CSR and Consilium. Declaratio, "Da qualche tempo." On liturgical changes being taken by private individuals. AAS 59 (1967) 85-86.

1967 JAN 01 Paul VI. Apostolic Constitution, "Indulgentiarum doctrina." On indulgences. AAS 59 (1967) 5-24.

1967 JAN 15 (Unsigned article in Notitiae). "Mecanique et Liturgie." The use of "mechanical" things (microphones, radio, records) in the liturgy. Not 25 (1967) 3-4.

1967 MAR 05 CSR and Consilium. Instruction, "Musicam sacram." AAS 59 (1967) 300-320.

Instruction of the Congregation of Rites on Music In the Liturgy. USCC. Published with a "Clarification and Exhortation" by Frederick R. McManus.

1967 MAY 04   CSR and Consilium. Instruction, "Tres abhinc annos." AAS 59 (1967) 442-448.

"A further Instruction on the correct implementation of the Constitution on the Sacred Liturgy." USCC.

1967 MAY 18   CSR and Consilium. *Variationes in Ordinem Missae inducendae, ad normam Instructionis S.R.C. diei 4 maii 1967.* Typ. Pol. Vat. 1967. pp. 39.

1967 MAY 25   CSR and Consilium. Instruction, "Eucharisticum mysterium." AAS 59 (1967) 539-573.

"Instruction on Eucharistic Worship." USCC.

1967 JUN 18   Paul VI. Apostolic letter, "Sacrum Diaconatus Ordinem." AAS 59 (1967) 697-704.

"General Norms for Restoring the Permanent Diaconate in the Latin Church." USCC.

1967 SEP 03   CSR and Consilium. *Graduale simplex in usum minorum ecclesiarum.* Typ. Pol. Vat. 1967. pp. 431.

1967 OCT 08   Consilium. Communication to the presidents of the Episcopal Conferences on the translation of the Roman Canon. Notitiae 34 (1967) 326-327.

1967 OCT 15   Paul VI. Apostolic Constitution, "Regimini Ecclesiae." On the reform of the Roman Curia. AAS 59 (1967) 885-890; 903-908; 928.

1967 NOV 12   (United States) Bishops' Committee on the Liturgy. "The Place of Music in Eucharistic Celebrations." Revised 1972 with the new title: "Music in Catholic Worship."

1968 MAY 23   CSR and Consilium. *Preces Eucharisticae et Prefationes.* Typ. Pol. Vat. 1968. pp. 53.

"Guidelines for the Episcopal Conferences for a Catechesis of the Faithful Concerning the Anaphoras of the Mass, prepared by the Consilium for the Implementation of the Constitution on the Sacred

Liturgy, June 14, 1968 and the Decree of the Sacred
Congregation of Rites, May 23, 1968." USCC.

Bishops' Committee on the Liturgy. *The New
Eucharistic Prayers and Prefaces.* ICEL-NCCB. 1968.
pp. 72.

1968 JUN 18 Paul VI. Apostolic Constitution, "Pontificalis Romani." Approving the new Rite of Ordination.
AAS 60 (1968) 369-373. English trans: see below.
1968 AUG 15.

1968 AUG 15 CSR and Consilium. *De Ordinatione Diaconi, Presbyteri et Episcopi.* Pontificale Romanum ex decreto
Sacrosanti Oecumenici Concilii Vaticanii II Instauratum auctoriatate Pauli PP. VI promulgatum.
Editio Typica. Typ. Pol. Vat. 1968. pp. 133.

Ordination of Deacons, Presbyters, and Bishops.
ICEL. NCCB. 1973.

1968 OCT 14 Paul VI. Allocution to the members of the Consilium. AAS 60 (1968) 732-737.
The control of the liturgy pertains to the Church
and not to individuals.

1969 JAN 00 Consilium. Descriptio et specimina Officii Divini
iuxta Concilii Vaticani II Decreta instaurati. In
Civitate Vaticana. 1969. pp. 79.
A description and example of the divine office
was sent to the bishops of the world. see Not 45
(1969) 74-85.

1969 JAN 25 Consilium. Instruction to the presidents of the
Episcopal Conferences on the translation of liturgical
texts.
The text used in this study is the text published
in Notitiae 44 (1969) 3-12 (in French.) "Instruction
sur la traduction des textes liturgiques pour la
célébration avec le peuple."

1969 FEB 14 Paul VI. Apostolic letter, "Mysterii paschalis."
Approving the general norms for the liturgical year
and the new Roman Calendar. AAS 61 (1969)
222-226.
English is printed in the Sacramentary; see below
1969 APR 06.

1969 MAR 19 CSR and Consilium. *Ordo celebrandi matrimonium.* Rituale Romanum ex decreto Sacrosancti Oecumenici Concilii Vaticani II instauratum auctoritate Pauli PP. VI promulgatum. Editio typica. Typ. Pol. Vat. 1969. pp. 40.

Rite of Marriage. ICEL. USCC. 1969.

1969 MAR 21 CSR and Consilium. *Calendarium Romanum* ex Decreto Sacrosancti Oecumenici Concicii Vaticani II instauratum auctoritate Pauli PP. promulgatum. Editio Typica. Typ. Pol. Vat. 1969. pp. 179.
    English is printed in the Sacramentary; see below 1969 APR 06.

1969 APR 03 Paul VI. Apostolic constitution, "Missale Romanum." Approving the new Roman Missal. AAS 61 (1969) 217-222.
    English is printed in the Sacramentary; see below 1969 APR 06.

1969 APR 06 CSR and Consilium. *Ordo Missae.* Missale Romanum ex decreto Sacrosancti Oecumenici Concilii Vaticani II instauratum auctoritate Pauli PP. VI promulgatum. Editio typica. Typ. Pol. Vat. 1969. p. 173.

    English quotations are from: *The Sacramentary: The Roman Missal* revised by decree of the Second Vatican Council and published by authority of Pope Paul VI. ICEL. NCCB. Catholic Book Publishing Co. New York. 1974.

1969 MAY 08 Paul VI. Apostolic constitution, "Sacra Rituum Congregatio." AAS 61 (1969) 297-305.
    Divides the Congregation of Sacred Rites (CSR) into two congregations, one for the Causes of the Saints, and one for Divine Worship (CDW) The Consilium is integrated into the CDW.

1969 MAY 15A CDW. *Ordo Baptismi parvulorum.* Rituale Romanum ex decreto Sacrosancti Oecumenici Concilii Vaticani II instauratum auctoritate Pauli PP. VI promulgatum. Editio typica. Typ. Pol. Vat. 1969. pp. 93.

Rite of Baptism for Children. USCC. ICEL. 1969.

1969 MAY 15B   CDW. Instruction, (de Missis pro coetibus particularibus), "Actio pastoralis." Original text was dis-
tributed to the Episcopal Conferences. ˙Emended
and definitive text: AAS 61 (1969) 806-811.

"Instruction on Masses for Special Gatherings."
USCC. 1969.

Published at the same time as the instruction
in France:

Commission episcopale francaise de liturgie. "Les
Messes de petits groupes." DC 15 mars 1970,
numero 1559. 278-283.

1969 MAY 25   CDW. *Ordo lectionum Missae.* Missale Romanum
ex decreto Sacrosancti Oecumenici Concilii Vaticani
II instauratum auctoritate Pauli PP. VI promulgatum. Editio typica. Typ. Pol. Vat. 1969. pp. 434.

Lectionary for Mass. USCC. ICEL. 1969. 2nd
Edition, with revision indicated by CDW on July
24, 1970.

1969 MAY 29   CDW. Instruction, (de modo Sanctam Communionem ministrandi), "Memoriale Domini." AAS
61 (1969) 541-545.

"Instruction on the Manner of Administering Holy
Communion." USCC. 1969. The English translation
contains only the first part of the instruction.
For those countries which received permission to
distribute Communion in the hand there is a second
part of the instruction. This second part was sent
to the Episcopal Conferences in the pertinent
languages. The text quoted in this study is that
published in Notitiae 48 (1968) 351-353.

1969 AUG 15   CDW. *Ordo exsequiarum.* Rituale Romanum ex
decreto Sacrosancti Oecumenici Concilii Vaticani
II instauratum auctoritate Pauli PP. VI promulgatum.
Editio Typica. Typ. Pol. Vat. 1969. pp. 91.

Rite of Funerals. USCC. ICEL. 1971.

1970 FEB 02   CDW. *Ordo professionis religiosae.* Rituale Romanum ex Decreto Sacrosancti Oecumenici Concilii Vaticani II instauratum, auctoritate Pauli PP. VI promulgatum. Editio typica. Typ. Pol. Vat. 1970. pp. 126.

Rite of Religious Profession. USCC. ICEL. 1971.

1970 MAR 26   CDW. *Missale Romanum* ex Decreto Sacrosancti Oecumenici Concilii Vaticani II instauratum auctoritate Pauli PP. VI promulgatum. Editio typica. Typ. Pol. Vat. 1970. pp. 966.
English translation: see 1969 APR 06.

1970 MAR 31   Paul VI. Motu proprio, "Matrimonia mixta." AAS 62 (1970) 257-263. The regulation of mixed marriages.

1970 MAY 31   CDW. *Ordo consecrationis virginum.* Pontificale Romanum ex Decreto Sacrosancti Oecumenici Concilii Vaticani II instauratum auctoritate Pauli PP. VI promulgatum. Editio typica. Typ. Pol. Vat. 1970. pp. 64.

The Revised Order of Blessing an Abbot or Abbess, of Consecration to a Life of Virginity, and of the Blessing of Oils. ICEL. 1971.

1970 JUN 29   CDW. Instruction, "Sacramentali Communione." AAS 62 (1970) 664-666.

"Instruction on the Extension of the Faculty to Distribute Holy Communion under Both Kinds." USCC, 1970.

1970 SEP 05   CDW. Instruction, "Liturgicae instaurationes." AAS 62 (1970) 692-704.

"Third Instruction on the Correct Implementation of the Constitution on the Sacred Liturgy." USCC. 1970.

1970 SEP 30   CDW. *Lectionarium.* Missale Romanum ex Decreto Sacrosancti Oecumenici Concilii Vaticani II instauratum, auctoritate Pauli PP. VI promulgatum. Editio typica. Typ. Pol. Vat. 1970-1971.

1970 OCT 18   CDW. *Missale parvum,* e Missali Romano et Lectionario exceptum. Editio iuxta typicam. Typ. Pol. Vat. 1970. pp. 168.

1970 NOV 01 Paul VI. Apostolic constitution, "Laudis Canticum." Promulgating the new Liturgy of the Hours. AAS 63 (1971) 527-535.
English: see below 1971 FEB 02.

1970 NOV 09 CDW. *Ordo benedictionis abbatis et abbatissae.* Pontificale Romanum ex Decreto Sacrosancti Oecumenici Concilii Vaticani II instauratum, auctoritate Pauli PP. VI promulgatum. Editio typica. Typ. Pol. Vat. 1970. pp. 31.
English: see above 1970 MAY 31.

1970 DEC 03 CDW. *Ordo benedicendi oleum catechumenorum et infirmorum et conficiendi chrisma.* Pontificale Romanum ex Decreto Sacrosancti Oecumenici Concilii Vaticanii II instauratum, auctoritate Pauli PP. VI promulgatum. Editio typica. Typ. Pol. Vat. 1971. pp. 17. English: see above 1970 MAY 31.

1971 FEB 02 CDW. *Institutio generalis de Liturgia Horarum.* Officium Divinum ex Decreto Sacrosancti Oecumenici Concilii Vaticani II instauratum, auctoritate Pauli PP. VI promulgatum. Typis Pol. Vat. 1971. pp. 93.

"General Instruction of the Liturgy of the Hours." *The Liturgy of the Hours.* The Divine Office revised by decree of the Second Vatican Ecumenical Council and published by authority of Pope Paul VI. ICEL. Catholic Book Publishing Co. New York. 1975. 4 Vols.

1971 APR 11 CDW. *Liturgia Horarum iuxta Ritum Romanum.* Officium Divinum ex Decreto Sacrosancti Oecumenici Concilii Vaticani II instauratum, auctoritate Pauli PP. VI promulgatum. Editio typ. Typ. Pol. Vat. 1971-1972. 4 Vols.

1971 JUN 14 Cardinal Tabera, Prefect CDW. "Notification on the Roman Missal, the Liturgy of the Hours, and the Calendar." Notitiae 64 (1971) 215-217.

1971 AUG 15 Paul VI. Apostolic Constitution, "Divinae consortium naturae." On the Rite of Confirmation. AAS 63 (1971) 657-664.
English: see below 1971 AUG 22.

1971 AUG 22 CDW. *Ordo Confirmationis.* Pontificale Romanum ex Decreto Sacrosancti Oecumenici Concilii Vaticani II instauratum, auctoritate Pauli PP. VI promulgatum. Editio typica. Typ. Pol. Vat. 1971. pp. 51.

Rite of Confirmation. ICEL. NCCB. 1972.

1972 JAN 06 CDW. *Ordo initiationis christianae adultorum.* Rituale Romanum ex Decreto Sacrosancti Oecumenici Concilii Vaticani II instauratum, auctoritate Pauli PP. VI promulgatum. Editio typica. Typ. Pol. Vat. 1972. pp. 185.

Rite of Christian Initiation of Adults. Provisional text. Study Book Edition. USCC. ICEL. 1974.

Rite of Reception of Baptized Christians into Full Communion with the Catholic Church. USCC. ICEL. 1973.

1972 JUN 01 Secretariat for Promoting Christian Unity. "Instruction Concerning Cases when other Christians may be Admitted to Eucharistic Communion in the Catholic Church." AAS 64 (1972) 518-525. English: USCC.

1972 JUN 16 Congregation for the Doctrine of the Faith. "Normae pastorales circa Absolutionem Sacramentalem Generali modo impertiendam. AAS 64 (1972) 510-514. Pastoral norms concerning General Sacramental absolution.

1972 JUN 24 CDW. *Ordo Missae.* Missale Romanum ex Decreto

1972 JUN 24 CDW. *Ordo Cantus Missae.* Missale Romanum ex Decreto Sacrosancti Oecumenici Concilii Vaticani II instauratum, auctoritate Pauli PP. VI promulgatum. Editio typica. Typ. Pol. Vat. 1972. pp. 246.

1972 AUG 07 CDW. Declaration, "In celebratione Missae." AAS 64 (1972) 561-563.

"Declaration on Concelebration." USCC. 1974. Published together with the "Commentary" found in Notitiae 77 (1972) 327-332.

1972 AUG 15A Paul VI. Motu proprio, "Ministeria quaedam." AAS 64 (1972) 529-534.

"An Apostolic Letter in Motu Proprio Form Laying Down Certain Norms Regarding the Sacred

Order of the Diaconate." USCC. 1972.

1972 AUG 15B Paul VI. Motu proprio, "Ad pascendum." AAS
64 (1972) 534-540.

"An Apostolic Letter in Motu Proprio Form by
which the Discipline of First Tonsure, Minor Orders
and Subdiaconate in the Latin Church is Reformed."
USCC. 1972.

1972 NOV 30 Paul VI. Apostolic Constitution, "Sacram Unctionem
infirmorum." AAS 65 (1973) 5-9.
English: see below 1972 DEC 07.

1972 DEC 03 CDW. *De institutione Lectorum et acolythorum.
De admissione inter candidatos ad diaconatum et
presbyteratum. De sacro caelibatu amplectenda.*
Pontificale Romanum ex Decreto Sacrosancti Oecumenici Concilii Vaticani II instauratum, auctoritate Pauli PP. VI promulgatum. Editio typica. Typ.
Po. Vat. 1972. pp. 38.

*Rite of Institution of Readers and Acolytes. Admission
to Candidacy for the Diaconate and Presbyterate.
Ordination of Deacons, Presbyters, and Bishops.*
Provisional Text. ICEL. NCCB. 1973.

1972 DEC 07 CDW. *Ordo unctionis infirmorum eorumque pastoralis curae.* Rituale Romanum ex Decreto Sacrosancti Oecumenici Concilii Vaticani II instauratum,
auctoritate Pauli PP. VI promulgatum. Editio typica.
Typ. Pol. Vat. 1972. pp. 81.

Rite of Anointing and Pastoral Care of the Sick.
Provisional text. ICEL. NCCB. Catholic Book
Publishing Co. New York. 1974.

1973 JAN 29 Congregation for the Discipline of the Sacraments.
Instruction, "Immensae caritatis." AAS 65 (1973)
264-271.

"Instruction on Facilitating Sacramental Communion
in Particular Circumstances." USCC. 1973.

1973 APR 27 CDW. Letter to the presidents of the Episcopal
Conferences, "Eucharistiae Participationem." AAS
65 (1973) 340-347.

"Letter to the Presidents of the National Con-

ferences of Bishops Concerning Eucharistic Prayers."
USCC. 1973.

1973 JUN 21   CDW. *De sacra communione et De cultu mysterii eucharistici extra missam.* Rituale Romanum ex Decreto Sacrosancti Oecumenici Concilii Vaticani II. Editio typica. Typ. Pol. Vat. 1973. pp. 69.

Holy Communion and Eucharistic Worship Outside of Mass. ICEL. NCCB.

1973 JUN 22   Paul VI. Allocution to the College of Cardinals on the 10th anniversary of his election. Italian text: OR 22-23 June 1973. French text: DC 15 juillet 1973. N° 1936. pp. 651-652.

1973 AUG 29   CDW. Second typical edition of the *Rite of Baptism for Children.* Notitiae 85 (1973) 269-272.

1973 OCT 25   CDW. Letter to the presidents of the Episcopal Conferences concerning the translation of the essential sacramental formulas.
The letter is not published in the AAS or Notitiae. I have examined the Latin text through the courtesy of Rev. Pierre-Marie GY, O.P.

1973 NOV 01   CDW. *Directorium de missis cum pueris.* Typ. Pol. Vat. 1973. pp. 20.

"Letter to the Presidents of the National Conferences of Bishops Concerning Directory for Masses with Children." ICEL. USCC. 1974.

1973 DEC 02   CDW. *Ordo Paenitentiae.* Rituale Romanum ex Decreto Sacrosancti Oecumenici Concilii Vaticani II. Editio typica. Typ. Pol. Vat. 1974. pp. 121.

Rite of Penance. Study Edition. ICEL. USCC. 1974 and 1975.

1974 JUN   CDW. *Jubilate Deo:* Cantus Gregoriani faciliores quos fideles discant oportet ad mentem Constitutionis Concilii Vaticani II de Sacra Liturgia. Typ. Pol. Vat. 1974.

1974 JUN 13   Paul VI. Apostolic letter "Firma in Traditione." AAS 66 1974.

"Faculties Concerning Mass Stipends." USCC. 1974.

1974 NOV 01 CDW. *Preces Eucharisticae pro missis cum pueris et de reconciliatione.* Typ. Pol. Vat. 1974.

Eucharistic Prayers for Masses with Children and for Masses of Reconciliation. Provisional Text. ICEL. NCCB. 1975.

1975 MAR 27 CDW. Publication of the second typical edition of the Roman Missal. (The changes in the General Instruction are listed in Notitiae 111-112 (1975) 297-337. The French Missal of 1974 contains the second edition of the Instruction. The ICEL Sacramentary of 1974 contains the first edition.)

1975 JUL 11 Paul VI. Apostolic Constitution, "Constans Nobis Studium." AAS 67 (1975) 418-420.

The Congregation for the Discipline of the Sacraments and the Congregation for Divine Worship are suppressed and a new Congregation for the Sacraments and Divine Worship is formed. (CDW becomes CSDW.)

2. Alphabetical Summary

ANOINTING OF THE SICK. see SICK

BAPTISM. see INITIATION

BISHOP. see also, ORDERS

1963 NOV 30 Faculties and privileges of bishops
1966 AUG 05 Statutes for Episcopal Conferences
1968 JUN 21 Pontifical insignia

CALENDAR. see YEAR

CANONIZATION and BEATIFICATION

1968 SEP 12 Celebrating saints and blessed during the year of their canonization or beatification.

1969 MAY 08 The Congregation of Rites is divided into two congregations, one for Divine Worship, and one for the Causes of Saints.

1969 APR 06 Order of Mass, number 76 and 158.
1972 AUG 07 Declaration on Concelebration, number 1 and 2.
1973 JAN 29 Instruction faciltating Communion. Lists 8 categories of times.

COMMUNION UNDER THE FORMS OF BOTH BREAD AND WINE

1963 DEC 04 Constitution, article 55. States principle and gives 3 examples.

1965 MAR 07 Rite for Communion under both kinds. Lists 11 occasions.

1965 JUL 08 Decision of CSR. Religious profession parallel to Secular Institute.

1965 SEP Decision of CSR restricts number 15 of Rite for Concelebration in this regard.

1967 MAY 25 Instruction on Eucharistic Worship. 13 examples.

1969 APR 06 General Instruction on the Missal. Numbers, 240, 241, 242. Enlarge principles and repeat list of 1967 MAY 25.

1969 MAY 15 Instruction for Mass celebrated for particular groups. States that Communion may not be received under the forms of both bread and wine when Mass is celebrated in homes. Statement of French Bishops on Masses are a good time to explain and introduce the practice of Communion under both kinds.

1970 MAY 31 Rite for the Consecration to a life of virginity.

1970 JUN 29 Instruction for the wider use of the faculty of receiving Communion under both species. Wider principles given. 14 examples listed.

1970 SEP 05 Third Instruction. Article 6. Tone more restrictive than instruction of 1970 JUN 29. Repeats the same list.

1970 NOV USA Bishops receive permission to extend the faculty to all present in the cases listed previously, and to funerals, special family masses, days of special religious or civic significance,

Holy Thursday, Easter Vigil, and all week day Masses.

1972 JAN   06 Rite of Initiation for Adults, suggests a Mass celebrated later with the bishop at which the newly baptized may receive under both species.

1975 MAR 27 Second typical edition of the missal takes account of legislation since 1969.

CONCELEBRATION.

1965 MAR 07 Rite for Concelebration
1972 AUG 07 Declaration on Concelebration

CONFESSION. see PENANCE

CONFIRMATION. see INITIATION

CURIA

1963 SEP   21 Paul VI announces the reform of the Curia
1964 JAN   25 Sacram Liturgiam establishes the Consilium
1964 FEB   29 Letter to Cardinal Lercaro indicating the specific competence of the Consilium ad exsequendam Constitutionem de sacra Liturgia
1967 OCT 15 Regimini Ecclesiae—reassigns the division of work

between the congregation of the Doctrine of the Fath, Congregation for the Discipline of the Sacraments, and the Congregation of Rites.

1969 MAY 08 Congregation of Rites divided into Congregation for Divine Worship and the Congregation for the Causes of the Saints

1974 JAN 26 Cardinal Knox becomes prefect of both the Congregation for Divine Worship and the Congregation of the Discipline of the Sacraments

1975 JUL 11 The two congregations become one: The Congregation for the Sacraments and Divine Worship

DEACON. see ORDERS

DIVINE OFFICE. see HOURS

ENGLISH. see LANGUAGE

EUCHARIST. see also, COMMUNION, COMMUNION MORE THAN ONCE A DAY, COMMUNION UNDER THE FORMS OF BOTH BREAD AND WINE, CONCELEBRATION, HOMILY, LANGUAGE, LITURGY, MUSIC, ORDERS, YEAR.

1960 JUL 25 Code of Rubrics
1961 JUN 23 New typical edition of the missal
1965 JAN 27 Ordo Missae; and new Rite of Mass
1965 SEP 03 Encyclical on the Holy Eucharist
1966 APR 17 The prayer of the faithful
1967 MAY 18 Variations in the Ordo Missae
1967 MAY 25 Instruction on Eucharistic Worship
1968 MAY 23 The new Eucharistic Prayers and prefaces
1969 APR 03 Apostolic constitution approving new missal
1969 APR 06 General Instruction on the missal
1969 MAY 15 Instruction on Masses for special gatherings
1969 MAY 25 Instruction on the Lectionary
1970 MAR 26 The text of the new missal
1970 SEP 30 Typical edition of the Lectionary
1970 OCT 18 Abbreviated missal

1973 APR 27 Letter to the bishops concerning the Eucharistic Prayers
1973 NOV 01 Directory for Masses with children
1974 JUN 13 Faculties concerning Mass stipends
1974 NOV 01 Eucharistic Prayers for Masses with children and for Masses of reconciliation.
1975 MAR 27 Second typical edition of the Roman missal

FUNERALS.

1969 AUG 15 Rite of Funerals

HOLY OILS. see OIL

HOLY ORDERS. see ORDERS

HOLY WEEK. see YEAR

HOMILY.

1947 NOV 20 Mediator Dei lists the homily among the liturgical actions
1955 NOV 16 Holy Thursday rubrics mention the homily
1960 JUL 25 Code of Rubrics states homily is to be given, iuxta opportunitatem, on Sundays and feasts.
1963 DEC 04 Constitution on the Liturgy states that the homily is an integral part of the liturgy
1964 JAN 25 Sacram Liturgiam calls for the homily on Sundays and Holy days.
1964 SEP 26 First Instruction prescribes the homily for Sundays and feasts and says "no exception is to be made."
1965 JAN 27 Ordo Missae mentions homily.

1967 MAY 25 Priest is not only to give a homily but to make sure all he says is clear and understandable

1969 APR 06 General Instruction strongly recommends homily as integral part of the liturgy and a necessary source of nourishment for the Christian life.

HOURS. THE LITURGY OF THE HOURS.

1961 MAY 15 Consultation of the bishops

1969 JAN 01 Description of new Hours sent to the bishops

1970 NOV 01 Apostolic constitution promulgating the Hours

1971 FEB 02 General instruction on the Hours

1971 APR 11 First volume of the text of the Liturgy of the Hours.

INITIATION. CHRISTIAN INITIATION.

1961 APR 16 Modified rite for the baptism of adults.

1969 MAY 15 Rite of Baptism for Children

1971 AUG 15 Apostolic Constitution promulgating the Rite of Confirmation

1971 AUG 22 Rite of Confirmation

1972 JAN 06 Rite of Christian Initiation of Adults

1973 AUG 29 Second typical edition of the Rite of Baptism for Children

INDULGENCES.

1967 JAN 01 Apostolic constitution on indulgences

LANGUAGE. LITURGICAL LANGUAGE.

1962 FEB 22 Apostolic Constitution "Veterum Sapientia" on the excellence and merits of Latin

1964 OCT 16 Letter on a unique liturgical translation for each language

1965 JUL 17 List of those parts of the Ordination Rite which may be said in the vernacular

1965 NOV 09 to 13 International Congress in Rome on liturgical translations

1965 NOV 23 Instruction on the language to be used in the office and community Mass

1967 OCT 08 Translating the Roman Canon

1969 JAN 25 Instruction on translating liturgical texts

1971 JUN 14 Notification that the entire Mass and Hours may be celebrated in the vernacular whether with or without a congregation

1973 OCT 25 Letter on the translation of the essential sacramental formulas

LECTIONARY. see EUCHARIST.

LITURGY. (General Documents)

1944 MAY 10 Beginning of the liturgical commission of Pius XII

1947 NOV 20 Mediator Dei

1948 DEC 30 The Memoria

1950 MAR 25 Memoria, supplement I. Classification of feasts

1959 MAY 17 Beginning of ante-preparatory phase of the Council—gathering suggestions which will be formed into the Constitution.

1960 JUN 05 Beginning of the preparatory phase. The formation of schemata.

1961 APR 12 A first schema for the liturgy is prepared

1961 AUG 10 Schema revised and theological chapter added

1961 NOV 15 Schema revised again

1962 JAN 11 Schema revised again, and approved by the commission

1962 FEB   01 Schema signed by Cardinal Cicognani
1962 MAR 23 Schema studied by Central preparatory commission
1962 JUL   13 Schema printed and sent to the Council Fathers
1962 OCT 11 Council opens
1962 OCT 22 Discussion of the Schema begins
1963 NOV 18 to 22 Final votes on the Emendations and Modi
1963 DEC 04 Promulgation of the Constitution on the Liturgy
1964 JAN 25 Motu proprio on the implementation of the Constitution
1964 SEP 26 First instruction on proper implementation
1967 MAY 04 Second instruction
1970 SEP 05 Third instruction

MATRIMONY.

1969 MAR 19 Rite of Marriage
1970 MAR 31 Motu proprio regulating mixed marriages

MUSIC.

1955 DEC 25 Encyclical on Sacred Music
1958 SEP 03 Instruction on Sacred Music and the liturgy
1964 APR 02 USA bishops permit English texts to be used at the offertory and Communion at a high Mass
1964 DEC 14 Typical edition of "Music desired in the Roman Missal"
1964 DEC 14 Kyriale Simplex
1967 MAR 05 Instruction on Sacred Music
1967 SEP 03 Graduale Simplex
1967 NOV 12 USA bishops. The place of music in Eucharistic celebration.

1972 JUN   24 Ordo Cantus Missae.
1974 JUN   Jubilate Deo. Book of easy Gregorian chants

OFFICE. see HOURS

OIL.

1965 MAR 04 Faculty to carry oil of the sick while traveling
1970 DEC   03 Rite for blessing of oils

ORDERS.

1967 JUN   18 General norms for restoring the permanent diacon-
              ate in the Latin Church.
1968 JUN   18 Approval of the new Rite of Ordination.
1968 AUG   15 Rite of Ordination of Deacons, Presbyters, and
              Bishops
1972 AUG   15 Apostolic letter giving norms for the diaconate
1972 AUG   15 Apostolic letter reforming the discipline of first
              tonsure, minor orders and the subdiaconate
1972 DEC   03 Rite of institution of readers and acolytes. Ad-
              mission to candidacy for the diaconate and
              Presbyterate. Rite for the commitment to celibacy.

OBEDIENCE TO LITURGICAL LAW

1963 DEC 04 Constitution on the Liturgy, article 22 3
1964 JAN 25 Motu Proprio, article 11
1964 SEP 26 First instruction, article 20
1966 DEC 29 Declaration of CSR: liturgical change by individuals
1967 MAY 04 Second instruction, preface
1967 MAY 25 Instruction on the Eucharist, article 45
1968 OCT 14 Allocution of Paul VI to Consilium: control of the liturgy pertains to the Church and not to individuals
1970 SEP 05 Third instruction, articles 1 and 3

PENANCE

1966 FEB 17 Apostolic constitution on Penance.
1972 JUN 16 Norms for giving General Sacramental Absolution
1973 MAY 24 First Penance before First Communion
1973 DEC Rite of Penance

RELIGIOUS PROFESSIONS

1970 FEB 02 Rites of religious profession
1970 MAY 31 Consecration to a life of virginity
1970 NOV 09 Rite for blessing an abbot or abbess

SICK. RITE OF ANOINTING AND PASTORAL CARE OF THE SICK.

1965 MAR 04 Faculty to carry the oil of the sick when traveling.

1966 FEB 14 The reception of Holy Communion by the Sick

1972 NOV 30 Apostolic constitution promulgating the rite of anointing

1972 DEC 07 Rite of anointing and pastoral care of the sick

YEAR. THE LITURGICAL YEAR. HOLY WEEK. CALENDAR.

1950 APR 21 Memoria, supplement II.

1951 FEB 09 Restoration of the Paschal Vigil

1951 JUN 19 Memoria, supplement III. Historical material for the reform of the calendar.

1955 MAY 25 Background for the reform of Holy Week.

1955 MAR 23 Simplification of the rubrics

1955 MAY 25 Background for the reform of Holy Week

1961 FEB 14 Instruction on particular calendars

1965 MAR 07 Variations in the order of Holy Week

1969 FEB 14 Apostolic letter approving the general norms for the reform of the calendar

1969 MAR 21 The Roman Calendar

A Select Bibliography, Part Two: Secondary Sources

1. Books

Abbott, Walter M. *The Documents of Vatican II.* New York: Herder, 1966.

Beguerie, Ph., and Evenou, J. *Eucharisties de tous pays.* Paris: Centre National de Pastorale Liturgique, 1975.

Bouix, D. *Tractatus de Jure Liturgico.* Parisiis: Apud Jacobum Lecoffre, 1853.

Bugnini, A. *Documenta Pontificia ad instaurationem liturgicam spectantia.* Vol. 1. 1903-1953. Vol. 2. 1953-1959. Rome, 1953, 1959.

Congar, Y. *Jalons pour une Theologie du Laicat.* Unam Sanctam N° 23. Paris: Cerf, 1953.

Dhôtel, Jean Claude. *Les Origines du Catéchisme Moderne.* Paris: Aubier, 1966.

Dix, Dom Gregory. *The Shape of the Liturgy.* 2nd Ed. London: Dacre Press, 1945.

Frutaz, A. *La Sezione storica della Sacra Congregazione dei Riti: Origini e metodo di lavoro.* Typ. Pol. Vat., 1963.

Germain, Elisabeth. *Languages de la foi a travers l'histoire.* Paris: Fayard-Mame, 1972.

Jung, Hans-Erich. *Le renouveau de l'année liturgique dans son enracinement historique.* Thése. Institut Catholique de Paris, 1975.

Jungmann, Josef Andreas, S.J. *Missarum Sollemnia: Eine Genetische Erklarung der Romischen Messe.* 2 vol. 3rd ed. Vienne: Herder, 1952.

Laurentin, Rene. *L'Enjeu du Concile.* Paris: Seuil, 1962.

_____. *L'Enjeu du Concile. Bilan de la Premiere Session.* Paris: Seuil, 1963.

_____. *Bilan de la Deuxième Session.* Paris: Seuil, 1964.

_____. *Bilan de la Troisième Session.* Paris: Seuil, 1965.

_____. *Bilan du Concile: Histoire, Textes, Commentaires avec une Chronique de la Quatrième Session.* Paris: Seuil, 1966.

Lengeling, J. *Die Konstitution des Zweiten Vatikanischen Konzils uber die heilige Liturgie.* Reihe *Lebendiger Gottesdienst,* N° 5/6. Munster, 1965.

Levillain, Philippe. *La Mécanique Politique de Vatican II: La Majorité et l'Unanimité dans un Concile.* Paris: Editions Beauchesne, 1975.

McManus, Frederick. *The Congregation of Sacred Rites.* The Catholic University of America Canon Law Studies, N° 352. Washington: The Catholic University Press, 1954.

Marliangeas, Bernard Dominique. *In Persona Christi: In Persona Ecclesiae: Etude de vocabulaire théologique.* Thése: Institut Catholique de Paris, 1966.

Martimort, A.G. (ed.) *L'Eglise en Prière: Introduction a la Liturgie.* 3rd Ed. Paris: Desclee, 1965.

Martimort, A.G., et Picard, F. *Liturgie et Musique: traduction de l'Instruction De Musica sacra et sacra Liturgia, 3 septembre 1958.* Lex Orandi, N° 28. Paris: Cerf, 1959.

Oury, Dom Guy. *La Messe de S. Pie V à Paul VI.* Solesmes, 1975.

Rahner, Karl, and Häussling, Angelus. *Die vielen Messen und das eine Opfer.* Freiburg: Herder, 1966.

Roguet, A.M. *The Liturgy of the Hours: The General Instruction on the Liturgy of the Hours with a Commentary.* Translated by Peter Coughlan and Peter Purdue. London: Geoffrey Chapman, 1971.

Schmidt, H. *Die Konstitution über die heilige Liturgie: Text-Vorgeschichte-Kommentar.* Herder-Taschenbuch, N° 218. Freiburg: Herder, 1965.

Souplesse et adaptation. Notes de Pastorale Liturgique, 117. Paris: Cerf/CNPL, 1975.

Woywod, Stanislaus, O.F.M. *A Practical Commentary on the Code of Canon Law.* Revised by Callistus Smith, O.F.M. New York: Joseph Wagner, 1962.

2. Articles

Botte, Dom Bernard, O.S.B. "La libre composition des prières liturgiques," Questions Liturgiques, 282 (1974) 211-215.

Bouyer, L. "L'improvisation liturgique dans l'Eglise ancienne,"

LMD 111 (1972) 7-19.

Cann, H. "Changing Emphases in the Concept of Authority in the Church," The Jurist, 23 (1963) 391-393.

Chenu, M.-Dominique, O.P. "Sauver les principes," LMD 12 (1947) 131-132.

————. "Anthropologie et liturgie," LMD 12 (1947) 53-65.

Cimetier, F. "La liturgie et le droit canonique," Liturgia. (Editor: Aigrain). Paris: Bloud et Gay, 1935. 29-58.

Congar, Yves, O.P. "Faits, problèmes et reflexions a propos du pouvoir d'Ordre et des rapports entre le presbytérat et l'épiscopat," LMD 14 (1948) 107-128.

————. "L'Eglise comme peuple de Dieu," Concilium 1 (1965) 15-32.

————. "L'ecclesia ou communauté chrétienne, subjet integral de l'action liturgique," La Liturgie apres Vatican II. Unam Sanctam N° 66. Paris: Cerf, 1967. 241-282.

————. "Autorite, initiative, coresponsabilité. Elements de reflexion sur les conditions dans lesquelles le problème se pose aujourd'hui dans l'Eglise," LMD 97 (1969) 34-57.

————. "Initiatives locales et normes universelles," LMD 112 (1972) 54-69.

————. "Rudolf Sohm nous interroge encore," RSPT 57 (1973) 263-294.

————. Les Fausses Décrétales, leur réception, leur influence," RSPT 59 (1975) 279-288.

Dalmais, Henri-Irenee, O.P. "La liturgie, acte de l'Eglise," LMD 19 (1949) 7-25.

————. "La liturgie comme lieu théologique," LMD 78 (1964) 97-105.

————. "Tradition et liberté dans les liturgies d'Orient," LMD 97 (1969) 104-114.

Davies, H. "Priere liturgique et prière spontanée dans le debat entre anglicans et puritains," LMD 111 (1972) 31-42.

De Clerck, Paul. "La fréquence des messes. Réalités économiques et theologiques," LMD 121 (1975) 151-158.

————. "Liturgie de l'Eglise particuliere et liturgie de l'Eglise universelle," LMD 123 (1975) 153-159.

Dell'Oro, Ferdinando, S.D.B. "I Documenti della Riforma Liturgica del Vaticano II (1963-1973): elenco cronologico con bibliografia," Rivista Liturgica 59 (1974) 102-163.

DeLubac, H. "Les eglises particulières dans l'Eglise universelle," DC 1602 (1972) 126-133.

Dekkers, E. "Créativité et orthodoxie dans la 'Lex Orandi,' " LMD 111 (1972) 20-30.

Gelineau, J. "La relation du prêtre avec le group célébrant," Bulletin du Comite des Etudes, 59 (1969) 439-442.

————. "Une technique à retrouver: le bon usage d'un modele dans les prières liturgiques," LMD 114 (1973) 85-96.

Gy, Pierre-Marie, O.P. "Esquisse historique de la Constitution "De Sacra Liturgia, "LMD 76 (1963) 7-17.

————. "Commentaire de la Constitution conciliaire 'De Sacra Liturgie,' " LMD 77 (1964).

————. "La responsabilité des évêques par rapport au droit liturgique," LMD 112 (1972) 9-24.

————."L'unification liturgique de l'Occident et la liturgie de la curie romaine," RSPT 59 (1975) 601-612.

————. "Typologie et ecclésiologie des livrcs liturgiques médié-vaux," LMD 121 (1975) 7-21.

————. "La nouvelle Congregation pour les sacrements et la culte divin," LMD 124 (1975) 7-13.

Hameline, D. "La créativité. Fortune d'un concept, ou concept de fortune?" LMD 111 (1972) 84-109.

Hanson, C. "The Liberty of the Bishop to Improvise Prayer in the Eucharist," Vigiliae Christianae 15 (1961) 173-176.

Hoffmann. J. "Pourquot un droit liturgique," Bulletin du Comite des Etudes 59 (1969) 443-456.

Jounel, Msgr. Pierre. "La composition des nouvelles prières euchar-istiques," LMD 94 (1968) 38-76.

_____. "La Liturgie des Heures dans le renouveau liturgique de Vatican II," Notitiae 97 (1974) 310-320; 98 (1974) 334-343.

Kelly, Walter J. "The Authority of Liturgical Law," The Jurist 28 (1968) 397-424.

McManus, Frederick. "The Scope of Authority of the Episcopal Conferences," The Once and Future Church. (Editor: Coriden). New York: Alba House, 1971. 129-178.

_____. "Liturgical Law and Difficult Cases," Worship 48 (1974) 247-336.

Martimort, A.-G. "L'obligation de l'office," LMD 21 (1950) 129-153.

_____. "Sedentes ascultant," LMD 31 (1952) 150-151.

Miller, John H. CSC. "The Nature and Definition of the Liturgy," Theological Studies 18 (1957) 325-356.

Montini, (Pope Paul VI) "Sur l'education liturgique," Lettre pastorale pour le Careme 1958. LMD 55 (1958) 141-170.

Nocent, A. "Soupless et adaptation de la liturgie depuis Vatican II," LMD 97 (1969) 76-94.

Noirot, Marcel. "Liturgique (Droit)," Dictionaire de Droit Canonique, IV, 535-594.

_____. "Le droit du Saint-Siège, des évêques et des fideles en matière liturgique," LMD 42 (1955) 34-55.

_____. "Reflexions canoniques sur des lois liturgiques récentes," LMD 46 (1956) 137-153.

Orsy, L. "Towards a theological conception of Canon Law," The Jurist 24 (1964) 383-392.

Roguet, A.-M. "De generibus literariis textum liturgicorum eorum interpretatione eorumque usu liturgico," Notitiae 15-16 (1966) 106-117.

Ruguet, A.-M. et Martimort, A.-G. "Le nouveau décret sur la Vigile pascale," LMD 29 (1952) 89-100.

Rotelle, John E. "Liturgy and Authority." Worship 47 (1973) 514-526.

Semmelroth, Otto, S.J. "The Priestly People of God and Its Official Ministers," Concilium 31 (1967) 87-100.

Turck, A. "Le problème de la loi: Reflexions pastorales," Paroisse et Liturgie 47 (1965) 3-13.

Vagaggini, Cipriano, O.S.B. "L'Evêque et la Liturgie," Concilium (French edition) 2 (1965) 13-27.

Vanhengel, M.C. "De celebrerende priester en de heiligende symboliek der sacramenten," Tijdschrift voor Theologie 3 (1963) 111-138.

Vismans, Thomas. "Liturgy or Rubrics?" Concilium 12 (1966) 83-91.

LIST OF ABBREVIATIONS
USED IN THIS STUDY

AAS ....*Acta Apostolicae Sedis.* The official bulletin of the Holy See. Before 1908 the title was *Acta Sanctae Sedis.*

Abbott ....*The Documents of Vatican II.* Edited by Walter M. Abbott, S.J. New York: Herder and Herder, 1966. English translations of the Council documents indicated "Abbott" are taken from this edition.

ADVat II..........*Acta et Documenta Concilio Oecumenico Vaticano II Apparando.* Series I. Antepraeparatoria. See Bibliography 1959 JUNE 18. Series II. Praeparatoria. See Bibliography 1960 JUNE 05.

ASS ....*Acta Sanctae Sedis.* See AAS.

ASVat II...........*Acta Synodalia Sacrosancti Concilii Oecumenici Vaticani II.* See Bibliography 1962 OCT 11.

CD.................*Christus Dominus.* Decree on the Bishops' Pastoral Office in the Church. See Bibliography 1965 OCT 28.

CDW..............Congregation for Divine Worship. See CSR.

CIC.................*Codex Iuris Canonici.* The *Code of Canon Law,* which was promulgated by Pope Benedict XV on Pentecost 1917, and which went into effect on Pentecost 1918.

Consilium ....Consilium ad exsequendam Constitutionem de Sacra Liturgia. Commission for the implementation of the Constitution on the Liturgy. See "Sacram Liturgiam" 1964 JAN 25, preface. Exists until it is absorbed into the Congregation for Divine Worship; see 1969 MAY 08.

CSR ....Congregation of Sacred Rites. Origin: 1588, Pope Sixtus V. 1969 MAY 08: becomes Congregation for Divine Worship. (CDW). 1975 JUL 11: becomes Congregation of the Sacraments and Divine Worship. (CSDW).

CSDW..............Congregation of the Sacraments and Divine Worship. see CSR.

DC...................*La Documentation Catholique.* Paris: Bayard Presse.

DCC...............*Dictionaire de Droit Canonique.* R. Naz, director. Paris: Librairie Letouzey et Ané. 1935-1965.

EL...................*Ephemerides Liturgicae.* Rome.

EP...................*L'Eglise en Priere.* A.G. Martimort, editor. Paris: Desclee. Unless otherwise noted, references are to the third edition, revised and corrected, 1965.

ICEL ....The International Commission on English in the Liturgy. The Constitution of ICEL is published in Notitiae 108-109 (1975) 245-248. See also: Notitiae 11 (1965) 339-345.

LG...................*Lumen Gentium.* Dogmatic Constitution on the Church. See Bibliography 1964 NOV 21B.

LMD...............*La Maison-Dieu.* Quarterly review published under the direction of the National Center for Pastoral Liturgy, Paris. 1945 and following.

MD.................*Mediator Dei et hominum.* Encyclical on the Sacred Liturgy. See Bibliography 1947 NOV 20.

NCCB..............The National Conference of Catholic Bishops. A canonical entity operating in accordance with the Conciliar decree, *Christus Dominus.*

NCWC.............The National Conference of Catholic Bishops. In May, 1967, the NCWC was reorganized and became the UCSS. Publications which were formerly handled by the NCWC then became the responsibility of the USCC Publications Department, 1312 Massachusetts Ave. N.W., Washington, D.C. 20005.

Not ....*Notitiae.* The journal of the Consilium. Numbers 1 to 45 were issued by the Consilium ad exsequendam Constitutionem de Sacra Liturgia. Numbers 46 to 107 were issued by the Sacra Congregatio pro Cultu Divino. 108 and following, by the Sacra Congregatio pro Sacramentis et Cultu Divino—Sectio pro Cultu Divino.

OR ....*L'Osservatore Romano,* Citta del Vaticano.

PO ....*Presbyterorum Ordinis.* Decree on the Ministry and Life of Priests. See Bibliography 1965 DEC 07.

RSPT...............*Revue des Sciences philosophiques et theologiques.* Journal of the professors of the faculties of philosophy and theology of the Saulchoir. Paris. 1914 and following.

SC..................*Sacrosanctum Concilium.* The Constitution on the Liturgy. See Bibliography 1963 DEC 04.

Typ. Pol. Vat. ...Typis Polyglottis Vaticanis. or: Tipografia Poliglotta vaticana.

USCC..............The United States Catholic Conference. A civil entity of the American Catholic Bishops assisting them in their work by uniting the People of God where voluntary, collective action is needed. See also: NCCB and NCWC.

INDEX

Thomas Richstatter was born in 1939 and grew up in Wichita, Kansas. He entered the Franciscan Order in 1958 and was ordained priest in 1966. After teaching and working in parishes of the archdiocese of Cincinnati, he obatined an MA in theology from the University of Notre Dame in 1971. He then studied liturgy and sacramental theology for five years at the Institut Catholique in Paris France and received the Maitrise in liturgy in 1974 and the degree Doctor of Theological Science in 1976. He is currently teaching liturgy at the Franciscan seminary in Dayton, Ohio.